ROYAL MYSTERIES
AND PRETENDERS

BLANDFORD HISTORY SERIES
(General Editor R. W. Harris)

PROBLEMS OF HISTORY

THE DISSOLUTION OF THE MONASTERIES	G. W. O. Woodward
THE EXPANSION OF EUROPE IN THE EIGHTEENTH CENTURY	Glyndwr Williams
FRANCE AND THE DREYFUS AFFAIR	Douglas Johnson
COLONIES INTO COMMONWEALTH	W. D. McIntyre
PAPISTS AND PURITANS	Patrick McGrath
THE CHURCH AND MAN'S STRUGGLE FOR UNITY	Herbert Waddams
THE REIGN OF HENRY VII	R. L. Storey

HISTORY OF EUROPE

RENAISSANCE, REFORMATION AND THE OUTER WORLD 1450–1660	M. L. Bush
ABSOLUTISM AND ENLIGHTENMENT 1660–1789	R. W. Harris
THE AGE OF TRANSFORMATION 1789–1871	R. F. Leslie
THE END OF EUROPEAN PRIMACY 1871–1945	J. R. Western
RUIN AND RESURGENCE 1939–1965	R. C. Mowat

THE HISTORY OF ENGLAND

REFORMATION AND RESURGENCE 1485–1603 England in the Sixteenth Century	G. W. O. Woodward
THE STRUGGLE FOR THE CONSTITUTION 1603–1689 England in the Seventeenth Century	G. E. Aylmer
ENGLAND IN THE EIGHTEENTH CENTURY 1689–1793 A Balanced Constitution and New Horizons	R. W. Harris
REACTION AND REFORM 1793–1868 England in the Early Nineteenth Century	John W. Derry
DEMOCRACY AND WORLD CONFLICT 1868–1965 A History of Modern Britain	T. L. Jarman

HISTORY AND LITERATURE

THE TRIUMPH OF ENGLISH 1350–1400	Basil Cottle
REASON AND NATURE IN 18TH-CENTURY THOUGHT	R. W. Harris
ROMANTICISM AND THE SOCIAL ORDER 1780–1830	R. W. Harris

Royal Mysteries and Pretenders

STANLEY B-R POOLE

*Formerly Assistant Editor of Debrett
and late Senior History Master
at the King's School, Canterbury*

BLANDFORD PRESS
LONDON

First published in 1969
© 1969 Blandford Press Ltd,
167 High Holborn, London W.C.1

SBN 7137 0502 7

*Set in 11 pt Times, Printed in Great Britain by
Richard Clay (The Chaucer Press), Ltd.,
Bungay, Suffolk*

Contents

	Preface	vii
	Acknowledgments	viii
	List of Illustrations	ix
Chapter 1	The Princes in the Tower	1
Chapter 2	Lambert Simnel and Perkin Warbeck	13
Chapter 3	Carlos of Spain	23
Chapter 4	The Casket Letters	35
Chapter 5	The False Dimitrys	45
Chapter 6	The Tsarevitch Alexis	54
Chapter 7	Peter III and Pugachov	67
Chapter 8	The Riddle of the Temple	81
Chapter 9	Alexander I of Russia and Feodor Kuzmich	95
Chapter 10	The Kaspar Hauser Story	109
Chapter 11	Stella Chiappini: A Princess of Orleans?	121
Chapter 12	The Mystery of Lake Starnberg	131
Chapter 13	Mayerling	143
Chapter 14	The Disappearance of John Orth	156
Chapter 15	Anastasia	167
	Genealogical Tables Nos. 1–18	181
	Bibliography	199
	Index	204

To Lallie Rimmer
who inspired this book
and to Ian Holness
who encouraged me
to write it

Preface

History is full of unsolved mysteries and those connected with the royal families of Europe have a particular fascination, as until comparatively recently monarchy remained the prevailing form of government in most of the continent.

I have endeavoured here to outline some of the best known of these mysteries. I lay no claim to originality, save possibly in assembling so many diverse 'cases' in the compass of one volume. Judging by the number of books and films that continue to appear dealing with some of the better known of these problems, public interest in them remains undiminished. Some, like the drama of Mayerling and the identity of Anastasia, have been the subject of much contemporary interest, but I trust that this collection will also focus attention on others perhaps less well known but in their own way equally absorbing.

If the contents of this book seem to confirm Gibbon's famous verdict that: 'history is indeed little more than the register of the crimes, follies and misfortunes of mankind'. I hope, nevertheless, that it may also evoke the sentiments expressed by Sir Walter Raleigh in the Preface to his *History of the World*: 'We may gather out of history a policy no less wise than eternal; by the comparison and application of other men's forepassed miseries with our own like errors and ill deservings.'

I am grateful to the Editor of Debrett, Mr. Patrick W. Montague-Smith, and to Kelly's Directories Limited for permission to re-produce much of an article on Anastasia written by me in *Debrett's Peerage* in 1967.

I am also indebted to Mr. R. W. Harris, the general editor of this series and my erstwhile colleague at the King's School, Canterbury, for kindly reading through the manuscript and making many valuable suggestions.

My publishers—and in particular Miss Vera Frampton and Mr. Roy Knightley—have been not only most helpful but also most forbearing, and my final thanks are due to them.

LITTLEBOURNE   STANLEY B-R POOLE

Acknowledgments

THE illustrations are reproduced by permission of the following:

Nos. 15 and 22 reproduced by gracious permission of H.M. the
    Queen
Austrian State Tourist Department, No. 55
Bulloz, Paris, No. 32
Cliché des Musées Nationaux, Nos. 28, 29, 30
Hessische Landes- und Hochschulbibliothek, Darmstadt, No. 20
National Portrait Gallery, Nos. 1, 3, 8, 14
Opera Mundi (Great Britain) Ltd., No. 61
Prado Museum, Madrid, Nos. 10, 11
Radio Times Hulton Picture Library, Nos. 2, 4, 5, 6, 7, 9, 12, 13,
    21, 23, 24, 25, 26, 27, 31, 33, 34, 35, 37, 38, 39, 40, 41, 42, 43,
    44, 45, 46, 47, 48, 49, 50, 51, 52, 53, 54, 56, 57, 58, 59, 60
Scottish National Portrait Gallery, Nos. 16, 17, 18, 19

List of Illustrations

(*Appearing between pages* 148 *and* 149)

1 Edward IV
2 Elizabeth Woodville
3 Richard III
4 The Princes in the Tower
5 Edward V
6 Lambert Simnel
7 Perkin Warbeck
8 Henry VII
9 Philip II of Spain
10 Isabelle de Valois
11 Don Carlos of Spain
12 Don John of Austria
13 The Palace of the Escurial
14 Mary, Queen of Scots
15 Lord Darnley and his brother, Charles
16 James VI
17 4th Earl of Bothwell
18 Earl of Moray
19 4th Earl of Morton
20 Dimitry of Russia
21 Ivan IV of Russia
22 Peter the Great of Russia
23 Alexis, Tsarevich of Russia
24 Peter III of Russia
25 Catharine the Great of Russia
26 Ivan VI of Russia
27 Grigori G. Orlov

28 Louis XVI of France
29 Marie Antoinette
30 The Dauphin, Louis XVII
31 Karl Wilhelm Naundorff
32 The Tower of the Temple
33 Alexander I of Russia
34 Elizabeth of Baden
35 Death of Alexander I
36 Tomb of Feodor Kuzmich
37 Kaspar Hauser
38 Kaspar Hauser at the home of his tutor
39 Kaspar Hauser
40 Family of Philippe Egalité
41 Maria Stella Chiappini
42 Philippe Egalité
43 Louis-Philippe, King of the French
44 Ludwig II of Bavaria
45 Schloss Neuschwanstein
46 Lake Starnberg
47 Crown Prince Rudolf of Austria
48 Rudolf and his wife
49 Baroness Marie Vetsera
50 Hunting lodge at Mayerling
51 Rudolf on his deathbed
52 The arrival of Rudolf's body in Vienna
53 Archduke John Salvator
54 John Orth and his crew on board the *Santa Margherita*
55 Schloss Orth
56 Nicholas II of Russia
57 The last Tsarina of Russia
58 The children of the Tsar
59 Nicholas II and his family in captivity
60 Anna Anderson
61 The burial place of the Romanovs

1

The Princes in the Tower

THE disorders in England in the fifteenth century, known as the Wars of the Roses, had their origin in the deposition of Richard II in 1399 by his cousin, Henry Bolingbroke. Richard II, who was conveniently murdered in Pontefract Castle five months after his deposition, had no children. According to strict hereditary right his heir was Edmund Mortimer, 5th Earl of March, who was a great grandson of Lionel, Duke of Clarence, the younger brother of Richard's father, the Black Prince. On the other hand, Richard's nearest heir in the male line was the new king, Henry IV, for his father, John of Gaunt, was a younger brother both of the Black Prince and of the Duke of Clarence.

The Earl of March died in 1424 without children and his heir was his nephew, Richard Duke of York, son of Anne Mortimer and Richard, Earl of Cambridge. He was also a Plantagenet prince, for he was a grandson of Edmund Duke of York, Edward III's fifth son (see Table No. 1).

While Henry IV and his son, Henry V, lived they were able to fight off any possible challenge from their Yorkist rivals, but when the latter died in 1422 his son and successor, Henry VI, was only eight months old.

The long minority of Henry VI, his periodic fits of insanity, his unpopular marriage with Margaret of Anjou (a marriage involving the surrender of the provinces of Anjou and Maine), the incapacity of his ministers and finally the loss of Normandy led to an outbreak of civil war in 1455 which lasted off and on for the next thirty years.

In 1461 Edward of York decisively defeated the Lancastrians and ascended the throne as Edward IV. Margaret of Anjou fled to France and Henry VI became a prisoner in the Tower.

This was not however the end of the story, for in 1470–1, with the help of Warwick 'the King Maker', who had changed sides, the Lancastrians made a final bid to recover their position. Henry VI was brought out of the Tower and once again became nominal ruler of England, but the Lancastrian hopes proved short-lived, for six months later two decisive battles—one at Barnet where Warwick was killed and one at Tewkesbury where Margaret was captured and her only child, Edward Prince of Wales, disposed of[1]—restored Edward IV to power. A few weeks later Henry VI, now once again back in the Tower, was murdered and thus there were no Plantagenet Lancastrians left.

The Yorkist triumph seemed complete but, as we shall see, the premature death of Edward IV in 1483 once again changed the picture. The murder of his two sons, the princes in the Tower, and the usurpation of the throne by his brother, Richard Duke of Gloucester, ushered in the last chapter of this long and bloody drama. The Lancastrians had found a candidate for the throne in the person of Henry Tudor, Earl of Richmond, a descendant of John of Gaunt on the distaff side and then an exile in Brittany (see Table No. 2). In 1485 he felt strong enough to challenge Richard III and in August of that year he landed on the coast of his native Wales. Three weeks later he defeated Richard at Bosworth in Leicestershire. The king was killed on the battlefield and Henry now became undisputed master of England.

Richard III's only child had died a year previously and the rightful heir in 1485 was—if he was still alive—the deposed Edward V and after him his younger brother, Richard Duke of York. They had both disappeared while prisoners in the Tower during the summer of 1483 and their fate has remained a mystery ever since. To understand the circumstances of their disappearance it is necessary to go back to 1464, the year in which their parents, Edward IV and Elizabeth Woodville[2] were married.

Edward IV, who was then twenty-three years of age and still a bachelor, had been on the throne three years, and in the April of that year decided to go and stay at the Abbey of St. Albans. On the last day of the month, on the pretext of hunting, he rode to Stony Stratford on the Buckinghamshire–Northamptonshire border. He stayed the

---

[1] The eighteen-year-old prince was either killed on the battlefield or murdered shortly afterwards.

[2] This name is indifferently spelt Woodville, Widvill, Wydevill, Wydville.

night there and early the next morning (1 May) rode five miles over the border to Grafton, an estate belonging to the Woodville family. There he married Elizabeth Woodville. The only people present at this clandestine ceremony besides the bride and bridegroom were the bride's mother, the priest and his assistant, and two witnesses. A few hours later the king returned to Stony Stratford and no one was any the wiser. For some months the marriage was kept secret. The king did return later on to Grafton, this time openly, but ostensibly simply as a guest of Lord and Lady Rivers and not (as he was) their son-in-law.

Inevitably, however, the news began to leak out and by mid-September, as Elizabeth was then four months pregnant, the king felt obliged to reveal it to his Council. There the marriage was greeted with almost universal disapproval. The ancient baronial families regarded the Woodvilles as upstarts, while the Yorkists were horrified because the new queen was the widow of a Lancastrian knight, Sir John Grey, who had been killed four years previously,[3] while fighting for Henry VI. In fact Elizabeth had been a lady of the Bedchamber to Margaret of Anjou, Henry VI's unpopular queen. This had come about because Elizabeth Woodville's mother, Jacquetta, had had as her first husband John Plantagenet, Duke of Bedford, a younger brother of Henry V. Jacquetta was a daughter of the Count of St. Pol in Flanders and belonged to the House of Luxembourg, which had produced the famous blind king of Bohemia who was killed at Crecy and had provided the Holy Roman Empire with several distinguished rulers (see Table No. 3).

A year after Bedford's death Jacquetta, to the indignation of her relations on both sides of the Channel, had contracted a second alliance with a comparatively unknown knight, Sir Richard Woodville, who had served under her first husband in the French Wars. Woodville was said to be the handsomest man in England, but in the eyes of Jacquetta's family this did not compensate for the misalliance. As the marriage took place without proper licence, the couple were punished by a fine of one thousand pounds before they could establish their rights to Jacquetta's property. Later, however, Woodville was created a Knight of the Garter and raised to the peerage as Baron Rivers.

Thus by background and temperament Jacquetta was disposed to

[3] At the second battle of St. Albans in 1460.

view with sympathy Edward IV's infatuation and ready to aid and abet her daughter's ambition to become queen. She found her prospective son-in-law—like her husband—to be an exceedingly good-looking man. The French chronicler, Philippe de Comines, who was no friend of Edward IV, declared that he was the handsomest prince he had ever seen. He was tall—when his coffin at Windsor was opened in 1789 the skeleton measured six feet three inches in length—well-proportioned and possessed of charm and ability.

What possessed Edward to marry Elizabeth must remain a matter of conjecture. He was a man of strong sexual passions and had several mistresses both before and after his marriage and it is said that he had originally attempted to include Elizabeth in their number, but that she had firmly indicated that the only way to her bed was via the altar. She was a beautiful woman, but had little else to recommend her. Unlike her affable and easy-going husband, she does not appear to have made friends easily and was never popular. Her life was bound up with her family. Edward may have thought that by raising up the Woodvilles and the Greys to position and power—rather in the manner that the Tudors in the next century created a new aristocracy—they might constitute a counter-balance to the old nobility. But this proved not to be so. They were detested by everyone.

A further objection to the marriage was that Elizabeth was four years older than her husband, and already the mother of two children. Indeed, according to some it was her concern for the welfare of her two fatherless sons that first brought her into contact with Edward. As it happened her age proved no impediment, for she bore her second husband nine children—three sons and six daughters.

The final affront to the king's advisers, and particularly to Warwick the Kingmaker, was that at the very moment when Edward got married at Grafton the earl was busily negotiating with the King of France to secure as queen Louis XI's sister-in-law, Bona of Savoy.

Elizabeth Woodville was crowned at Westminster Abbey in May 1465 and thereafter the advancement of her relations was rapid. Already, in the same year as Elizabeth's own marriage, one of her sisters was married to the heir of the Earl of Arundel. Soon after her father was given an earldom, and promoted to be Lord Treasurer, while her eldest son, Sir Thomas Grey, became Marquis of Dorset and was married to the heiress of the Duke of Exeter. Elizabeth's other sisters were married into the ancient families of Bourchier,

Strange, Herbert and Stafford. Of her brothers, one became Bishop of Salisbury and another, Sir John Woodville—to the scandal of many—became, at the age of twenty, the fourth husband of the Dowager Duchess of Norfolk, who was close on eighty and old enough to be his grandmother. This swift elevation of the queen's relations excited universal jealousy, and thus in 1469, when Warwick at last broke with his master and raised the standard of revolt in favour of Henry VI, both her father and Sir John Woodville were seized and executed.

On 9 April 1483—no doubt hastened by his dissolute way of life—Edward IV died suddenly in his Palace at Westminster at the early age of forty-two. As his son, Edward, Prince of Wales, was only twelve and a half years old, in his final will he entrusted the kingdom to his brother Richard, Duke of Gloucester, who was to govern on behalf of the young Edward V till that prince should come of age. Just how much power Richard would be left to wield clearly depended to some extent on the attitude taken up by the King's Council. In a somewhat similar situation in 1422, when Henry V died leaving his infant son to the care of his youngest brother, Humphrey Duke of Gloucester, in the ensuing struggle the Council, led by the Beaufort family, had succeeded in wresting control from the Protector. The Woodvilles probably hoped to repeat this, while Richard, of course, was determined to be the real ruler.

In 1483 the position of the Woodvilles appeared quite strong. Edward V was at Ludlow with his maternal uncle, Lord Rivers, who had been Governor of his household since 1473: the rest of the royal family was in the palace of Westminster. The queen's eldest son (by her first marriage), the Marquis of Dorset, was Constable of the Tower, and as such had control both of the late king's armaments and his treasure, and her brother, Sir Edward Woodville, was in command of the fleet.

On the other hand the ultimate custody of Edward V was due to go to his paternal uncle, the Duke of Gloucester. The latter was at Middleham Castle, his estate in Yorkshire, when his brother died, but he had a powerful ally in London, in the Council, in the person of Lord Hastings, and was thus kept informed of all that went on in the capital. It was in fact Hastings, and not the queen, who had sent messengers to Middleham to give the news of Edward IV's death. It was vital for Richard to get possession of his nephew as soon as possible and break the power of the queen's party: in this he had the support both of those magnates who detested the Woodvilles and of the populace at large. Equally important for the Woodvilles was to push on with the young king's coronation and thus give him a status independent of Richard's position as his guardian, and make it possible for the Council to rule in his name.

Once again Hastings was of service to Richard when it was announced in Council that the king would come to London for his coronation on 4 May. The Woodvilles planned to give him a large armed escort—no doubt hoping that a show of force would overawe their enemies, but Hastings threatened to retire to Calais, where he was Governor, unless the number was reduced to two thousand.

On 24 April the young king, accompanied by his uncle, Lord Rivers, and his half brother, Sir Richard Grey (Dorset's younger brother), left Ludlow. On the 29th Richard, who was coming south from Yorkshire hoping to intercept the royal party, and accompanied by the Duke of Buckingham, who although married to Elizabeth Woodville's youngest sister detested the whole family,[4] arrived at Northampton to find that Edward had just passed through the town in the direction of Stony Stratford. Lord Rivers, rather unwisely, returned to Northampton to greet Richard. This was Richard's chance. He seized Rivers and then went on to Stony Stratford where he arrested Grey, in the king's presence, explaining that both men had conspired to threaten his (Richard's) life. The king perforce had to see his kinsmen sent to Yorkshire where, a month later, they were executed without trial outside Pontefract Castle.

As soon as she had learnt what had happened, the queen, with her younger son, Richard Duke of York, her five daughters, her son Dorset and her brother, the Bishop of Salisbury, sought sanctuary in Westminster Abbey. This was a convenient refuge, as it adjoined the Palace, and she had stayed there before for six months during Warwick's rising and had given birth to Edward V there. But in her haste this time she had part of the dividing wall knocked down to accommodate her goods and chattels.

Meanwhile Richard proceeded to London with his nephew. On arrival the young king was first lodged in the Bishop of London's palace near St. Paul's and then transferred to the royal apartments in

---

[4] Buckingham, who enjoyed precedence before all dukes other than those of the blood royal, had been a ward of Edward IV and had had no choice in his marriage.

the Tower. It should be remembered, in the light of what ultimately happened, that the Tower was still used as a palace as well as a prison and there was nothing necessarily sinister in sending the princes there. Their sister, Elizabeth of York, Henry VII's wife, often stayed there and in fact died (in childbirth) there. By a mixture of bribery and blandishments the navy was prevailed upon to desert Sir Edward Woodville, who fled to Brittany. The Council recognised Richard's right to be Protector of the Realm and to have the custody of the king. The coronation, originally fixed for 4 May, was postponed till 22 June.

So far all had gone well for Richard and so far he had behaved quite correctly. There was nothing as yet so far to suggest that he was the monster that Shakespeare and the Tudor apologists made him out to be. Unlike his brother Clarence, he had been consistently loyal to Edward IV, who would never have left him the custody of the young king had he believed Richard to be a bloodthirsty fiend. But perhaps the ease with which the Protector had got his own way with the Council and overcome the Woodvilles now awakened his dormant ambition to be king. Some of his early supporters such as Hastings began to have qualms at the trend of events, but Richard acted swiftly to forestall any opposition. On 13 June he denounced Hastings to the Council and had him summarily executed. He also accused the queen of conspiring with Jane Shore, Edward IV's last mistress, to practise witchcraft and even attributed his withered arm to their machinations.

Three days later the Archbishop of Canterbury (Cardinal Bourchier) went to Elizabeth and persuaded her to let Richard Duke of York leave the Sanctuary and join his brother in the Tower. Jane Shore did public penance at St. Paul's, but the queen was left exposed to Richard's wrath. Clearly she had misgivings about surrendering her younger son, but she was afraid that if she did not agree then he would be taken by force. Edward V's coronation was further postponed, this time till 2 November.

Four days after Jane Shore had publicly confessed her sins, Dr. Shaw, who was a brother of the Lord Mayor and thus an influential prelate, used the cathedral to preach a sermon on a text from Wisdom iv. 3: 'Bastard slips shall not take deep root.' He repeated the story, apparently got from Bishop Stillington of Bath and Wells, that Edward IV's marriage was null and void because of a pre-contract

to marry Lady Elizabeth Butler, a daughter of the Earl of Ormonde.[5]
Remarks were also made about the irregular nature of the ceremony
at Grafton in 1464.

On 26 June Richard felt able—after a decent show of reluctance—
to accept the Crown[6] and his coronation took place on 6 July. From
this time onwards little was seen of the princes in the Tower.
They were no longer observed playing in the garden or even star-
ing out of the windows. They gradually disappeared from public
view and if they were murdered it probably happened about this
time.

Soon after Richard's coronation the new king set out on a
progress that took him across most of his kingdom and it was during
this journey, according to the 'official' Tudor account that he planned
the murder of his nephews. First, he sent a servant, John Green, to
Sir Robert Brackenbury, the Constable of the Tower, with a message
commanding him to put them to death. Brackenbury refused and so
Richard then sent Sir James Tyrell, telling Brackenbury to surrender
the keys of the Tower to him. This done, Tyrell sent in his groom,
John Dighton, who with one of the gaolers, Miles Forest, entered
the princes' room while they were asleep and smothered them with
pillows. Tyrell then supervised their burial at the foot of a staircase.
Tyrell is said to have confessed his part in the crime on the eve of his
execution in May 1502. He was beheaded for having surrendered
the fortress of Guines near Calais, of which he was governor, to
Richard III's nephew, the Earl of Suffolk. This story, popularised by
Sir Thomas More in his *History of Richard III* and by Shakespeare in
his play *Richard III*, held the field till recent times. But there is much
that is suspect about it—Tyrell's confession does not survive; he was
executed for treason and not regicide[7] and More seems to have derived his information from Cardinal Morton in whose household he
spent part of his youth. Morton, who was violently anti-Yorkist, had
played a significant part in the conspiracy against Richard III and

[5] There was no truth in this. The Ormondes were firm Lancastrians. Lady Elizabeth,
who died in 1473, married the 2nd Earl of Shrewsbury, whose family were also Lancastrians.

[6] Offered to him the previous day by an assembly of Lords and Commons at Westminster who were apparently satisfied with his claims.

[7] Tyrell had been included in a general pardon from Henry VII on 16 June 1486
and again 16 July 1486. Some of those who believe Henry VII to have been responsible
believe the murder took place between these two dates.

after the battle of Bosworth became Henry VII's Archbishop of Canterbury and Lord Chancellor.

A different version of how they died is supplied by a contemporary Burgundian chronicle [8] which says that the princes were walled up in a room in the Tower and then left to suffocate or starve.

In July 1674 some workmen, who were pulling down a staircase outside the White Tower which led from the royal apartments to the Chapel, unearthed a wooden chest containing the skeletons of two children. These were sent to the king's surgeon who identified them as the bones of two boys aged about eight and thirteen.[9] They were deemed to be the remains of the two princes, and Charles II ordered that they be put in a marble urn (to be designed by Sir Christopher Wren) and placed in Westminster Abbey. This was done in 1678.

In July 1933 this urn was opened and examined by a team of doctors and anatomists, but their findings did not really solve anything as all they could say was that the bones represented the remains of two children of the right age and sex. However, their findings were challenged some twenty years later and it would now seem, in the light of the best anatomical knowledge, that they could have been the bones of any children between seven and fourteen years of age, of either sex. Nor could it be established for certain that these were the right bones. There is indeed evidence that during the four years that elapsed between the date of their discovery and their final interment, some of the bones disappeared and Wren's urn was found to contain the bones of animals as well as of human beings.[10]

Thus when the two princes died and how they died still remains a mystery. They certainly disappeared in the summer of 1483 and were never seen or heard of again. It is highly doubtful if they survived beyond 1485,[11] and probably they were dead before then.

As to how they died, natural causes cannot be completely ruled out, although they are most unlikely. It is possible that, confined to rooms in the Tower and treated with negligence or subjected to even

---

[8] *Chronique des ducs de Bourgogne* by Jean Molinet.

[9] For a full discussion of the problems raised by these bones see Mr. Geoffrey White's article in *The Complete Peerage*—Vol. XII, Part ii, Appendix J.

[10] These appear to have included fish and poultry as well; it serves to remind us that the Tower was used as a palace as well as a prison.

[11] Henry VII married their eldest sister, Elizabeth of York, on 18 January 1486. Presumably if he was responsible for their death he would have removed them before then.

harsher measures, they did not long survive. Life for everyone was precarious in those days and especially for young children. Two of their sisters and their only brother had died young, while their cousin Edward (Richard III's only child), who must have had every care and attention, died at the age of ten or eleven. Nevertheless the speed and convenience of their disappearance must inevitably give rise to the gravest suspicions. Had they died naturally, whoever was king at the time had only to announce the fact and arrange to give them a public funeral and so convince everyone that this was the end of the matter. This may not have stopped rumours of foul play but it would have prevented any further mystery.

If—as is likely—their death was violent, then it could have been by suffocation, by starvation, by being immured or perhaps by being stabbed. The only medical clue, if indeed it is one, is provided by a stain on one of the skulls from Westminster Abbey. This, if it was caused by congestion of the blood, might support the theory of suffocation.

If we knew the date of their death then it would be comparatively simple to fix the responsibility for it. Until 22 August 1485 (the date of the battle of Bosworth) the princes' fate was in the hands of Richard III: thereafter Henry VII was in control. There is no firm evidence to connect either monarch with what happened. No credence can be placed on the Tyrell story as reported by Sir Thomas More. It is mere hearsay evidence and comes from a biased source (Morton). Henry VII never openly accused his predecessor of the princes' murder. The Act of Attainder passed by the Parliament of 1485–6, which set out Richard's misdeeds, did contain a reference to 'the shedding of infant's blood', but did not specify the victims. But gradually the Tudor apologists built up a picture of Richard III as a monster of iniquity. With his deformed back and withered hand he was an ideal target for their every slander. He was the 'wicked uncle' of popular folklore and he was described as cruel and bloodthirsty, cunning, unscrupulous and perfidious. It was recalled that he had despatched, without proper arraignment or legal proceedings, not only old enemies like Rivers and Sir Richard Grey[12] but also his trusted friends like Hastings[13] and Buckingham[14] to whom he owed

[12] Executed before Pontefract Castle, 13 June 1483.
[13] Executed Tower Hill, 13 June 1483.
[14] Executed Salisbury market place, 2 November 1483.

his throne. And his detractors not only blamed him for the death of the princes but also (quite unjustly) held him responsible for the death of his own brother, the Duke of Clarence,[15] and even the murder of Henry VI.[16]

No one now believes this is a true picture of Richard III, who with all his faults was both brave and cultured and could on occasion be generous. What in the end counts most against him is that his nephews disappeared while they were in his custody and were never seen or heard of after July 1483. All contemporary historians—notably the Italian Mancini who was in England in the summer of 1483 and the Chronicle of Croyland which was written early in 1486—speak of their disappearance and clearly hold Richard responsible for it.

As far as character is concerned Henry VII was scarcely any improvement on Richard III. Just as ambitious and unscrupulous as his predecessor, the fact that he was more skilful in concealing his plans and intentions made him a more successful monarch, but scarcely a more endearing one. He was a cold, calculating, miserly man, and the execution of the Earl of Warwick (see pages 21–2) shows that he was just as capable of judicial murder as Richard was. Richard could strike down Hastings and Buckingham but spare Warwick, while Henry could spare Lambert Simnel but execute Warwick and Perkin Warbeck. There was an essential likeness between the two kings when it came to distinguishing between those who appeared to threaten their position and those who did not—whether that position had its origin in usurpation, as in the case of Richard, or in victory on the field of battle, as in the case of Henry.

No one seems to have thought much the worse of Henry IV because he allowed the gaolers at Pontefract Castle to starve Richard II to death, or of Edward IV for consenting to the death of his brother Clarence and the murder of Henry VI. But what made the princes unique was that they were mere children and, unlike Richard II, Clarence or Henry VI, had done nothing to forfeit the regard of others. Thus, if Richard III was their murderer, as their uncle and appointed guardian he does indeed become a monster and deserves the same sort of opprobrium accorded to King John for murdering his nephew Arthur, but if Henry VII was responsible the crime

---

[15] Drowned in the Tower, 18 February 1477.
[16] Stabbed in the Tower, 21 May 1471.

may seem a little less frightful in that he was but a distant kinsman.

The general verdict as far as Richard III goes must remain nonproven, and unlovable though Henry VII was, there is nothing to connect him with the death of the princes, other than mere speculation. The matter remains in dispute between members of the Bosworth Society, who still see in Richard III the villain of the piece, and members of the Richard III Society who hold the contrary view. There is little prospect of any further evidence coming to light which could decide the matter once and for all.

Interest in the princes' fate was recently revived when in December 1964 some workmen discovered a small lead coffin on a building site in Stepney. From the Latin inscription affixed to it, the coffin clearly contained the remains of Anne Mowbray, the child wife—she was only just over five years old when she married and only eight years and eleven months when she died—of the younger of the princes, Richard Duke of York. She was the only daughter and heiress of the last Mowbray Duke of Norfolk and had been married with great pomp in Westminster Abbey in 1478. She did not of course live with her husband (who was eight months younger than she was) and died at Greenwich in 1481. Originally she had been buried in Westminster Abbey but at some juncture her coffin had been removed to the Abbey of the Minories (Minoresses) at Aldgate where, in the Nun's Choir, her mother Elizabeth, Duchess of Norfolk, who died in 1507, had chosen to be buried. The remains of the child Duchess, after being examined by doctors, anatomists, dentists, osteologists and radiologists, were re-interred—in the same casket in which they had been found—in Westminster Abbey in May 1965.

2

Lambert Simnel and Perkin Warbeck

THE death of Richard III on the field of Bosworth did not bring with it the extinction of the Plantagenet dynasty. Richard's own son—his only child—Edward, Prince of Wales, had predeceased his father and died in 1484, at the age of eleven. The obvious heir was Edward, Earl of Warwick, the son of Richard's elder brother, the ill-fated Duke of Clarence. He had been born in February 1475 and at first Richard designated him heir-apparent.[1] But later the king changed his mind and substituted instead his older nephew John de la Pole, Earl of Lincoln, son of his sister, Elizabeth Plantagenet, Duchess of Suffolk. He was some ten years older than Warwick and was obviously a better choice (see Table No. 4).

One cannot, however, help feeling sorry for Warwick, who was the last male Plantagenet. Before he was two years old he had lost both his parents[2] and after 1483 he became virtually a prisoner simply because he had a better right to the throne than either Richard III or Henry VII. Richard kept him in close confinement at Sheriff Hutton, one of his Yorkshire estates, and after the battle of Bosworth he was transferred to the Tower where he spent the rest of his life.

The uncertainty surrounding the fate of the princes in the Tower and the continued existence of Warwick and other Plantagenet heirs inevitably produced a crop of pretenders to the throne. The two best known are Lambert Simnel and Perkin Warbeck. Neither of them amounted to very much.

Lambert Simnel, who was probably born about the same year as

[1] It cannot be argued from this that the princes in the Tower were already dead, for Richard could never acknowledge their rights, as to support his own claims he had proclaimed them to be bastards.

[2] The Duke of Clarence had been murdered in the Tower in February 1477: the Duchess had died in childbirth two months previously.

the Earl of Warwick (1475), was a man of the people whose father has been variously described as a joiner, a shoemaker, a baker and an organ builder. No doubt Simnel likewise would have been content to follow one of these callings but for a chance encounter with a certain Richard Simons, an ambitious priest from Oxford who saw great possibilities for himself if Lambert Simnel could be passed off as a Plantagenet prince. Lambert Simnel was a personable young lad with a natural sense of dignity that impressed those he met and thus made the imposture possible. Simons, who acted as Simnel's tutor, introduced him to Yorkist circles and declared that he was in fact the young Earl of Warwick who had successfully escaped from prison. He took him to Ireland where Richard III, his 'uncle', had been popular and where the Fitzgeralds of Kildare were always prepared to welcome anyone who could strike a blow at the government in London. Kildare, who was Lord Deputy, and his brother Thomas, who was Lord Chancellor, came out in favour of Simnel who was crowned as Edward VI by the Bishop of Meath in Christ Church Cathedral on Whitsunday 24 May 1487.[3]

Assisted by the youngest sister of Edward IV and Richard III, Margaret, Duchess of Burgundy, who persuaded Maximilian of Austria (the husband of her stepdaughter) to send a band of fifteen hundred German mercenaries, Simnel's supporters decided to try their luck in England. They landed on the Lancashire coast near Furness and marched southwards. On 16 June (1487), at Stoke-on-Trent, the rebels found their way blocked by the royal army. The ensuing battle was a hard fought one and lasted three hours—mainly because the German mercenaries gave a good account of themselves—but Simnel's forces were finally routed and the Pretender himself taken prisoner. Among those who fell on the battlefield were Kildare's brother, Sir Thomas Fitzgerald (Lord Chancellor of Ireland) and Richard III's nephew and heir, the Earl of Lincoln.[4]

[3] John Payne, Bishop of Meath 1483–1507. He was pardoned after the battle of Stoke.

[4] Another victim of the battle was Richard III's former Chamberlain, Lord Lovel, who after Bosworth had made his way to Burgundy. He had accompanied the German mercenaries first to Ireland and then England. He was last seen trying to escape across the River Trent on horseback. He is said to have reached his house at Minster Lovel in Oxfordshire and taken refuge in a secret room where by accident or treachery he became immured. In 1708, when alterations were being made at Minster Lovel, a skeleton of a man sitting at a table was said to have been found in an underground vault. His fate may have suggested to some a similar fate for the princes.

Kildare himself was captured, but pardoned and allowed to retain his Deputyship.

Thus ended Simnel's bid for the throne. From the beginning the imposture had been a clumsy one, for, as Henry VII had the real Earl of Warwick locked up in the Tower, all he had to do was to parade his captive through the streets of London to show everyone how baseless Simnel's claims really were. So one Sunday morning the unfortunate Warwick was taken out of his cell and made to attend mass at St. Paul's Cathedral where he could be seen by all and sundry.

Henry VII does not appear to have been greatly disturbed by Simnel's bid for the throne. It was obvious that Simnel had not the makings of a successful king, nor Simons the necessary qualifications to become Archbishop of Canterbury. The real threat came from Lincoln who was now dead. Henry obviously regarded Simnel as of little consequence, a young lad led astray by others, and he showed unexpected clemency (and perhaps a touch of contempt) by despatching him to the royal kitchens, there to serve as a scullion: Simons the priest, who was also captured at Stoke, was imprisoned for life. According to Polydore Virgil (Archdeacon of Wells), the Italian cleric and historian who was still living in England in 1525, Simnel later became a falconer and was transferred to the service of Sir Thomas Lovell.[5] The latter, who was an extremely wealthy man, had been one of the executors of Henry VII's will and had served both that monarch and Henry VIII as chancellor of the exchequer. When Lovell died in 1525 Lambert Simnel was present at his master's funeral, which took place with great pomp in a chantry chapel that Lovell had built in a nunnery at Shoreditch. On this occasion Simnel is described as a yeoman. This is the last mention made of him and he disappears for ever from the stage of history.[6] There was a man named Richard Simnel who is mentioned as being an inmate of the priory of St. Osyth in Essex when that monastery surrendered to the crown in 1539, but what relation, if any, he was to Lambert it is impossible to say.

One of the casualties of the Simnel rising in 1487 was Henry VII's mother-in-law, Elizabeth Woodville. She and her daughters

---

[5] No relation of the Viscount Lovel referred to on page 14n, and came of a family of Lancastrian allegiance.

[6] Most authorities place the date of his death as 1534.

had emerged from the Sanctuary at Westminster in March 1484 after a stay there of eight months. She was unmolested by Richard III who granted her a pension.[7] She was officially styled Dame Elizabeth Grey. On the succession of Henry VII, who married her eldest daughter, Elizabeth,[8] in January 1486, she became the Queen Dowager and returned to court life, but Henry found her presence an embarrassment and took the opportunity of getting rid of her as soon as he could. At a Council held at Sheen in February 1487 it was decided that she should terminate her public life for good and all and retire to the abbey of Bermondsey. There she died in June 1492, at the age of fifty-five, and was buried at Windsor beside her second husband.[9]

The next Pretender, Perkin Warbeck, constituted a more serious threat. He was superior to Lambert Simnel both in intelligence, social position and education. He was born about 1474 and, according to his confession written when he was a prisoner in the king's hands, he was the son of a Fleming, John Osbeck of Tournai. His father is described as Controller of Customs, though it was also asserted that he had once been a boatman on the River Scheldt which flows through the town.[10] His Christian name was Peter but he is always remembered in history by his nickname of Perkin or Peterkin.

Flanders at this time formed part of the vast duchy of Burgundy and the Duchess Margaret, as a sister of Edward IV and Richard III, welcomed to her court at Malines all those Yorkists who disliked the rule of Henry VII and who still hoped to be able to reverse the verdict of Bosworth Field. As she was childless[11] all her hopes were concentrated on her kinsmen in England.

Warbeck, whose early life was spent amidst the trading circles of

[7] Her relations with Richard III, 1484–5, are indeed strange if he was the murderer of her two sons.

[8] She was the only Queen of England to have been the daughter of one king (Edward IV), the sister of a second king (Edward V), the niece of a third (Richard III), the wife of a fourth (Henry VII), and the mother of a fifth (Henry VIII).

[9] Sir Francis Bacon, in his *History of the Reign of King Henry the Seventh* (published in 1622) asserts that she encouraged Simnel, but there is no proof of this.

[10] Tournai was an ancient Roman town and a flourishing trade centre. Its marble sculptures, tapestries and carpets were sought after all over Europe and its cathedral, one of the best in Flanders, reflected the city's prosperity. Henry VIII captured it in 1513 but sold it to the French five years later.

[11] She was the third wife of Charles the Bold who had been killed at the battle of Nancy in 1477. His only child, Mary, the first wife of the Emperor Maximilian, had died in 1482.

Tournai and Antwerp, came in contact both with merchants from London (from whom he learnt to speak English) and with Yorkist exiles. His mother, Catherine de Faro, was a native of Portugal and possibly of Jewish descent, and as a young lad he visited that country in the service of Lady Brampton whose husband, Sir Edward, was himself a partisan of the House of York. From there he transferred himself to the employ of a Breton silk merchant named Pregent Meno, whose principal trade was with Ireland. There Warbeck acted—in modern parlance—as something between a salesman and a male model.

When, in 1491, he first appeared in the streets of Cork—a city strongly Yorkist in sympathy—in all his finery, his handsome features, dignified bearing and general air of being a person of some consequence (not to speak of his acting ability and plausible tongue) led to a rumour that he was a Plantagenet prince. At first it was thought that he was the Earl of Warwick,[12] then it was suggested that he was a bastard son of Richard III, and finally that he was Richard, Duke of York, the younger of the princes murdered in the Tower. At first he denied that he was any one of these three and later said that he took an oath before the mayor of Cork to that effect, but when the Yorkists in Ireland (particularly the Fitzgerald Earls of Desmond and of Kildare) and those in exile in France assured him of their support, he was persuaded to change his mind.

From Ireland he went to France to get support from her king, Charles VIII, who supplied him with a suitable residence in Paris and gave him a guard of honour. However, in November 1492, a treaty of friendship between England and France[13] compelled him to return to Tournai. Back in Flanders he cultivated the friendship of the Dowager Duchess who recognised him as her nephew and in turn found for him a place to live, together with the usual guard of honour. There is no doubt that she helped to coach him in his new rôle. Their alliance was cemented by his promise to restore to her her estates in England (confiscated by Henry) and resume payment of her allowance.

It was in vain for Henry to threaten economic sanctions against the

---

[12] The Irish had a particular regard for Warwick because his father, the Duke of Clarence ('a goodly and well-featured prince' according to Sir Thomas More) had spent close on nine years as Lieutenant of Ireland.
[13] Signed at Etaples, 3 November 1492.

Flemish merchants unless Warbeck was banished, or to send the Garter King of Arms to Malines to denounce him as an impostor and supply proofs of his parentage. Margaret was well aware of his origins, but was equally determined to make what use of him she could, so she continued to recognise him as 'The White Rose of England'.

Warbeck also made an impression on the Archduke Philip, who, as a grandson of Margaret's husband, was nominal ruler of Flanders.[14] In August 1493 Warbeck went to Vienna to attend the funeral of Philip's paternal grandfather, the Emperor Frederick III, and there he met the new Emperor (Philip's father), the Emperor Maximilian. Maximilian for his part also saw possibilities in supporting Warbeck who seemed a much more likely candidate than Lambert Simnel had been. So he installed him in a house in Antwerp as his guest and allowed him to make preparations to invade England.

By the summer of 1495 Warbeck's expedition was ready but Henry VII had already taken effective counter-measures. In Ireland he had replaced Kildare by Sir Edward Poynings, on whose ability and loyalty he could count, and in England he had rounded up all the prominent Yorkists and other disaffected persons, including his own chamberlain, Sir William Stanley[15] and sent them to the block. Thus when early in July, Warbeck with fourteen ships and some fourteen hundred men attempted to land on the Kentish coast at Deal the affair proved a complete fiasco; Warbeck lost three of his ships and over three hundred men.[16]

Without ever himself landing, Warbeck sailed away with the rest of his forces to join the Earl of Desmond in besieging the city of Waterford. This was a lamentable choice for it was a stronghold of the Butler family, Earls of Ormonde, who were the principal rivals in Ireland to the Fitzgeralds and had consequently always been fervent Lancastrians, and it was a town that had already successfully rebuffed

---

[14] Philip, who was the son of Mary of Burgundy and the Emperor Maximilian I, was born in 1478, and till he came of age Margaret was the real ruler of Flanders. Philip later married Joanna of Spain and became the father of the Emperor Charles V.

[15] Stanley had played a decisive part in the victory of Bosworth where he is said to have saved Henry's life, while his brother, the first Earl of Derby, was at this time the husband of Henry's mother, Margaret Beaufort, Countess of Richmond. As he was reputed to be the richest man in England this may well have had something to do with his downfall.

[16] Most of the prisoners, who represented half the casualties, were executed.

Lambert Simnel. After eleven days Waterford showed no signs of capitulating and so Warbeck was once again obliged to seek his fortunes elsewhere.[17]

This time he went to Scotland where James IV welcomed him to his court at Stirling Castle. They had been in contact by letter for some years, but this was the first time they had met. Of all the monarchs that Warbeck had so far had dealings with James proved easily the most sympathetic. A genuine affection sprang up between the two men and the Scottish king gave Warbeck in marriage the hand of his kinswoman, Lady Catherine Gordon, a daughter of the Earl of Huntly.[18] James gave them both a magnificent wardrobe which must have delighted Warbeck, as it was his love of clothes that had started him off on his career of imposture. He stayed in Scotland, as an honoured guest, for the next two years and now openly exchanged the title of Duke of York for that of King Richard IV.

In September 1496 he made an attempt to make good his claim by invading Northumberland. But the brutal conduct of his Scottish allies, to whom the whole affair was just another border raid in which slaughter and looting were the order of the day, alienated what little support from the English Warbeck might have hoped to gain. The whole affair lasted only three days and the invading force never penetrated beyond four miles.

Warbeck remained in Scotland for a further nine months, but as it was clear that Henry was now determined to take action against his northern neighbour and was making open preparations for war, James allowed Warbeck and his wife and a small flotilla to sail from Ayr in July 1497. Inevitably they went to Ireland—still the Mecca for all Yorkists—but this time chose Cork. However, neither Kildare nor Desmond was prepared to take any further risk on his behalf. Apart from John Walters, a former mayor, no one of substance rallied to his support and his principal counsellors had sunk to people of the calibre of Heron, a grocer who had absconded for debt, Skelton, a tailor, and Astley, a copy clerk.

At this juncture, however, a revolt of Cornishmen—mainly due to discontent at the heavy taxation imposed by the Parliament which

[17] As a reward for its resistance Henry VII gave the city the right to the devise 'Intacta manet Waterfordia'.

[18] Huntly's second wife had been a daughter of James I. His third wife, Catherine's mother, was a descendant of Robert I.

met in January 1497 to vote subsidies for the impending war with Scotland—and a renewal of hostilities in Northumberland gave promise of better things. So after spending a month in Cork Warbeck sailed for Cornwall. He made the voyage in a Spanish ship and he and his companions, after narrowly escaping on the high seas,[19] landed at Whitesand Bay, near Land's End, on 7 September. Unfortunately for him this was a month too late, for the powerful rebel force of Cornishmen, led by Lord Audley, had marched to London and already been defeated (17 June) at Blackheath, while in the north James IV was about to sue for peace.

Nevertheless there was still plenty of discontent in the West country and when Warbeck raised his standard in Bodmin he received a warm welcome. It was decided to march on Exeter, but here his untrained and ill-equipped forces met stout resistance. Without proper siege artillery they could gain no entry into the walled city. To avoid encirclement by a royalist army marching to relieve the city, Warbeck abandoned the siege and passed on to Taunton. Here matters were, if anything, worse, for there were two armies, one led by Lord Daubeney (who had defeated the rebels at Blackheath) and one by Henry himself were converging on the area. Warbeck's nerve broke and with a few companions including Heron, Skelton and Astley he fled for sanctuary to Beaulieu Abbey. Here, surrounded by the king's forces and on promise of clemency, he surrendered. He was brought back to Taunton for a confrontation with the king. Henry extracted a complete confession from him, took him back to London and paraded him through the streets as a self-confessed impostor.

Despite the fact that he had given much more trouble than Lambert Simnel and enjoyed patronage in much more exalted quarters, Henry was disposed to be magnanimous. Warbeck was allowed to remain at court in a sort of protective custody, but on the night of 9 June 1498 he escaped his keepers and made for the coast. However, he got no farther than the monastery of Sheen. He was brought back and, by way of punishment, was made to sit in the stocks, first in the courtyard of the Palace of Westminster and then in Cheapside. After that he was imprisoned in the Tower in a cell beneath that occupied by the Earl of Warwick.

In February 1499 Henry had to put to death yet another Pretender,

[19] His ship was actually boarded by Henry's men but Warbeck, successfully concealed in a barrel, evaded capture.

a certain Ralph Wilford or Wulford, a London shoe-maker's son who, like Lambert Simnel, had been persuaded by his ambitious tutor (an Augustinian friar) to declare himself to be the Earl of Warwick. He was hanged on Shrove Tuesday and his tutor imprisoned for life.

By now Henry was convinced that both Warbeck and Warwick in their different ways constituted a threat to the Tudor dynasty and there was nothing he wanted to see more than them both permanently out of the way. Negotiations had been afoot for some time to marry his elder son, Arthur, Prince of Wales, to Catherine of Aragon[20] and they wanted no pretenders around to frighten off the Spaniards or imperil the prospect of a handsome dowry from the treasury at Madrid.

So, with the connivance of their gaolers,[21] Warbeck and Warwick were encouraged to meet and talk over their prospects. By November Henry felt that he had the evidence he wanted and both Warbeck and Warwick were accused of plotting to escape, with the intention of killing the Lieutenant of the Tower, stealing the treasury, blowing up the powder store and escaping to Flanders. Their trials were separate, for Warwick had to be arraigned before his peers in a court at Westminster, presided over by the High Constable of England, the Earl of Oxford, whereas Warbeck was tried at Whitehall in the Court of the King's Bench. They both pleaded guilty and were both executed. Their difference in rank was given final recognition in that, whereas Warbeck was hanged, drawn and quartered at Tyburn on 23 November, the Earl (five days later) was beheaded on Tower Hill. Others executed were Astley and John Walters.

So Warwick's miserable life came to an end. Of his brief life of close on twenty-five years only the first nine had been spent in freedom: his only crime was that he was the last male Plantagenet.[22] He was no match for the Tudors, for he had received no proper education, was of mediocre intelligence (if not a simpleton) and suffered from grave defects of character. Life would have had to deal him a completely different set of cards for him either to have been

---

[20] They were married by proxy on 19 May 1499.

[21] One of Warbeck's gaolers was his erstwhile friend and counsellor, Astley.

[22] Edward IV left an illegitimate son, Arthur Plantagenet, Viscount l'Isle, who died in 1541 leaving three daughters. The famous General Monk, who brought about the restoration of Charles II, was one of his descendants. L'Isle, who was Governor of Calais under Henry VIII, had no political pretensions.

B

able to play any satisfactory part in national life or achieve any sort of personal happiness.

Warbeck, although he was in the end no less of a pawn in the hands of others, had his freedom during most of his life, had had a varied and interesting career and known moments of triumph and joy.

His widow, Lady Catherine Gordon, never shared in his disgrace. She was well treated by Henry VII, who brought her from St. Michael's Mount where Warbeck had left her after the debacle of 1497, and attached her to his court and gave her a pension.[23] To this Henry VIII added an estate in Berkshire, which had formerly belonged to the de la Pole family, and there she died in 1537. She made three further marriages, two of them to gentlemen ushers of the Court.[24]

[23] She was present (under her maiden name which she resumed) at the betrothal ceremony of Henry's daughter, Margaret, to James IV of Scotland in 1502.

[24] These were her second and fourth husbands, James Strangways and Christopher Ashton. Her third husband, Sir Matthew Cradock (who died in 1531) was a prominent landowner in Glamorgan. There is an effigy of her in Swansea Church.

3

Carlos of Spain

DON CARLOS, the only child of Philip II of Spain, by his first wife, Maria of Portugal, was born at Valladolid on 8 July 1545. He was born lame, with one leg shorter than the other, and from early days suffered from epileptic fits. As his mother died four days after his birth, the infant prince was entrusted to Philip's younger sister, Joanna. She herself was not the stablest of characters and could in no way effectively replace the child's mother. Later she was joined in the task of bringing him up and educating him by Don Honorato Juan (later Bishop of Cartagena) and Don Garcia de Toledo, a cousin of the Duke of Alba and later Spanish Viceroy of Sicily. But none of the trio was able to make much impression on the child, who from early days displayed a wayward and obstinate streak.

Unfortunately indifferent health and the loss of his mother were not the only disadvantages the young Don Carlos had to contend with. His ancestry was also against him. Cut off by the Pyrenees in the north and the presence of the Moors in the south, Spain and Portugal had been rather isolated from the rest of Europe during the Middle Ages and this had resulted in a great deal of inter-marriage between the different Iberian kingdoms—Castile, Aragon, Navarre, Portugal, etc. And even before the foundations of modern Spain by the union of the two principal kingdoms of Aragon and Castile (through the marriage in 1469 of Don Carlos's great, great grandparents, Ferdinand of Aragon and Isabella of Castile) the same family had been ruling in them both for over half a century: Ferdinand's grandfather and Isabella's grandfather were themselves half-brothers.

A glance at Table No. 5 shows just how much a product of inbreeding the unfortunate Don Carlos was. Whereas a normal person would have eight different great grandparents he had only four, and

of these four, two, Joanna and Maria of Spain, were sisters. They in turn, like Joanna's husband, Philip of Austria, were themselves children of second cousins, while the fourth great grandparent, Maria's husband, Manuel I of Portugal, was the child of first cousins. This heavy concentration of blood might not perhaps have mattered had the original stock been healthy and sound, but unfortunately it was not. There was madness in the royal house of Castile. Don Carlos's great grandmother (twice over) Joanna (whose own grandmother, Isabella of Portugal, Queen of Castile, had died insane) was an hysteric, prone to religious melancholy which was increased, first by the numerous infidelities of her husband, Philip of Austria, and then by his premature death at the age of twenty-eight. Her mental condition so disturbed her mother, Queen Isabella, that when the latter died in 1504 she entrusted in her will the government of Castile to her husband, Ferdinand, instead of to the rightful heir, her daughter. Joanna had been passionately in love with her blond handsome husband, and although her frantic jealousy had made their marriage a stormy affair[1] his early death[2] completely prostrated her. She made an extravagant display of her grief. She insisted that her dead husband should not leave her side and she absolutely refused to be parted from his corpse. Dressed partly as a widow and partly as a nun, she set out in December 1506 to accompany Philip to his last resting place in the royal mausoleum at Granada.

Preceded by a magnificent hearse, drawn by four horses, surmounted by candles and tapers and accompanied by a retinue of priests and servants, she made her way to the south. At every stop (usually a wayside monastery), she had the coffin opened, the bands removed from her dead husband's face and feet so that she could kiss and fondle them. At Torquemada she had to stop in January 1507 to give birth to a posthumous daughter. She never resumed the journey to Granada, but she did wander from place to place, still with the coffin. Her travels now took place exclusively at night and her condition visibly deteriorated. She grew increasingly careless about

---

[1] She had on one occasion tried to disfigure one of his mistresses by attacking her with a pair of scissors. Fortunately she only succeeded in cutting off her rival's hair.

[2] Officially Philip died of a fever caused by drinking water after playing a game of pelota on a hot September's day. People then, and historians since, have suspected that he had been poisoned on the orders of his father-in-law. Certainly his death was very convenient for Ferdinand, who could then rule in Castile undisturbed, as Philip and Joanna's elder son, Charles, was only six years old.

her appearance and person, and became dirty in her habits. Finally her father prevailed on her to go and live in the small and remote Castilian town of Tordesillas on the River Douro, some twenty miles south-west of Valladolid.

There, in a building half palace half fortress, she lived in virtual seclusion for the next forty-seven years. From her windows she could look down at Philip's coffin at the convent of St. Clara opposite till at last her son, Charles V, persuaded her to have the body buried at Granada. The Emperor also managed to see that the unfortunate Infanta Catherine,[3] who had been with her mother since her birth, was given a proper education. For a brief moment Joanna emerged (not from her palace, but into politics) during the revolt of the Communes in 1520–1, but the rebels found her of little real use as she was clearly too feeble-minded even to be a satisfactory figure-head for their movement.

After the royal troops re-entered Tordesillas and drove out the insurgents, Charles V intensified the surveillance kept over his mother. To the end she remained violent and abusive to her servants, frequently tried to starve herself and refused to change her clothes or linen. But what gave greatest offence to her family were the anti-religious sentiments she developed as she grew older. However, finally, she was persuaded to be reconciled to the Church just before she died in April 1555 at the age of seventy-five.[4]

Her lack of self-control and her fits of unbridled rage were to appear again and again among her descendants and to prove a tragic legacy to the Habsburgs in Spain. Nowhere was this more obvious than in the case of Don Carlos. From his early years his violent temper and vindictive disposition began to cause considerable misgivings in his family. Both his grandfather and his father must have been reminded of the mad queen at Tordesillas. The Emperor Charles V, who saw Don Carlos for the last time as he passed through Valladolid in 1558 on the way to his retirement, was worried about him and thought that his aunt paid too much attention to the child's physical health and not enough to the formation of his character. He found him too wilful and headstrong.

---

[3] She remained, however, at Tordesillas till her marriage with John III of Portugal in 1525.

[4] Her grandson, Philip II, who was more sympathetic to her plight than his father, Charles V, sent the Jesuit, St. Francis Borgia, to be present at her bedside.

In 1559, when he was fourteen years old, Don Carlos attended his father's marriage to Elisabeth de Valois, the eldest daughter of Henry II of France and Catherine de Medici. At that time she was the same age as the young prince and had in fact at one time been formally betrothed to him. This had happened three years previously following one of the many temporary truces that punctuated the long struggle between France and Spain. Like most king's daughters, Elisabeth was simply a pawn in the diplomatic armoury of her country, and had at one time also been suggested as a bride for Edward VI of England. In 1559 the situation changed and Elisabeth's destiny with it, for France and Spain signed a definite peace treaty (at Cateau Cambresis) and through the death of Mary Tudor Philip once again found himself a widower. To cement the new agreement with France he decided to marry the young princess himself. Despite this inauspicious beginning and despite the disparity of age— Philip was eighteen years older than his new bride—it proved to be a happy, if shortlived, marriage. Although Elisabeth—or Isabella (of the Peace), as she was called in Spain—was unable to provide Philip with a male heir, he was grief-stricken when she died in October 1568, soon after giving birth to a third daughter who did not survive her. She was only twenty-three years of age.

It was natural in view of what happened to Don Carlos that many should try and find an explanation for his death in the supposed jealousy of father and son over a bride the age of the son and originally intended for him. She treated Don Carlos with sympathy to which, as he had never encountered much of it in his life, he responded with affection. But there was no suggestion of impropriety in her attitude. Indeed, at the bidding of her ambitious mother, she tried to interest him in her sister Marguerite or, failing that, in his aunt Joanna who, although she was his aunt and had brought him up, was considered to be a matrimonial possibility. She had just emerged from a brief and childless marriage with a prince of Portugal.

In 1560 Don Carlos was presented to the Cortes at Toledo as Prince of the Asturias and heir to the throne, and the next year he was sent to the university of Alcalá de Henares to complete his education. It was here that he had an accident which had the most serious affect both on his mind and his body. While he was on the way to keep a secret assignation with a college servant's daughter, with whom he was temporarily infatuated, he lost his footing and

accidentally fell downstairs and fractured his skull. He became critically ill and every expedient, both natural and supernatural, was tried out to cure him. He was bled and purged without any noticeable improvement and he even failed to respond to a trepanning operation performed by the distinguished Flemish surgeon Vesalius to relieve pressure on the brain. As a last expedient the dead body of St. Diego[5] was laid on the bed beside the unconscious patient and the saint's cold shroud was allowed to cover Don Carlos's face. This was the turning point in the prince's illness: the fever abated and from that time Don Carlos began to recover his strength.

Unfortunately the same could not be said of his mental powers. For, whatever was the state of his mind before the accident there is no doubt at all that thereafter his eccentricity became more marked and his vicious and uncontrollable temper more in evidence. Stories of his peculiarities, his sadistic attacks on courtiers, his nocturnal excursions through the streets of Madrid insulting young girls and beating up young men, and his strange physical habits (and probable impotence) fill the reports sent from the Spanish capital by Count Dietrichstein, the Imperial ambassador[6] and his Venetian colleagues. They also attracted the attention of casual visitors to Madrid such as the French writer, Brantôme. Moreover, the Venetian ambassador noted the growing antipathy between Philip and his son. Philip had up to now been a devoted, if disapproving, parent and had not left Don Carlos's bedside during the crisis of 1562 till the prince was on the way to recovery. But in 1563 he brought from Vienna his nephews Rudolf (later the Emperor Rudolf II) and Ernest (later Governor of the Spanish Netherlands), the sons of his cousin (and brother-in-law) the Emperor Maximilian II. Their conventional and virtuous behaviour was in sharp contrast to that of Don Carlos and should anything happen to him they were Philip's closest male heirs.

However, Philip did not yet completely despair of his son and in 1567, in the hope that perhaps some political responsibility might assist him, he appointed Don Carlos President of the Council of State.

[5] He had died at Alcala in 1463 and was canonised in 1588, mainly at the instigation of Philip II, who was grateful for the favour done to his son.

[6] Negotiations were afoot betwen Madrid and Vienna for a possible marriage between Don Carlos and his cousin the Archduchess Anna (1549–80), the daughter of the Emperor Maximilian II. Two years after the death of Don Carlos, Anna became the fourth wife of her uncle, Philip II, and was the mother of Philip III.

But this did not work out satisfactorily for, either out of ambition or from sheer contrariness, Don Carlos began to display a strong sympathy for the rebels who were challenging Spanish rule in the Netherlands. In fact he made it plain that he would like to go to the Netherlands as Viceroy to succeed Margaret of Parma [7] whose term of office was about to expire. There could, of course, be no question of entrusting so important a post to such a headstrong and unstable person, and Philip appointed the Duke of Alba to replace Margaret. Carlos's reply to this was an attempt to stab Alba when the duke came to take leave of him before taking up his new appointment. He told Alba that he would not suffer him to go and ruin a country so dear to him and then lunged at him with a dagger, but the duke seized him and held him so closely that the weapon was useless. Don Carlos then attempted to turn the tables on Alba by maintaining that it was the duke who was trying to assassinate him. This Philip refused to believe.

Don Carlos next planned to escape from Spain and wrote to certain grandees to tell them that it was his intention to go to Germany. On Christmas Day 1567 he spoke to his kinsman, Don John of Austria, [8] about this project and tried to enlist his support. Don John, after trying to dissuade the prince, passed the information on to Philip, who was spending Christmas at his newly built palace, the Escurial, twenty-five miles out of Madrid. The crowning folly—if we are to believe the French historian de Thou—came on the evening of the same day (Christmas Day), when Don Carlos confessed to the Prior of Atocha that he had resolved to kill a man. [9] The priest thereupon refused absolution and, by dint of further questioning, came to the conclusion that it was the prince's intention to murder the king. A message to this effect was duly relayed to the Escurial. There, in retreat—the Escurial is half palace and half monastery [10]—

[7] She was a daughter of Charles V by his Flemish mistress, Katharina van den Gheynst.

[8] He was an illegitimate son of Charles V and was later (1571) famous as the victor of the battle of Lepanto. He became Governor of the Netherlands in 1576 and died at Namur in 1578.

[9] de Thou got this information from his compatriot, Louis de Foix, the inventor and engineer who was one of the architects of the Escurial. Foix also said Don Carlos had asked him to design a book covered in steel and gold which could kill a man at one blow.

[10] Built in the shape of a gridiron in memory of the manner in which St. Lawrence had been martyred, it was part palace, part monastery, part church and part mausoleum.

the king, who never did anything in a hurry, spent the next three weeks considering what best to do. To do him justice he was not concerned about his own safety but rather about the effect of the prince's defection would have on Spain. The example of Louis XI of France,[11] who as Dauphin had fled from his father, Charles VII, whom he detested, to seek refuge at the court of the Duke of Burgundy (then France's most powerful enemy), filled him with the direst forebodings. Not that there was much similarity between Louis XI, who was to prove the ablest of the Valois kings, and the subnormal Don Carlos. Philip consulted his confessor, the Grand Inquisitor and some of the principal prelates and lawyers of the kingdom. Their advice, which survives in a document of one of them, the canonist Martin Azpilcueta ('Doctor Navarro'), was to urge the king to take any measures he thought fit to prevent Don Carlos from leaving the kingdom and placing himself at the head of the Flemish rebels—for both they and Philip felt that it was the Netherlands and not Germany that Don Carlos would make for—and perhaps provoking a civil war in Spain itself. So Philip took the reluctant decision to place his son under arrest.

The king returned to Madrid on 17 January 1568, and on the evening of the next day, while Don Carlos was asleep, his firearms were removed[12] and Philip, accompanied by his principal minister, Ruy Gomez de Silva, by the Duke of Feria (Alba's cousin) and other dignitaries and guards entered his son's room. When he awoke and saw his father, the prince is reported as having said: 'I am a dead man. Does Your Majesty wish to kill me?' and added, 'I am not mad, but reduced to despair by my sufferings.' The king is said to have replied, 'Calm yourself. I am not come to put you to death but like a father to bring you back to your duty', and to have reassured his son that what was being done was being done in the prince's own interest. But when Don Carlos saw his papers confiscated, his room stripped of all furniture save a single bed and mattress, bars put across the windows and guards stationed outside the door and he himself compelled to dress in funereal black, his rage and despair knew no

[11] Twice banished by his father, he finally fled to Burgundy in 1456 and remained there till Charles VII died in 1461.

[12] Don Carlos, among other things, suffered from a persecution mania and kept a veritable arsenal of weapons in his room, including two swords under his pillow and two loaded pistols by his bedside.

bounds, and he attempted to throw himself into the fire which burned on the open hearth, and had to be forcibly restrained.

Thereafter he disappeared from public view. He was held virtually incommunicado and apart from the king none of his family (not even his aunt Joanna with whom he had remained on reasonable terms) ever set eyes on him again. Six months later, on 24 July, it was announced from Madrid that he had died. Clad in a habit belonging to that St. Diego who had come to his rescue in 1562, he was buried, without the usual funeral sermon, in the convent of the Dominican nuns, El Real, at Madrid. Philip announced to the courts of Europe, and wrote personally to the Pope, that his son had died as a result of his own excesses.

This had a certain ring of truth about it, for the behaviour of Don Carlos in confinement was strongly reminiscent of that of his great grandmother, Queen Joanna of Castile, when she was detained at the castle of Tordesillas. The exact cause of death was said to be a malignant fever brought on by the prince's eccentric and intemperate habits. He appears to have tried to starve himself, confining his diet to ice water and then to have eaten one huge meal after another.[13] He also alternated between having his room overheated and then stripping off his clothes and lying down on the stone floor surrounded by blocks of ice. On one occasion he tried to set fire to his bed and there was something suicidal in his eating habits. Between them his doctor and his confessor were able to restore him to some kind of tranquillity so that he was able to prepare himself for his death and make his peace with God, if not with his father. They felt it inadvisable, however, that there should be a final confrontation between father and son. On the night before his death—he died at four o'clock the following morning—Philip did come to visit him, but as he was by then unconscious he was unaware of what was happening. Philip gave his son his blessing and withdrew weeping.

The imprisonment, in solitary confinement, and the mysterious death of the heir to the Spanish throne, caused a sensation in Europe. Speculation was rife and rumour had it that he had either been poisoned on his father's orders, or that he had been strangled, or even that his veins had been opened while he was taking a bath.

---

[13] Some years previously Dietrichstein had commented on his gluttony. Their protruding jaw is said to have made it difficult for some Habsburgs to masticate their food properly.

The death of his stepmother, the Queen of Spain, a mere three months later, though it was perfectly normal, served to increase gossip. It was remembered that she was the same age as the prince and had once been affianced to him. And so the life and death of Don Carlos became a favourite subject for fictional drama. The Englishman Otway (1651–85), the Frenchman Campistron (1656–1723), the Italian Alfieri (1749–1803) and the German Schiller (1759–1805) all found in him tragic inspiration.

Today his life and death raise two main problems—just how mad was he? and what part did Philip play in his son's death? Unfortunately it is not possible to give completely satisfactory answers to either of these questions.

It is clear from the evidence that Don Carlos was not mad in the sense of being a raving lunatic under perpetual restraint, but it is also equally clear that he was far from normal and was certainly totally unfit to control the destinies of Spain and her vast empire. He was obviously—to use a modern phrase—a very disturbed person, a psychopath. And as with many psychopaths his mental condition was not always apparent. In fact, once again to use a modern description, he had a split personality and was a schizophrenic. How far this was due to purely physical factors (such as he had inherited from his Spanish and Portuguese ancestors) and how far to psychological (the loss of his mother and the circumstances of his early upbringing) it is impossible to say. The study of mental abnormality is still in its infancy and even when in the past there is plenty of clinical evidence of insanity—as in the case of George III[14] for example—the exact nature of the malady is open to different interpretation. In the case of Don Carlos no such clinical evidence exists to help us.

Nor unfortunately have we Don Carlos's own defence of his actions. He was never brought to public trial and was never able to say anything on his own behalf. Philip entrusted the examination of his papers to a court presided over by Cardinal Espinosa, who was a state councillor, Grand Inquisitor and President of the Junta of Castile. In this court, the very existence of which Don Carlos knew nothing, the 'prosecution' was assigned to another member of the

---

[14] The latest medical research by Dr. Ida Macalpine and Dr. Richard Hunter ascribes the 'insanity' of George III to the disease of porphyria and traces the malady back to Mary, Queen of Scots—see *Porphyria, A Royal Malady*, 1968.

Council of Castile, Don Bribiesca de Mugnatones. The court, after
examining the prince's papers and interrogating witnesses, drew up a
report which found Don Carlos guilty of treason in that he plotted
to kill his father and to take over the government of Flanders. His
punishment was left to the king to determine. As the report was not
ready till July 1568 its value at once became purely academic, as
Don Carlos was already mortally ill. Thus no formal judgment was
ever arrived at and none was executed.

The only real victim of the report was the Baron de Montigny,[15]
who had been sent by the Flemish nobility to Spain in 1562 and again
in 1566 to acquaint Philip with their grievances. He was arrested in
Madrid a few months after the death of Don Carlos, was tried for
treason and was duly executed. No mention of Don Carlos was made
at Montigny's trial, but it was widely believed that the prince's papers
had revealed a connection between them. Among other things Don
Carlos, on the strength of his dislike of the Inquisition and his
sympathy for the Flemish insurgents, has been credited with 'liberal'
opinions, but his views on these, as on most other subjects, were
hopelessly disordered and incoherent. Even had he reached the Low
Countries it is highly doubtful if the rebels would have found in him
much more comfort than the communeros had found in his great
grandmother, Queen Joanna, in their hour of need.

The question of Philip's responsibility for his son's death is a complex one. Until January 1568 the king's conduct was correct and indeed without reproach, for in 1562, for example, when Don Carlos
was critically ill Philip had proved himself a devoted father and
stayed by his son's bedside till the boy was out of danger. Thereafter, though relations between them steadily deteriorated, they were
no worse than those existing between father and son in many other
cases. Since the time of David and Absalom there had been kings'
sons who had rebelled against their father. It is thus on Philip's conduct between the time of Don Carlos's arrest and his death six months
later that the king must be judged.

Philip clearly had to take action of some sort as he believed Don
Carlos intended to leave the country on 19 January. Some form of
detention was obviously necessary. But it would have been much
wiser either to have sent him to some distant castle, where like

[15] Floris de Montmorency, Baron de Montigny (1528–70) was a brother of the Count
Hornes whom, with Egmont, Alba had executed at Brussels, 5 June 1568.

Queen Joanna at Tordesillas he could have eked out his days in seclusion, carefully guarded but comfortably housed, under medical treatment if that were necessary, but accessible to members of his own family, or to have imprisoned him in some fortress where definite charges could have been brought against him in a proper judicial manner and justice could not only have been done but have been seen to have been done. To confine him to his room, strip it of its furnishings and allow no one to visit him save his guards, his accusers, the doctors, and the priests, was bound to raise the gravest suspicions as to Philip's motives.

Nor were these suspicions allayed when Philip announced that Don Carlos had died of his own excesses. Even the Emperor Maximilian II, who was Philip's cousin and brother-in-law and who was naturally concerned in the welfare of his relations in Madrid (especially as Don Carlos was his prospective son-in-law), confessed that he could not understand how these excesses could not have been controlled since Don Carlos was a prisoner in his father's hands. If Don Carlos's death was indeed brought about by his intemperate habits in the matter of diet, Philip can scarcely be acquitted of some of the blame. Even if it was difficult to prevent him from starving himself there was no need to provide him with copious draughts of ice water and allow him to consume immense meals. Inevitably there were those who suggested that Philip had used his knowledge of his son's gluttonous tastes to shorten the prince's life.

Philip might have escaped these suspicions but for his position and character. As leader of the Counter Reformation, as the patron of the Inquisition, as the oppressor of the Netherlands, as the man who sent the Armada to England and encouraged civil war in France, Philip had enemies all over Europe. But he also had them in his own country where his devious methods of government and his jealousy of his more gifted subordinates were resented. This was particularly true in the case of his half-brother, Don John of Austria, whose ability and gifts were freely used but distrusted by Philip. The king was said to have had a hand in Don John's death[16] and was certainly privy to the murder of Don John's secretary, Escovedo, who was murdered by hired assassins in the streets of Madrid.[17] Finally

---

[16] He seems to have died of peritonitis following a burst ulcer, but naturally poison was suspected.

[17] On the night of 31 January 1578, on the orders of Perez.

there was Philip's quarrel with his own Secretary of State, Antonio Perez, whom he suddenly arrested but who eventually managed to escape to reveal many of the king's secrets to the courts of England and France.[18]

One of Philip's troubles was that he had the mentality of a civil servant rather than that of a ruler and that he became absorbed in administration rather than in governing. His delaying tactics[19] concealed marked powers of dissembling which present him in an unfavourable light. For instance, the day of Perez's arrest he had worked all day with the king till 10 p.m. Philip then bade him goodnight and said he would see him in the morning. An hour later Perez was arrested. Similarly it was recalled that the very day Don Carlos was arrested Philip had gone to mass in a family party which included his son, Don John of Austria and his nephews, the Archdukes Rudolf and Ernest.

Such conduct is not endearing, but it does not necessarily make Philip a murderer. The Emperor Maximilian, who, in one way or another, knew all there was to know about Don Carlos, would scarcely have allowed his daughter Anna to become—as she did in November 1570—Philip's fourth wife. Before she died in childbirth in 1580 she bore Philip four sons, the youngest of whom, Philip (born 1578) survived to become Philip III. Of him his father is reported to have said: 'God, who has given me so many kingdoms, has denied me a son capable of ruling them. I fear that they will govern him.' Perhaps Philip was one of those fathers who would never have been satisfied with any kind of son he might have had. Philip himself lived on till 1598 when, after a long, agonising and putrefying disease, he breathed his last in the Escurial palace. Just how responsible he was for the tragedy that overtook his eldest son will always remain something of a mystery. The sins of the father were certainly visited on the third generation, Charles II of Spain, whose mental condition was little better than that of Don Carlos. There was no fourth generation, and on his death in 1700 the Habsburg kings of Spain came to an inglorious end.

[18] Arrested 28 July 1579, Perez escaped in 1591. He resided in London 1593–5 and died in Paris in 1611.
[19] 'Time and I will solve every problem', was one of his favourite expressions. Consequently there was a backlog of two years in much government business.

4

The Casket Letters

If England in the fifteenth century presented a picture of lawlessness, at times bordering on anarchy,[1] the plight of Scotland was far worse. For there the malady was much more deep-seated and was to last much longer.

The Scottish nobility were even more ambitious than their English counterparts and distinctly more lawless. Reinforced by the clan system which was not broken till after the Jacobite Rising of 1745, and divided by bitter feuds, such as that between the Douglases and the Hamiltons, their lives were consecrated to violence. The comparatively backward nature of the country, its almost complete absence of urban development and consequent lack of a powerful middle class left them in a position of unchallenged supremacy, while their wealth (far in excess of that of the Crown) and their armies of private retainers—the Earls of Douglas, for instance, rarely moved around with a retinue much under two thousand—gave them the status of semi-independent princes. And relations with England, punctuated as they were by constant border raids and frontier incidents, usually culminating in periodic invasions, only served to increase the atmosphere of endless crisis.

In this situation the monarch's position was never secure and Scottish rulers right down to the Gowrie Conspiracy in 1600 seem to have been a special target for violence and murder. Of Mary Queen of Scots' five immediate predecessors on the throne of Scotland only one, her father James V, died in his bed. James I, who had spent eighteen years as a prisoner in England—he had been captured by pirates while on the way to France to be educated there—was mur-

---

[1] The Paston and the Stonor Letters show, however, that the general population was less involved in the baronial disorders than might be supposed.

dered at Perth (1437) by a band of nobles led by his own uncle; James II, who had murdered the head of the Douglas family with his own hands, was killed by the explosion of a cannon while trying to recover Roxburgh Castle from the English (1460); James III was found murdered in a mill at Sauchieburn (close to Bannockburn) after a battle with his disaffected nobles, led by his own son (1488); James IV was killed by the English at the battle of Flodden (1513).

Between the accession of James I (1406) and that of Mary Queen of Scots (1542) only one reign, that of James IV, started without a regency. The minority or absence of their ruler provided the Scottish nobility with a golden opportunity to further their ambitions which they never neglected to seize, while the remarkable number of bastards fathered by Scottish kings—James IV had five illegitimate children and James V is credited with as many as nine—raised up a further brood of ambitious people anxious to carve out positions of power and influence consonant with their royal blood.

The Scottish nobility was a much smaller group than the English and much more closely interrelated. They enjoyed a monopoly of power and spent most of their time disputing it with one another. Treason, sedition, conspiracy, murder and assassination were an inseparable part of their way of life. It is against this turbulent background that we can best see and evaluate the reign of the only woman to occupy the Scottish throne—Mary Queen of Scots.[2] (See Table No. 6.)

Mary Queen of Scots is one of the best known and most controversial characters in history. To some—especially those fascinated by her beauty, her charm and her wit—she was the innocent victim of circumstances beyond her control and devised by the implacable malice of her enemies, to others she is little better than an adulteress and a murderess. In addition the Catholics have often saluted her as a martyr while the Protestants likened her to a whore from Babylon. The principal bone of contention between both sides has been the part she played in the murder of her second husband, Lord Darnley, and what credence, if any, can be given to the famous Casket Letters.

Before examining the problems raised by the Letters it is as well to

[2] One can hardly count Margaret, the Maid of Norway, who became Queen on the death of her grandfather, Alexander III, as she died as a child at Orkney (1290) while on her way to claim her inheritance.

recall the main events of her life. She was born in Linlithgow Castle on 7 or 8 December 1542, a fortnight after the English defeated the Scots at the battle of Solway Moss. She was the only child[3] of James V and his second wife, Mary of Guise. A week later her father died and she became Queen of Scotland, first under the regency of James Hamilton, 2nd Earl of Arran (who was next in line of succession) and then, in 1554, of her mother.

Her matrimonial future was settled the following July when the Treaty of Greenwich provided for her to come to England when she was ten years old and there, two years later, to marry Henry VIII's only son, Prince Edward. The English, however, were not satisfied that the Scots had any intention of carrying out this arrangement and so the prince's uncle, the Earl of Hertford (later Protector Somerset) was sent to harry and devastate the Lowlands. His decisive victory at Pinkie near Edinburgh in September 1547 alarmed the Scots and to prevent any possible English 'take over' they despatched Mary off to France to be brought up by her grandmother, the Duchess of Guise.

At the French Court Mary received an excellent education in the best Renaissance tradition and grew up to be one of the most accomplished women of the age. In April 1558 she married the Dauphin, and the sudden death of her father-in-law while jousting in July 1559 made her Queen of France as well as of Scotland. However, she did not long enjoy her new position, as her delicate young husband, Francis II, died of an ear infection in the December of the following year. As they had no children the throne passed to Francis' brother, Charles IX. He was only nine years old and effective power passed to his mother, Catherine de Medici, who now became Regent of France. Clearly there was no future for Mary in France and so she decided to return to Scotland, where her own mother, the Regent (Mary of Guise), had herself died in June 1560, leaving the country without any effective ruler.

Mary landed at Leith in August 1561. She was now eighteen years of age and faced with the task of governing the most factious kingdom in Christendom. There the situation was made worse in that, led by John Knox and aided by England, Protestantism had not only come to stay in Scotland, but had taken the form of extreme

---

[3] There had been two elder children but they died in infancy. James V left several illegitimate children—Lord James Stuart, afterwards Earl of Moray, who later played an important part in his half-sister's career was one of them.

Calvinism; religion now added a further complication to plague the rulers of Scotland. Mary's position was made even more delicate in that not only was she a Catholic but she was heir presumptive to the throne of England where her cousin Elizabeth was now ruling as the champion of Protestantism (see Table No. 7).

It was clear that a great deal of political wisdom was needed to deal with Scottish affairs, but unfortunately this was one of the qualities that the new ruler did not possess. It was also abundantly clear that, unlike Elizabeth, Mary required a partner to assist her to rule and ensure the succession. Having turned down Don Carlos of Spain (see Chapter III), an Austrian archduke and Elizabeth's favourite, Robert Dudley, she rather unexpectedly fell in love with her cousin Henry Stuart, Lord Darnley. He was a good-looking youth three years younger than her and, after her, next in succession to the English throne (see Table No. 7). They were married according to the rites of the Catholic Church in the chapel of Holyrood Palace on 29 July 1565.

For a time things went well and soon Mary became an expectant mother. Darnley was a Catholic, though not a very determined one, and the marriage provoked opposition from the Protestant Lords which, after a few skirmishes, resulted in a victory for Mary: the two principal malcontents, Moray and Arran, fled, the one to England and the other to France. Throughout these troubles, and for some time before, Mary had been taking the advice of her Piedmontese secretary, David Rizzio, whose qualities reminded her of the graces of Latin civilisation and the cultured life of the Renaissance. Close as was their relationship, there was nothing really harmful in it, but it did not strike Darnley in that light. He proved to be a jealous, arrogant, unstable person, who behaved more like a spoiled child than a grown man. In return for a promise of the crown matrimonial, which would give him royal power in her lifetime and real power should his wife die, he entered into a conspiracy with Moray, James Douglas, 4th Earl of Morton and other Protestant lords to get rid of Rizzio. The unfortunate Italian was dragged from the queen's presence and brutally stabbed to death by a host of assailants who took care to leave Darnley's dagger in the body. Mary, who was six months pregnant, never forgave her husband for what had happened, though she was careful enough at the time to win him back and force him to disavow his connection with the conspirators and betray them.

The birth of James VI in June 1566 made Darnley no longer necessary for any of her plans in the future.

Moreover, Mary had now fallen head over heels in love with James Hepburn, 4th Earl of Bothwell. He was far from being the bluff ruffian he is sometimes pictured as, but he was certainly passionate, masterful and vigorous, which neither Francis II nor Darnley had been. He had received a good education but was, first and foremost, a man of action. He was also reckless and foolhardy. Although a Protestant he was no friend of the English and had all the qualities to attract the queen. He was cordially disliked by many of his contemporaries, who did not hesitate to accuse him of witchcraft and sodomy. Just before Rizzio's murder he had married in a Protestant ceremony Lady Jean Gordon, who was a Catholic and a sister of the Earl of Huntly, and it was to Bothwell's castle at Dunbar that Mary and Darnley had gone to rally their forces against the conspirators.

After the baptism of his son in Stirling Castle in December 1566, Darnley, who had retired to Glasgow where the retainers of his father, the Earl of Lennox,[4] were strongly entrenched, fell ill—either of smallpox, or possibly syphilis. In January 1567 he was visited by Mary[5] where—if the Second Casket letter is to be believed—she complained of being almost killed by his breath although she was not sitting nearer to him than on a chair by his bolster and he was lying on the other side of the bed. His illness, whatever it was, only increased the loathing she now felt for him, but nevertheless she pretended to be fully reconciled to him and persuaded him to leave the Lennox stronghold and come to Edinburgh. He could not take up residence at Holyrood till he had been purged of his disease for fear of infecting his infant son, so it was arranged that he should be moved to Kirk o' Field, a house outside the city walls. They made the journey together, he on a horse litter with his face covered to hide the ravages of his complaint.

From time to time Mary stayed at Kirk o' Field, sleeping in a room below her husband's, but on the evening of 9 February she left the house to attend the wedding of one of her servants at Holyrood. While she was away, sometime about 2 a.m., the house was blown up with gunpowder (said to have been stored in the queen's room) and

[4] Lennox had a castle in Glasgow, close to the Cathedral.
[5] Mary had already had smallpox and was therefore immune.

the body of Darnley was found in the grounds, where presumably he had escaped, with marks on his throat suggesting strangulation.

Few murders in history have been so clumsily executed, and public opinion led to Bothwell's being arraigned before a court of his peers. His examination was a mere formality and he was acquitted. Actually any number of people were implicated in the elimination of Darnley and this is one of the reasons why the matter was never satisfactorily investigated or cleared up. The only ones punished were the agents who carried it out, the evidence against others more highly placed was simply suppressed.

There the matter might have rested but for Mary's determination to marry Bothwell. On 24 April, while returning from Stirling to Edinburgh, she was 'abducted' by Bothwell—with or without her consent no one knows—and taken as a 'captive' to Dunbar. They returned together to Edinburgh early in May and the next day Bothwell secured a divorce.[6] A week later Bothwell was created Duke of Orkney and on 15 May they were married in Holyrood Palace according to Protestant rites.

Mary's indecent haste to marry the man whom everyone regarded as her late husband's murderer provoked an explosion of wrath. The Confederate Lords led by Morton took the field against their sovereign and her new consort, and Mary was obliged to surrender to them without a fight at Carberry Hill near Musselburgh. Bothwell, who was allowed to escape, fled to the north, ultimately making his way to Denmark where he died, a prisoner and insane, in Dragsholm Castle in 1578. The Confederate lords then imprisoned Mary in the island fortress of Lochleven belonging to her enemies, the Douglas family, and where the mistress of the castle, Lady Douglas, was the mother of the Earl of Moray.[7] There, after a miscarriage, she is supposed to have given birth to dead twins. She was compelled to abdicate in favour of her son, James, and agree to the appointment of Moray as Regent.

[6] The confused religious situation in Scotland cannot be better illustrated in that Bothwell, a Protestant, secured an annulment of his marriage (on grounds of consanguinity, although a dispensation had been issued to cover this) from a Catholic court, on 7 May, while his wife, a Catholic, got her divorce (on grounds of her husband's adultery with one of her maids) from a Protestant one two days previously. She died in 1629, having married two further husbands.

[7] Margaret, daughter of James, 5th Lord Erskine. She had been the mistress of James V. Her husband, Sir Robert Douglas was killed at the Battle of Pinkie.

Mary spent a year Lochleven, but finally, in May 1567, with the help of Sir George Douglas, the younger brother of her captor and another member of the clan, Willie Douglas, [8] she managed to escape. Eleven days later her forces were decisively defeated at the battle of Langside, near Glasgow, and she fled across Solway Firth to Cumberland and threw herself on the mercy of Elizabeth. In England she remained in captivity, constantly shifted from one castle to another for twenty years till she was executed at Fotheringay in Northamptonshire in 1587.

Elizabeth's position was delicate. She did not approve of subjects deposing their rulers, but if she helped Mary to regain her throne she would alienate the Protestants in both kingdoms and perhaps drive Scotland once again into the arms of France. So she decided, as usual, to temporarise and suggested a Commission made up of Englishmen, led by the Duke of Norfolk, to enquire into the conduct of Moray and his associates who were to send representatives to state their case. Mary was also to send delegates to safeguard her interests. This mixed Commission met first at York in October 1568 and was later transferred to Westminster. What was meant as an enquiry soon turned into what was virtually a trial of Mary, for Moray's representatives accused her of complicity in Darnley's murder and produced the famous Casket Letters to prove it.

These had come into the hands of the Earl of Morton in June 1567 —conveniently enough a few days after Mary's surrender at Carberry Hill—when one of Bothwell's valets, Geordie Dalgleish, was arrested and was found to have in his possession (under his bed) a small silver gilt box which was locked. Before forcing the lock Morton took the precaution of summoning six witnesses, three Catholics (the Earls of Atholl and Home and Lord Sempill) and three Protestants (the Earls of Mar and Glencairn and Crichton of Sanquhar). The casket was found to contain eight letters, some poems and a few legal documents. These were what Moray's men showed to the English commissioners in York in December 1568, eighteen months later. They remained in Morton's possession till just before his death in 1581,[9] and were then taken by one of his servants to

---

[8] He remained with her till after the collapse of the Ridolfi plot in 1571 when he was sent back to Scotland and there executed.

[9] Morton, who was Regent of Scotland from 1572 to 1578, was overthrown by the intrigues of James VI's favourite, Esmé Stuart and executed on a charge of being privy to Darnley's murder.

William Ruthven, Earl of Gowrie, who with his father[10] had taken a leading part in the murder of Rizzio, and was in turn executed in 1584 following an attempt to seize the person of James VI in an affair known as 'The Raid of Ruthven'. From that time they disappeared altogether and have never been seen since. It is generally supposed that they came into James's possession and that he destroyed them.[11]

Thus the originals of the Casket Letters do not survive and cannot be subjected to modern examination. It is clear that they were written in French and have certain French phrases and idioms,[12] which have been literally translated into English, but only make real sense in the original language. The Scots, of course, had their own version in their own tongue, and when at last Moray produced the Casket Letters in their original form in December 1568 English translations were made (often hastily) in some cases direct from the French and in some cases from the Scots. Copies of the French originals can be found in the Calendar of Hatfield Manuscripts and copies of the English translations can be consulted in the State Papers related to Mary Queen of Scots in the Public Record Office. There were also French re-translations, such as those later produced by the Huguenots.

The English and Scottish versions differ in certain particulars and there appear to have been omissions, due either to haste and careless-ness on the part of the copyist or deliberate falsification. None of the letters bears any date or place of origin—except Letter I, which ends 'From Glasgow this Saturday Morning' (which may well have been a subsequent clerical interpolation)—and none of them is signed. They vary greatly in length—the most important of them, Letter II, runs to three thousand, one hundred and thirty-two words—while some of them are quite short (Letter VI is only two hundred and seventy-seven words). They are not necessarily arranged in chrono-logical order, as Letter I looks as though it may well have been written after Letter II. Although declared by their producers to be in

---

[10] After Darnley's murder he fled to England, where he died a few months later.

[11] This must inevitably give rise to the belief that James thought they were genuine.

[12] Such as the frequent use in the Scottish version of the word *summa* (translated into English 'to be short') which clearly derives from the French words *en somme*. Also the curious expression used in Letter II: 'I have taken the worms out of his nose' better rendered by the Scots: 'I have drawn it all out of him' must be the French idiom 'tirer les vers du nez'. When Mary was in captivity at Bolton Castle during the conference at York she writes to her commissioner, Leslie, Bishop of Ross, using the identical words: 'tirer les vers du nez' to describe an attempt by the English statesman, Sir Francis Knollys, to discover what was really in her mind.

Mary's handwriting, this cannot be proved. The Italian hand used by Mary was easy to forge, as one can see from genuine letters written by her to Elizabeth. The letters also vary considerably in style and content. They are nevertheless letters of a woman passionately in love and willing to risk all for her beloved.

Letter I reproaches her lover for not writing and says that she will 'bring the man Monday to Craigmillar'[13] and adds that 'he is more gay than ever you saw him; he puts me in remembrance of all things that may make me believe he loves me'. This is usually thought to refer to Darnley, but if, as is possible, the date and place were added subsequently by another hand, it could equally apply to a visit made in January 1567 by Mary to Stirling to see her son James.

Letter II, the longest and easily the most important of the whole collection, reports the author's journey to Glasgow, notes how well Darnley, whom she describes as 'this pocky fellow', is informed of what goes on at court, speaks of his desire for her pardon and a resumption of their proper married life. She tells Bothwell that Darnley spoke so well and so humbly that had she not had 'a heart as a diamond' she would have been obliged to take pity of him. She confesses that she does not like dissembling and that she 'do here a work that I hate much', that she cannot sleep for the thought that she might be in her lover's arms and tells him to 'burn this letter, for it is too dangerous'. She says that she is 'the most faithful lover that ever you had or shall have' and that he can rest assured that she will bring Darnley back with her. Neither Darnley nor Bothwell is specifically named in the letter, but it is easy to identify them both.

Letters III, IV and V, written in a totally different style, could be the letters of any woman passionately in love with a man and jealous of his every movement. Letters VI and VII have echoes in them of Mary's abduction by Bothwell and the pardon he can expect to receive for advancing himself in this way, with a warning to be more circumspect and to make sure of the (Confederate) Lords and see that he is free to marry. Letters VIII bids him to be certain that his forces are superior to those of the Earl of Sutherland (the husband of Bothwell's divorced wife) and could refer to events either before or after the confrontation at Carberry Hill.

On the face of it these letters are enough to establish the guilt of

[13] This was the place first decided on to bring Darnley to: it was later changed to Kirk o'Field.

Mary, who must have been aware of the conspiracy against Darnley and who led him from Glasgow to Edinburgh, where his murder could better take place. Whether she knew any of the details can never be established. Clearly Elizabeth and her Council felt she was guilty. They realised that, rightly or wrongly, her character was now irreparably ruined, but even so they were not prepared to subscribe to the new and dangerous doctrine that subjects could at will sit in judgment on their rulers. Thus when the Commissioners reached their final conclusion in January 1569—they could no longer go on because Moray was obliged to go back to Scotland—they devised a compromise formula whereby Moray and his associates were acquitted of all treasonable and disloyal actions against their rightful sovereign, but the charges against Mary were held to be not proven nor to warrant Elizabeth's withdrawing her confidence from her 'dear sister'. All the same Elizabeth still declined to meet Mary and kept her in captivity till at last events—in the form of a series of plots of mounting gravity—compelled her to send the Scottish queen to the block.

In the whole affair of the Casket Letters, which remains an unsolved mystery, it must be said that most of Mary's Scottish accusers were themselves deeply implicated in the plot to remove Darnley (though not to promote Bothwell to his place), and that in the eighteen months during which they had custody of the letters they had ample time to alter, falsify or even forge them. Mary was never formally tried, never had the opportunity of confronting her adversaries or cross-examining them and was badly served by her own commissioners[14] who were some distance from where she was compelled to stay.

Nevertheless it was Mary's action in bringing Darnley from Glasgow to Edinburgh that brought about his death. She was clearly aware of the plot against him; how far she was an accessory before the fact must remain an open question. No more information is to hand in 1968–9 than there was in 1568–9.

[14] Professor J. E. Neale in his *Queen Elizabeth* (Jonathan Cape, 1934) says of the Bishop of Ross, one of Mary's commissioners and then her ambassador, that he 'told a servant of Elizabeth's that Mary was not fit for any husband; "for first, he saith, she poisoned her husband the French King, as he hath credibly understood; again she hath consented to the murder of her late husband, the Lord Darnley; thirdly, she matched with the murderer!" . . . "Lord, what a people are these; what a Queen, and what an Ambassador!" the Englishman exclaimed' p. 173.

5

The False Dimitrys

THE period of history from the death of Feodor I, the last Tsar of Muscovy of the House of Rurik, in 1598, and the election of the first Romanov Tsar, Michael, in 1613, is usually referred to by Russian historians as the Time of Troubles. This phrase was invented before they had any experience of what the Revolution of 1917 was to do for them.

The person indirectly but really responsible for these troubled years was Ivan IV, the Terrible, who reigned as Tsar of Muscovy from 1533 to 1584. Abroad he added to Russia the vast lands of the Middle Volga region from Kazan to Astrakhan, and obtained the first foothold in Siberia, and at home he successfully asserted the complete ascendancy of the Crown over the landowning nobility (the boyars). He not only exchanged the title of Grand Duke for that of Tsar, but he was also the first Russian ruler to call himself Autocrat of all the Russias, a title his successors bore till 1917, to emphasise that he owed his power to himself alone and to no one else.

But he was a cruel as well as a licentious man and at times little short of a homicidal maniac. He established his rule on the blood of others. After the defection of Prince Kurbsky[1] Ivan instituted a veritable reign of terror. Hundreds of thousands of people (sixty thousand in the city of Novgorod alone) were done to death. Some were merely executed, some hanged, some flogged or beaten to death, some strangled (including the Archbishop of Moscow who ventured to protest at this blood bath), some forcibly drowned, others were impaled or disembowelled: the lucky ones got off with imprisonment or exile. Torture was freely used with every sadistic practice that the imagination could devise. The instruments of these 'purges' were

---

[1] He was one of Ivan's leading generals, who deserted to the Poles in 1564.

45

the Oprichniki, a sort of Praetorian Guard who were recruited from the lowest stratum of the population. They enjoyed a privileged existence and were rewarded with lands and treasure—usually at the expense of the boyars.

Revered by the Bolsheviks for his stern measures against the boyars, Ivan may very well have served as a model for Stalin. Both illustrate Lord Acton's famous dictum that all power tends to corrupt and absolute power corrupts absolutely.

Although married no less than seven times, Ivan only had issue by his first two wives and his last. By his first wife, Anastasia Romanov, to whom he was passionately attached and whom he playfully called his 'little heifer', he had six children, but only two survived—Ivan, the Tsarevich, and Prince Feodor. The second marriage, to a Circassian princess, produced only a son who died in infancy: the seventh, to Maria Nagaya, resulted in 1583 in the birth of a further son, Dimitry.

Prince Feodor was reputed to be simple-minded,[2] but the elder boy, Ivan (born in 1554), was both healthy and intelligent. He was a close and faithful associate of his father, who regarded him as his heir,[3] and played his part in the country's affairs, in so far as the Tsar permitted anyone to share his authority. He apparently accepted his father's activities without question and was present, for instance, at the sack of Novgorod in 1569. No one could question his loyalty to his father: in fact on him the real hopes of the dynasty rested.

These hopes, however, were doomed to disappointment, for one day in November 1581 a sudden altercation between father and son resulted in the Tsarevich's death. The Tsar had gone to visit his son in the latter's apartments and heated words were exchanged between them. Ivan flew into a sudden rage and struck his son with the iron-tipped staff that he always carried about with him. Boris Godunov, at that time Ivan's principal favourite, tried to intervene, but this only provoked the Tsar further and he struck the young prince a second time, this time on the head. There are two versions as to the cause of their quarrel. One view is that the Tsarevich asked if he could lead an army to relieve the fortress of Pskov, which for the last

---

[2] Some historians have suggested that this was a pose on the prince's part to avoid sharing in his father's way of life.

[3] By Ivan's will, dated 1572, the younger Ivan was nominated his successor.

three months had been besieged by the Poles, and that it was this implied criticism of the Tsar's leadership that sparked off the quarrel. Other historians, however, maintain that the Tsar criticised the dress of his daughter-in-law, who was expecting a child, as immodest and that the young Ivan resented this and said so. As soon as he saw what he had done the Tsar's mood changed and he did everything he could to save his son's life. He sent for doctors and, meanwhile attempted to staunch the flow of blood himself. He dropped down on his knees and begged his son's forgiveness. This the young Ivan, who had not lost consciousness, readily gave, but unfortunately a mortal blow had been struck. Four days later, despite every medical care, he was dead. A fit of temper caused the age-old dynasty of Rurik to be threatened with extinction.

At first Ivan, full of remorse, gave way to the most extravagant displays of grief[4] but gradually he recovered his vigour and energy. His seventh marriage provided him with another son—Dimitry— and he even made overtures to Queen Elizabeth to receive the hand of Lady Mary Hastings, who through her mother, Katharine Pole, was a descendant of Edward IV's brother, the Duke of Clarence. Fortunately for Lady Mary, who was terrified at the prospect of becoming the wife of such an ogre, the proposal came to nothing and she was able, as a spinster, to live out her life in undisturbed tranquillity. Eventually, however, his debaucheries caught up with him. He died—probably of syphilis—in March 1584.

As the late Tsarevitch Ivan, although married three times, had no children the successor was Ivan the Great's elder surviving son, Feodor, who had been born in 1557. Feodor took no interest in politics, indeed little in the world itself, for his sole passion was for church ritual and his favourite pastime was campanology. Although married—to a sister of Boris Godunov—Feodor had no children save a daughter who died when she was two years old and he was quite content to leave affairs of state to his brother-in-law. His heir was his half brother Dimitry, who had been born in 1583.

On the death of Ivan the Great his widow, Maria Nagaya, and her son, Dimitry, retired to the small town of Uglich on the Volga some eighty-five miles north of Moscow where they had an estate. Here in May 1591 Dimitry is said to have died in a rather mysterious fashion.

---

[4] He was completely unrestrained in his behaviour at his son's funeral and had to be forcibly separated from the coffin.

He was an epileptic and while playing with a knife in the courtyard of his mother's house he had a fit, cut himself badly and bled to death. His death meant that when Tsar Feodor died the direct line of the House of Rurik would come to an end. To escape responsibility for this his mother and his governess blamed some other boys with whom he happened to be playing. An enquiry, conducted by Prince Vassili Shuiski, himself a collateral descendant of Rurik and a future Tsar, established the true facts, but as these were never published the child's death was attributed by many to the machinations of Godunov, who stood to gain most by it. For when Feodor died in January 1598 it was Godunov who became Tsar. Others, however, preferred to think that it was one of the other children who had died at Uglich and who had been passed off as the dead prince. The Tsarevich, so they averred, had escaped his 'murderers' and was still alive.

Meanwhile, of course, Godunov reigned in the Kremlin. He was of a family of Tartar origin and had served his apprenticeship under Ivan the Terrible. He had married a daughter of Ivan's favourite, Malyuta Skuratov, and his sister had been the wife of Tsar Feodor. He is perhaps best remembered by most people today as the hero of Pushkin's play and Mussorgsky's patriotic opera: Chaliapin was singing in this rôle in 1917 when the mob broke into the Opera House and compelled him to sing the Red Flag. Boris was able but completely unscrupulous and soon made plenty of enemies. It was inevitable that sooner or later he would be challenged by someone claiming descent from the dynasty of Rurik which had ruled in Russia since the ninth century. And the mystery surrounding the death of Prince Dimitry was bound to encourage any adventurer who wished to claim the throne.

The first serious challenge came in 1603, when a young man did emerge to declare that he was the missing Dimitry. Briefly his story was that in the confusion that reigned at Uglich immediately after his 'death' he had not been mortally wounded and that he had been rescued and another child substituted in his place. He had been educated in a monastery and after the death of his rescuer and benefactor had stayed on there till he had made his way to Poland. He never claimed to have much personal recollection of his early childhood and his account was made plausible in that it was known that four days had elapsed between the date of his 'death' and the arrival of Shuiski's commission from Moscow. It was also known that during these four days there had been an outbreak of mob violence at Uglich and that several people, including some of the children playing with Dimitry, had been killed. It was therefore possible, since Shuiski could not have had much idea what Dimitry looked like,[5] to have substituted for the funeral the body of another child. It was also known that the Tsaritsa Maria had retired to nurse her grief and took little interest in the practical arrangements for her son's burial. She does not even seem to have been examined by Shuiski's commission.[6]

In 1603 the 'dead or missing' Dimitry was living as a servant in the household of a Polish nobleman, Prince Adam Wisniowiecki, and it was here one day that he revealed to his master his real identity and declared himself to be the Tsarevich supposed to have been killed at Uglich in 1591. Prince Adam, who had recently lost some of his lands in the Kiev area to Russia, was not only impressed by this claim but saw in it an opportunity to recover his estates. Poland had recently made peace with Russia, but there were plenty who, like Prince Adam, were only too anxious to renew hostilities. This was particularly true of the Palatine of Sandomierz, George Mniszech, whose eldest daughter was married to Prince Adam's cousin, Prince Constantine Wisniowiecki. It was at Mniszech's castle that Dimitry met his future bride, Marina Mniszech. The ready and promised help of the disaffected Cossacks of south Russia, who were only too willing to strike a blow at the central government in Moscow, made Dimitry's cause seem promising. Mniszech passed him on to the Papal Nuncio, who in turn brought him to the notice of the king (Sigismund III). Converted to the Catholic faith, he was backed by the Jesuits who saw in his candidature the possibility of converting Holy Russia to the Roman faith and thus undoing the schism of 1054.

Sigismund allowed him to equip an army in southern Poland and in October 1604 Dimitry invaded Russia. Many people flocked to his banner, but after some initial successes he was soundly defeated at Dobrynichi in January 1605: it looked as though Godunov would have no difficulty in retaining his throne. But in April 1605 quite suddenly, soon after a meal and not without suspicion of poison, Boris died. He had not had time to found a dynasty. His son Feodor

[5] Dimitry was only six months old when his father, Ivan IV, died and had soon after gone to live at Uglich.
[6] She was later forced into a monastery, probably on the orders of Godunov.

II was only sixteen years old and his widow, who was remembered as the daughter of Malyuta Skuratov, Ivan the Terrible's blood-thirsty favourite,[7] was Regent. There was a steady defection of ambitious courtiers to Dimitry, who now moved on to Tula. Two months later Feodor II and his mother were treacherously murdered in their apartments in the Kremlin:[8] the way to Moscow now lay open. Ten days later Dimitry was installed in the Kremlin in their place. The Tsaritsa Maria was brought out of the monastery, where she had been confined for the past fourteen years, and declared that Dimitry was in fact her long lost son, and on 21/31 July the new Tsar was crowned by the Patriarch in the Cathedral of the Assumption.

Dimitry ruled for scarcely a year, but during that time he displayed exceptional energy and intelligence combined with progressive ideas and a generous disposition. At home he stood up to the boyars, befriended the serfs (whom he even thought of emancipating), while abroad he toyed with the idea of leading an international crusade against the Turks. But what makes him an interesting and unusual figure is that he behaved rather like a character from one of the novels of Dostoievsky. He not only rewarded his friends but his enemies as well. When for instance the Shuiski family conspired against him he not only forgave them but restored them to favour. He appears to have hated bloodshed, cruelty and violence. In this respect as in many others he was considerably in advance of his age. He was a welcome contrast both to his 'father' and his predecessor.

But his position was from the beginning quite hopeless. He had forsaken the Orthodox religion of his forefathers and become a Catholic and he was no sooner established in Moscow than he sought to bring there as his bride another Catholic and a foreigner to boot. For while he was in Poland he had become affianced to George Mniszech's daughter, Marina. They were married by proxy at Cracow in November. The ceremony was a Catholic one performed by the Bishop of Cracow (Cardinal Maciejowski) and attended not only by the Catholic king of Poland but by the Papal Nuncio. In May 1606 Marina arrived in Moscow, accompanied by a large retinue of priests and by still more Poles. Dimitry had already scandalised his subjects by bringing with him some Jesuit fathers, and this fresh influx of heathens, as the Orthodox population regarded them, was watched

---

[7] He had strangled the Archbishop of Moscow with his own hands.
[8] Godunov's daughter was compelled to become a nun.

with mounting hostility. The couple were then married according to the Orthodox rites and Marina was crowned as Tsaritsa. However, both she and her husband undid any good this conformist behaviour might have had by not taking the Holy Communion customary on such occasions.

Marina was a staunch Catholic but Dimitry seems to have had ecumenical ideas. He numbered both Lutherans and Unitarians among his friends. The people of Moscow on the contrary were extremely bigoted. To them the Orthodox faith was the only faith and religious tolerance had no place in their hearts, and any deviation was not to be thought of. Combined with a rabid xenophobia this made them a dangerous element. They were already alienated by Dimitry's free and easy ways, his western ideas and his friendship with foreigners. It was not difficult to convince them that the 'Tsar' was an arch heretic and this is what the self-seeking and ungrateful Shuiskis did. A week after Marina's enthronement a mob stirred up by them broke into the palace, which they sacked, stripped Dimitry of his robes, beat him and then hacked him to pieces with every refinement of indignity and cruelty. His body, which bore twenty-one wounds, was thrown down into a courtyard and then taken to the principal square for everyone to see. There, with the corpse of Peter Basmanov, one of his principal counsellors who had carried the orb at Marina's coronation,[9] the body lay in the open for three days to be abused by anyone who cared to defile it. Finally it was burnt on a pyre outside the city walls and the ashes, mixed with gunpowder, were fired from a cannon pointing in the direction of the heretical country (Poland) from which he had come. This was thought to be the best way of laying his ghost.

Some two thousand other people, mainly Poles, Germans and other foreigners, were killed as the infuriated mob rampaged through the streets of the city. Marina, on the other hand, was let off with a short period of imprisonment and then told she could go back to her native country.[10] Prince Vassili Shuiski, who had engineered the coup against Dimitry, now took his place as Tsar. He was a lineal descendant of Rurik and now confessed that he had only pretended to believe Dimitry was Ivan IV's son in order to use him to rid the country of the tyrannical Godunov.

---

[9] Basmanov had played a leading part in deserting the Feodor II for Dimitry.
[10] Possibly to avoid reprisals from Poland.

Who was Dimitry? There is little doubt that Dimitry himself believed he was the person he claimed to be: there is no hint in anything he said—even as he was being mortally wounded he still reiterated his claim—or did to make anyone believe to the contrary. His beliefs, however, do not constitute proofs.

As to his 'mother', it is doubtful if she could recognise in the Tsar of 1605 the child of 1591 unless, as seems unlikely, she had from the beginning been a party to his escape from Uglich and was aware that the child buried there was not her son. She was still in the prime of life and may well have welcomed exchanging a life of monastic seclusion for the splendours of court existence. She outlived the deposition and death of Shuiski to die in July 1612.

Mr. Philip Barbour, in a new and fascinating biography of Dimitry,[11] mentions seven possibilities for Dimitry's identity, but inclines in the end to the traditional view that he was a member of the Otrepyev family, who were small landowners in Galich.

A certain Youri Otrepyev, who was a member of the minor nobility, had taken the name of Grigori (Grishka) when he entered the religious life in the Chudov monastery in the Kremlin. Many of the details of his life are obscure, but he seems to have spent a good deal of time in the household of various boyar families, notably the Romanovs who had supplied Ivan IV with his first wife. About 1600, possibly as the result of some indiscreet and treasonable words, he was either expelled from his monastery or ran away. He fled to Poland where officially he disappears from history. Boris Godunov certainly thought Dimitry was Grigori Otrepyev and this supposition might help to explain the otherwise odd fact that the Pretender should first declare himself in Poland. Although a servant there—a valet—Dimitry was an educated man, a fine horseman and a person of natural dignity. Contact with the Romanovs may have given him some insight into court life, while his monastic experiences, if they were disagreeable, may account for his conversion to Catholicism. But in the end he must remain something of an enigma.

Dimitry had not long been dead before a second pretender appeared. The second Dimitry, because he established himself in the village of Tushino, just outside Moscow, is often called the Thief or Brigand of Tushino. His real identity is a complete mystery and his

[11] *Dimitry, Tsar and Great Prince of All Russia, 1605–1606*, by Philip L. Barbour, Macmillan, 1967.

claims to be the missing Tsarevich did not deceive anyone: although once again there were those who found it convenient to accept him at his face value. He contrived to kidnap Marina as she was on her way back to Poland and she obligingly declared that he was her husband. As, however, she went through another marriage ceremony (privately) with him to quieten her conscience, not much store can be set by this identification. Soon after, a son was born to this marriage. The second Dimitry, like the first, enjoyed the support of the Don Cossacks and of the Poles and for a time his cause prospered, notably in the south. But his murder in December 1610 by one of his servants while he was out hunting put an end to his career. After a series of adventures his 'widow' was re-captured by the authorities in Moscow and brought back there. Her four-year-old son was publicly hanged and she was confined to a prison in Kaluga where she died soon afterwards.

No sooner was the second Dimitry gone than, in the spring of 1611, yet a third appeared. His real name was probably Sidorka and he was a former deacon from Ivanograd. With the help of the Cossacks he installed himself in Pskov—he is sometimes called the Thief of Pskov—but he only lasted a year when he was betrayed, taken to Moscow and in May 1612 executed.

Meanwhile the wretched Vassili Shuiski who had dethroned the first Dimitry, ruled miserably in Moscow, controlled by a small clique of boyars, while most of the country was occupied either by the Poles or the Swedes. The anarchy and confusion continued after Shuiski's deposition and death (in Warsaw) in 1612, and the Times of Troubles did not come to an end till 1613 when the young Michael Romanov—he was born in 1596—who was a great nephew of Anastasia, Ivan IV's first wife, was chosen as Tsar, and a new dynasty came into being. His father, Philaret Romanov, was the actual head of the family, but as an ecclesiastic he was automatically excluded from secular rule. He had been made Archbishop of Rostov by the First Dimitry and promoted to be Patriarch by the Second Dimitry. The Romanovs were held in high esteem because they had been unjustly oppressed by Boris Godunov whose reign had ushered in the disorders of the last two decades and they were additionally popular in that they were closely connected with the sacred line of Rurik and represented a guarantee of continuity with the past. Their descendants held the throne till the Revolution of 1917.

C

6

The Tsarevich Alexis

THE first three Romanov Tsars, Michael III, 1613–45, his son Alexis, 1645–76, and his grandson Feodor III, 1676–82, were men of mediocre ability, but Feodor's youngest brother, Peter I, was a person of very different calibre.

At first he had to share his authority with an elder half-brother, Ivan V (see Table No. 9), and, as Ivan was only sixteen years of age and Peter only ten, the real ruler was Alexis' daughter Sophia, who acted as Regent till 1689. In that year, however, Peter, who was now seventeen, was able successfully to challenge this arrangement and overthrow Sophia and relegate her to a monastery where, as Sister Susanna, she eventually died in 1704. Ivan V lived on till 1696 but was a mere cipher, and although he had five children they were all daughters. Thus, to all intent and purposes, Peter was the sole ruler of Russia from 1689 till his death in 1725.

A man of great physical strength and boundless energy, he was equally capable of days of prolonged hard work and nights of unbridled debauchery. Essentially a man of action, he was as much at home on the battlefield as in the council chamber. He was coarse in his manners, profligate in his life and united the same sort of ability and cruelty that had characterised Ivan the Terrible. His love of buffoonery might at times disguise but could never conceal his utter and complete ruthlessness. He was not only determined to brook no rivals in Russia but to make his country's influence felt all over Europe. His two consuming ambitions were to modernise his country by sheer force and bring it into line with the rest of Europe and to break the power of Sweden and, if possible, of Turkey, Russia's two neighbours, which blocked the country's expansion in the north and in the south. The Black Sea was a Turkish lake; the Baltic a Swedish one. Russia's only port was Archangel, which was ice-bound in winter. Peter's passion was the sea and at one time he worked as a common labourer in the dockyard at Zaandam in Holland and that of Deptford in England.

A war with Turkey in 1696–7 gave Russia the port of Azov at the head of the Azov Sea, but Russia had to wait for the reign of Catherine II before she was able to get possession of the north coast of the Black Sea. But on the other hand the long Northern War 1700–21 with the great victory over the Swedes at Pultava (1709) added Karelia, Ingrelia and Esthonia and Lithuania, which gave Russia her coveted access to the Baltic.

Peter the Great's visit to the West took place in 1697–8, and he was away from Russia for eighteen months. He visited Germany, Holland,[1] England and then finally Vienna.[2] His visit to England, which included a visit to the Houses of Parliament, a review of the fleet, the award of an honorary doctorate of laws at the University of Oxford, and a sitting to Sir Godfrey Kneller for his portrait, is illustrative of Peter both at his best and his worst. At his best was his determination to extract from his stay everything that could be extracted, as can be seen in his interviews with such people as Bishop Burnet, William Penn the Quaker and the Astronomer Royal. At his worst was his complete abandon to excessive drinking,[3] his gluttony[4] and his lechery. While working at the Royal dockyard at Deptford he was lodged at Sayes Court, which the government requisitioned for the purpose. It belonged to the famous diarist, John Evelyn, who had let it to Admiral Benbow. As the Admiral was away on active service at the time it was vacant. As a result of Peter's tenancy the house suffered such damage—to the windows and the woodwork on the inside and to the garden outside where Peter and his companions drove wheelbarrows through Evelyn's priceless box hedges—that the Treasury was obliged to commission Sir Christopher Wren to go down there and assess the damage in order to compensate the unfortunate owner.

[1] William III was at the time ruler of Holland and England.
[2] He had originally intended to go to Venice, whose maritime traditions attracted him, but the revolt of the Streltsi recalled him to Russia.
[3] He was in the habit of taking a boat from Greenwich to a tavern near the Tower of London which later became known as the 'Czar's Head'. A public house of that name existed on the same site till the blitz of 1940–1 when it was destroyed.
[4] When he stayed at an inn at Godalming on the way to review the fleet at Portsmouth, he consumed enormous quantities of food.

His wars and visits abroad gave Peter little opportunity—had he had the inclination which he had not—for family life.

A few months before he overthrew the Regent Sophia he had married, at the age of sixteen and a half, Eudoxia Lapoukhin, the daughter of a Muscovite boyar family. The bride, who had been chosen for Peter by his mother, the Tsarevna Natalia, was pleasant to look at, affectionate and not unintelligent. But she was a few years older than Peter, completely inexperienced, and by outlook and up-bringing—she had been educated in a convent—rigidly conventional and even conservative in her attitude to life. She was attached to the traditional ways of life and had little hope of coping with a man like Peter.

From the first he neglected her and almost immediately after the marriage returned to his bachelor quarters and to his boon companions, male and female, who were usually recruited from the lowest stratum of society. He was more interested in sailing ships on Lake Pereslavl and preparing his military forces than occupying himself with her. They cohabited—if it can be called that—for less than four years, and after his mother's death in 1694 he gave up any pretence of living with her.

There were three children, born between 1690 and 1693, but only the eldest, Alexis, survived infancy. On his return from his European tour in 1698 Peter took the opportunity of a rising of the reactionary forces in the country,[5] in which members of the Lapoukhin family were deeply implicated, to get rid of her permanently. She was divorced and confined to the Pokhrovsky monastery at Suzdal, some seventy miles from the capital, where she was made to take the veil. Peter had never been faithful to Eudoxia, but after their divorce he made no attempt to control his sexual appetites. He had a series of mistresses till finally he became so attached to the last of them, Catherine Scavronska (later Catherine I), a Lithuanian laundress of doubtful origin and even more doubtful morals, that he married her. Between 1707 and 1718 she bore him eight children.[6] They were privately married in 1707 and five years later she and Peter went

[5] Led by the Streltsi, Moscow's permanent garrison, who had placed Sophia in power. They were now severely dealt with, and after a further revolt in Astrakhan in 1705 Peter disbanded them altogether. They tried to play the part in the seventeenth century that was successfully adopted by the Imperial Guard in the eighteenth.

[6] Of these only two daughters survived, the Tsarina Elizabeth and Anna Duchess of Courland, the mother of Peter III.

through a public ceremony in the Church of St. Isaac in St. Petersburg. She was crowned Empress in May 1724, nine months before Peter's death. She was a woman after Peter's own heart, who could endure the hardships of military life and not only share his bed but share his bouts of drinking, his practical jokes, but could also participate whole-heartedly in all the brutish revels of his court. Before she had met Peter she had been the mistress of his favourite Menshikov, and like Menshikov had come up the hard way.[7] She may have looked like a German comedy actress, as Frederick the Great's waspish sister, the Margravine of Bayreuth, said she did but she was also a woman of considerable ability. Between such a person and her timid stepson there could be little sympathy or understanding.

Eudoxia's son, Alexis, had been born in February 1690. He spent his childhood with his mother and her Lapoukhin relations and scarcely saw anything at all of his father. Then in his ninth year he was abruptly taken away and entrusted to the care of Peter's youngest sister, Natalia, who had always disliked his mother. He was now to be educated in the way his father wanted. However, his first tutor, Prince Wiasemsky, had been appointed before Eudoxia's divorce and he continued the child's education along the lines of strict Muscovite orthodoxy despite the fact that he now had to make regular reports to the Tsar. If anything, he increased the growing gulf between father and son. His interests were almost exclusively theological and in Alexis, who remained devoted to him throughout his life, he found a willing and apt pupil.

When Peter at least realised what was happening, he replaced Wiasemsky by a German, Baron Heinrich von Huyssen.[8] The latter was a cultured man and he gave the prince a sound education in the classics and in foreign languages, with the result that Alexis was able to speak French, German and even Italian with tolerable ease. But he was a delicate boy and a very indolent one. He only became proficient in those subjects he really liked and had little powers of concentration and a strong aversion to any sustained effort. Thus he made no progress in mathematics or the practical sciences and still less in carpentry and engineering, despite the fact that his father always held these to be the most important part of a prince's make-up. Alexis

---

[7] Menshikov, who later helped to procure the succession of Catherine after Peter's death in 1725, started life as a vendor of meat pies in the gutters of Moscow.

[8] Originally appointed in 1703 he retired in 1705 but was recalled in 1708.

hated everything connected with war or violence and detested the sea. In him the Lapoukhin blood seemed to triumph and, in so far as he resembled any of the Romanovs, it was his grandfather and name-sake, the devout and gentle Tsar Alexis, who provided the model.

Moreover, his early years with his mother and her relations, all of whom were bitter opponents of Peter's westernising reforms and strong partisans of the old order, left an indelible impression on his mind. He remained in clandestine correspondence with his mother at Suzdal as long as he could and at least on one occasion went to see her. It is probable that Eudoxia had confided her sorrows to her son and to some extent poisoned the boy's mind against his father. Such a burden could well adversely affect any young child and quite early on Alexis, who was now obliged to share his life with his father, learned how to practise deceit. It is indeed possible that some of his indolence and also his dilatory nature, which increased with the years, were yet another result of his predicament. For all his life long he sought to escape the pressures put upon him. A stronger character might have profited from such experience and won through to a greater self-reliance. But not so Alexis: he was not built that way. Instead he sought consolation in drink—the only vice he really shared with his father—and a life of mild dissipation.

He still saw little of his father, whose sudden and occasional de-scents upon the Tsarevich's household terrified everyone and none more so than Alexis. As time went on Peter became more and more disquieted by the development of his son's character. He was com-pletely unimpressed by Alexis' intellectual attainments and distrust-ful of the influence of the young prince's companions. He would have preferred to send Alexis abroad to study western civilisation at first hand, but the long Northern War prevented this. As it was, he hoped to correct Alexis' obvious shortcomings by initiating him into the art of war and the serious business of governing an empire.

In 1702, when he was only twelve years old, Alexis had been taken to Archangel, Russia's only port, to see how important sea power was for Russia's future. The next year he had to join a military camp as a private to participate for a short time in the discipline of military life, and in 1704 he was made to go to Narva on the Baltic coast and watch the Russians besiege the Swedish garrison there. Three years later when the Swedes had penetrated deeply into Russian territory Alexis was entrusted with various military tasks in Moscow (which had to be put into a state of readiness to cope with a possible Swedish attack) and in the South of Russia, and he was allowed to be present at the meeting of the country's ministers. Partly because of ill-health, but partly because he clearly had no aptitude for military affairs, he took no part in the great victory of Pultava (1709)—which was the Stalingrad of the early eighteenth century and marked the end of Sweden as a Great Power.

Later the same year Peter, who was a great believer in what the West had to offer, ordered Alexis to go to Germany and become a student at Dresden.[9] Alexis, who was dismayed at the prospect of spending time in an infidel city away from the ministrations of the Orthodox Church, managed to put off the project till 1710, when at last he was obliged to go. He hated every moment of his enforced exile and refused to profit by it. Next Peter thought that a foreign princess, uncontaminated by Muscovite ideas, might help and so Alexis was married off in October 1711 at Torgau on the River Elbe, where Peter's ally, the King of Poland (and Saxony) then had his military headquarters. The bride was the seventeen-year-old Princess Charlotte of Brunswick-Wolfenbüttel, whose elder sister was married to the heir to the Holy Roman Empire, the future Emperor Charles VI. The young couple then had to trek from one military camp to another, as Peter insisted on his son's being present at the military operations then in progress in Pomerania and Mecklenburg.

Charlotte, who submitted to her fate with Christian resignation as befitted a princess married for reasons of state, did her best to make Alexis a good wife. But the Tsarevich was not greatly interested in her and did not hesitate to show it.[10] He increased his drinking habits, which now had a decisive hold on him, and installed his mistress, Eufrosina, a Finnish serf, originally belonging to his friend and erstwhile tutor Prince Wiasemsky, under the same roof. Her misery was not decreased by her eventual journey to Russia to find her destination was the new city of St. Petersburg, then, apart from a few modest houses, little better than a collection of mud huts in the middle of a swamp.[11] To emphasise her isolation Alexis took himself

[9] This was the capital of Peter's ally, the Elector of Saxony, who was also King of Poland.

[10] She was a Lutheran and Alexis regarded this with horror.

[11] In the winter of 1712–13 Charlotte fled back to her home in Brunswick and it took all Peter's powers of persuasion to induce her to go to Russia.

off—on grounds of health—to Karlsbad[12] for six months, despite the fact that his wife was eight months pregnant, and while he was away he never bothered to communicate with her at all. When he returned he found that he was the father of a daughter, Natalia.[13] A year later, in October 1715, a son was born, the future Peter II. Unfortunately, nine days after his birth, Charlotte—still only twenty-one years of age—died. To do him credit Peter, who was ill at the time, bestirred himself to visit his daughter-in-law on her deathbed and showed her much more affection than did her husband.

Eight days later, Peter's second wife, Catherine, gave birth to a son, who was also named Peter. These two births meant that Alexis, although still heir to the throne, was no longer indispensable for the continuance of the dynasty, and could, if necessary, be by-passed in favour of either of the two infant Peters.

Peter, who was much upset by Charlotte's death, took the occasion to address to his son a long letter reproaching him with his behaviour and commanding him to turn over a new leaf and either take some interest in military and public affairs or be cut off as 'a gangrenous limb'. To his chagrin Peter received a reply in which Alexis confessed that he was unequal to the tasks set before him and would be quite willing to renounce the throne if Peter so desired. Peter, disgusted that anyone should be prepared so light-heartedly to renounce his inheritance, then sent a further letter making it quite clear that if Alexis were not to succeed he need not think that he would be allowed to retire into comfortable seclusion but instead would be required to go into a monastery as a monk.[14] He then visited Alexis, who was pretending to be ill in bed, and gave him some six months grace to think things over. Peter made it clear that he expected Alexis to join him in his projected invasion of Sweden and give him his answer then. Throughout these interchanges Alexis had discussed his every move with his friends—the long beards, as Peter contemptuously called them.[15] It was part of Alexis' tragedy that through temperament

---

[12] Alexis had first gone to Karlsbad for health reasons while he was at Dresden and it was there that he had first met Charlotte.

[13] She died in 1728, at the age of fourteen.

[14] This was an occupational hazard for all unsuccessful Russian rulers, male and female.

[15] The day after his return from the west Peter had commanded the Muscovites to shave off their beards and had himself taken part in the execution of his ordinance. The clergy and the conservatives bitterly opposed this measure and took pride in

and circumstances he became the focal point of all the opposition to Peter's policy of reform at home: his associates all hoped for the day when Anti-Christ, as they stigmatised Peter, would at last die and Alexis rule in his place. He would then be able to restore the old Russia, the Russia of before 1689.

His principal adviser was a certain Alexander Kikine who, although he had been promoted by Peter to be secretary of the Admiralty, was underneath an implacable enemy of the regime.

Alexis' counsellors all advised flight before the six months was up and after some delays the Tsarevich, accompanied by his mistress Eufrosina (disguised as his page), her brother and three servants, set off for Germany. On the pretext of joining Peter, who was then at Lübeck in Mecklenburg, they left for Riga in September 1716. From Riga Alexis made his way secretly to Vienna, where he turned up two months later, to seek asylum with his brother-in-law, the Emperor Charles VI.

Later in the evening of 10 November the Imperial Chancellor, Count Schönborn, was surprised to receive a visit from a distracted and almost hysterical young man who said he was the Tsarevich of Russia. The Court of Vienna, both on grounds of relationship and humanity, were disposed to listen with sympathy and they were not unmindful that the presence in Austria of the heir to the Russian throne might well prove to be of considerable diplomatic value. Therefore, after a brief stay outside the capital, Alexis was conducted to the remote and impregnable fortress of Ehrenberg in the Tyrol.

It took Peter and his agents five months before they discovered where Alexis was, but in April 1717 Rumiantzev, who was the Captain of Peter's guard, managed to track him down. Peter then made representations to the Emperor for his son's return. By this time the Empress, who remembered the way Alexis had treated her sister, and the Emperor's ministers, who were scandalised by the presence of Eufrosina (whose disguise by now had been penetrated), had adopted a much more reserved attitude to their guest. The Court of Vienna was by no means anxious to risk an open breach with St. Petersburg, so to gain time they advised Alexis to go to Naples (then Austrian territory), where he would be safer till matters could be sorted out.

There, in the Castle of St. Elmo, overlooking the famous bay,

retaining their beards—which they could do under payment of tax—as a protest against such westernising apostasy.

Alexis spent the next six months, and in many ways these were probably the happiest months of his life. He had no responsibilities, he had Eufrosina and he had the Mediterranean sun.

But Peter, who was deeply offended by the turn of events, was determined to get Alexis back to Russia. As his principal agent he sent Count Peter Tolstoy[16] to achieve this end. The Emperor allowed Tolstoy to go to Naples and deliver a letter from Peter to his son, but, to salve his conscience, insisted that the prince must be free to make his own decision. Tolstoy, by bribery, threats and cajolery, managed to persuade Alexis that the Emperor was about to withdraw his protection (which was not altogether true), that the Tsar was about to invade Austria and come and claim Alexis by force (which was even less true) and that the Viceroy of Naples, Count Daun, had received instructions from Vienna to remove Eufrosina, which was again not true. Alexis was intelligent enough to see that his cause was probably lost but still felt that he was in a position to bargain on the terms of his return. Finally he extracted from Tolstoy a promise that he would be allowed to marry Eufrosina and retire to one of his estates in the provinces if he went back to Russia. Tolstoy, who had not the actual authority to do so, nevertheless gave the necessary guarantee. He was able to quote Peter's original letter (dated from Spa 22 July) which read: 'If you will submit, you may hope all things from us, and by divine justice I swear that no punishment shall await you; on the contrary, all my affection will be restored to you if you will only obey me and return.' The rest of the letter made it clear that if Alexis did not come back he would be treated as a traitor and treated without mercy.

So on 14 October the party left Naples. Eufrosina because of her health—she was pregnant—travelled separately and in a more leisurely fashion. The journey took some four months, but at last on 31 January Alexis arrived in Moscow and was lodged in the Kremlin. There on 3 February father and son confronted one another for the first time for over a year. There in the presence of the Notables of the city Alexis was made to sign an Act of Renunciation and swear to accept his half-brother—Peter, the son of Catherine Scavronska—as the new Tsarevich and ultimate successor. Alexis was formally pardoned, but only after agreeing to supply the names of all his accomplices and sympathisers. The next day, the 4th, he was given a

[16] An ancestor of the famous nineteenth-century writer.

long questionnaire requiring him to name all who had helped him to flee and those with whom he had been in correspondence with since he left Russia.[17]

Alexis, still trusting that all would turn out well for him, gave the necessary information, with the result that some fifty people were promptly arrested and put in gaol. A sort of inquisition was instituted which followed the pattern later copied by Stalin in the Great Purges. Torture of one sort or the other was freely used and the victims were invited to denounce others who in turn implicated more people. Eudoxia was fetched from Suzdal where it was discovered that so far from living modestly as Sister Helena she kept considerable state, was prayed for as the Tsaritsa and behaved accordingly. Also she had a lover, Stephen Glebov, a major of the Imperial Guard. Peter did not take his revenge on her personally beyond sending her to a remote convent on the shores of Lake Ladoga.[18] Her immediate associates were not so fortunate. Glebov, after torture, was impaled on a gibbet in the Red Square at Moscow. He took three days to die and was several times visited by Peter who enjoyed taunting his victim. Sister Capteline who had acted as a go-between for Eudoxia and Glebov, and Eudoxia's sister, Princess Troiekurov, were stripped and flogged in the presence of a jeering audience of soldiers. Her friend the Bishop of Rostov, who had once prophesied that Eudoxia would again occupy the throne, was solemnly unfrocked, then broken on the wheel and finally beheaded.

Most of Alexis' close friends suffered death in some form or other. Kikine, who had escaped to St. Petersburg, was brought back by Menshikov, tortured and then cruelly put to death. Alexis' valet was executed and a host of people were tortured, beaten and either killed or sent to Siberia. Neither age nor sex was allowed to interfere with the sentences. A few escaped comparatively lightly like Wiasemsky, for example. He defended himself with unexpected vigour, was acquitted and merely exiled to Archangel. Some were incredibly hardy, such as Prince Stcherbatov who, despite the fact that he had his nose cut off and his tongue pulled out by the roots, somehow survived to end his days in peace as a monk.

---

[17] Such as any Orthodox priests who may have given him the sacrament.
[18] Catherine I transferred her to the fortress of Schüsselburg where she lived in pleasanter circumstances. Peter II, who was her grandson, allowed her back to Moscow, but she preferred in the end to retire to her former convent where she died in 1731.

After this holocaust at Moscow Peter returned to St. Petersburg. There on 30 April he had an interview with Eufrosina who by this time had come back and been arrested. In return for her life she was induced to betray her lover and give the Tsar a full account not only of Alexis' movements but all he had ever said by way of criticism of his father and the present régime, and to provide him with the names of all those both in Russia and abroad whom Alexis had either seen or written to. Alexis was then brought to the Peterhof Palace and confronted both with Eufrosina and her disastrous revelations.[19] She told Peter that it was the intention of Alexis when he came to the throne to destroy St. Petersburg and make Moscow the capital once again and to disband the fleet. Alexis' behaviour at this point strongly reminds one of people caught up in a similar situation in a modern totalitarian state. He readily confessed to these new 'crimes' and seemed to take an almost masochistic pleasure in doing so.

The next few days Alexis was frequently interrogated—Peter entrusted this task to the wily Tolstoy who had ensnared Alexis at Naples—and made to confess to further indiscretions. He had to answer a fresh questionnaire which among other things demanded a list not only of those who had helped Alexis in the past but also those in the kingdom on whose support he was relying to place him on the throne. When he had got what he considered sufficient evidence of the Tsarevich's treasonable intentions Peter issued a manifesto to the leaders of the Church asking them what he should do with a rebellious son like Alexis who was bent on playing the part of an Absalom.

The bishops, however, were not anxious to take the responsibility for condemning Alexis and returned an equivocal answer, pointing out that while there were plenty of Old Testament precedents for any severity Peter might care to mete out there was also the example set by Christ in the Parable of the Prodigal Son.

Alexis was then formally arrested and placed in a dungeon in the fortress of St. Peter and St. Paul,[20] and on the 17th he was brought before the High Court which was made up of the Senate and most of the Notables of the kingdom. It was in no real sense a trial but

[19] She disappears from history at this point and seems to have been the only person who got off scot free. Nothing is known of her child by Alexis. Even his birthplace is not known for certain.

[20] This was one of the first buildings Peter had erected in St. Petersburg. It was part fortress, part palace and part prison. Later it was to be a prison for Dostoievsky and Bakunin and the place where Lenin's brother was executed.

simply a means of giving legality to what was a foregone conclusion. The hundred and twenty-seven people making up the court acted both as judge and jury and the verdict was reached by vote. On 24 June they voted unanimously condemning Alexis of having conspired against his father and been in treasonable contact with Russia's enemies abroad; they then condemned him to death.

Meanwhile, on 19 June in the Troubetzkoy Bastion of the fortress[21] where Alexis was confined, the Tsarevich had his first taste of torture. He was given twenty-five lashes with the knout and was confronted with his former confessor, Jacob Ignatiev, who had received many letters from Alexis when the latter was abroad. On the 22nd Peter sent Tolstoy to see Alexis and to ask him—no torture was to be used on this occasion—why he had so opposed his father and why he had been so obstinate. Alexis' reply was revealing. He ascribed his downfall to his early years spent exclusively with women and priests and his early initiation into debauchery. He recalled the well-known incident when in answer to his father's request for certain plans to be drawn up which Alexis knew that he was incapable of providing, he had taken a pistol and shot himself in the right hand so that he could have an excuse for his failure. On the 24th Alexis received a further fifteen strokes of the knout and was told of the death sentence pronounced by the Court. On the 26th Peter, accompanied by Tolstoy, Menshikov, Golovkin,[22] Rumiantsev and others, again went to see Alexis, and he was again tortured. Peter was with him from 8 a.m. to 11 a.m. and then left. In the early evening between 6 and 7 p.m. the Tsarevich died. Indeed, considering his frail physique and poor health it was a miracle that he had survived so long. The next day Peter informed the Russian diplomatic representatives abroad that his son had died of apoplexy, but after the attack he had regained consciousness, confessed his sins, asked for forgiveness and had made a Christian end.

This was not the opinion of the Diplomatic Corps in St. Petersburg. Pleyer, the Austrian Minister—and he had been in St. Petersburg for over twenty years—said Alexis had been killed with either a sword or an axe (decapitated) while the Dutch Minister reported that to hasten the end and on his orders Peter's minions had cut the

[21] The Fortress of St. Peter and St. Paul had eight such bastions, most of them named after Russian families who had served Peter well.

[22] The Imperial Chancellor whom Alexis blamed for his marriage.

Tsarevich's veins and let him bleed to death. Neither Pleyer nor de Bie (the Dutch Minister) were eye-witnesses, but no one could acquit Peter of some blame. It was said that he had taken an active part in the torture of Alexis on the last day of the Tsarevich's life and clearly he was anxious to avoid the public execution demanded by the High Court.

Alexis was buried on the 30th. As a traitor he could not be buried inside the church proper and yet as a royal prince he could not be buried outside. As a compromise he was buried in a spot under a staircase leading to the belfry. No one will ever know how exactly he died and what part, direct or indirect, Peter played in the final drama. Alexis' death remains an awful lesson on the dangers inherent on neglecting one's children and then suddenly demanding that they resemble the pattern laid down by the parent. There is for the psychologist a terribly modern ring about this awful story.

7

Peter III and Pugachov

PETER THE GREAT's murder of his son Alexis had many, if at the time unforeseen, results for the Romanov dynasty, and almost equally harmful for Russia was his unstatesmanlike decision, taken four years later, to alter the law of succession to enable a ruler to nominate his successor. Until Tsar Paul re-defined the succession in 1797 in terms of primogeniture the Russian throne remained an open prize to be taken possession of by palace revolution or by *coup d'etat*. For the most part, whoever controlled the principal guard regiments was likely to emerge the victor. Thus between Peter's death in 1725 and Paul's accession in 1796 Russia had seven rulers—Catherine I, Peter II, Anna, Ivan VI, Elizabeth, Peter III and Catherine II—and in no case did the succession follow any established pattern.

Despite his ukase of 1722 Peter the Great died without nominating a successor, but with the help of Menshikov, Tolstoy and other of her husband's friends and cronies, his widow, Catherine I, was able to seize power. She had been publicly crowned as Empress eight months before Peter's death and she seemed the best guarantee of a continuation of his policy. However, worn out by her debaucheries, she died two years later. The crown then reverted to Peter II, the only son of the ill-fated Alexis. He reigned only three years and died of smallpox on the eve of his marriage. With him the male line of the Romanovs came to an end. His closest relatives were the children of Peter the Great and Catherine I. Originally there had been eight of them but only two—both daughters—survived infancy. The elder, Anna, who had renounced her rights on marrying the Duke of Holstein, had died in childbirth in 1728, the younger, Elizabeth, was just over twenty years of age. But the Golitzin and Dolgoruki families—Peter II was to have married a Princess Dolgoruki—who were in control at the time, passed her over in favour of Anna, Duchess of Courland, a daughter of Peter the Great's half-brother, Ivan V (see Table No. 9). Anna, who ruled from 1730 to 1740, was childless, and so on her death there was once again a succession problem. She had used her right of nomination to choose as successor her great nephew, Ivan VI, a prince of Brunswick, who was only two months old. To act as regent she designated her much disliked favourite, Biron. The Russians, who looked askance at Biron as a German and the son of a stable boy, soon sent him packing to Siberia and Ivan's mother, Anna Leopoldovna, assumed control. However, she was also heartily disliked as a foreigner, and as she possessed no ability whatsoever it was not difficult for Elizabeth, Peter the Great's only remaining daughter, who did possess ability and who had won over the Preobrazhenski Guards, to dislodge her. Anna Leopoldovna and her husband, who had been kidnapped from their beds at night, were eventually exiled to a remote fortress near Archangel,[1] while the infant Ivan, who was separated from his parents, was deposed after a reign of fifteen months and imprisoned on his own. His final place of incarceration was the grim fortress of Schlüsselburg on the shores of Lake Ladoga, some twenty miles east of St. Petersburg. There he was kept in solitary confinement in an inner bastion, separated from the rest of the fortress by a moat. It was forbidden to refer to him by name and he was just called the nameless prisoner. Like the unfortunate Earl of Warwick (see page 21) his whole life was spent in confinement. He spoke slowly and with apparent difficulty and struck the few who ever saw him as little better than a simpleton. He had received no education and his world was bound by the four walls of his lonely cell. Nevertheless he remained a focal point of conspiracy for the disaffected.

His end, when it came in July 1764, was something of a mystery. There was, among the guards in the outer fortress at Schlüsselburg, a certain Lieutenant, Mirovich. He came of an aristocratic but impoverished family from the Ukraine and found himself seriously in debt with little prospect of ever extricating himself from his plight. But some chance remarks caused his thoughts to turn to another guardsman, Grigori Orlov, who had also once been just as humble and obscure a soldier as himself, but who, by seizing his opportunity to help place Catherine II on the throne, had become one of the richest

[1] Anna Leopoldina died there in 1746. Her husband survived till 1775.

and most powerful men in the kingdom. What Orlov had done for Catherine II, Mirovich could do for Ivan VI. But gradually a project undertaken for self-advantage became a sort of crusade and Mirovich felt that he had been chosen by God to restore to his throne the rightful Tsar. And so, in the early hours of a July morning, Mirovich attempted to put his plan into effect. Having won over some of the guards and overcome the Governor of the fortress, Mirovich and his companions crossed over to the inner fortress. Here at first they met with some resistance but before long they were allowed in, and there in his cell they found Ivan VI already dead. At the first sound of the attack the two guards watching over him had plunged their swords into the body of the sleeping prince, who, mortally wounded, expired almost immediately. So perished the unfortunate ex-Tsar in his twenty-fourth year. He had never even seen Mirovich or known of his existence, let alone been privy to any conspiracy to secure his freedom. He was quietly buried in the grounds of his fortress prison, as Catherine could scarcely have risked a state funeral in the Cathedral of St. Peter and St. Paul. Ivan's only crime was that he had a better claim to the throne than anyone else. The official explanation that he had died as the result of an accident deceived no one. Ivan's death, like that of Peter III two years previously, was so convenient for Catherine that rumours of her complicity abounded. Mirovich was brought to trial and publicly executed, and though he took all the blame for what had happened people were not convinced—especially as the two guards who had actually killed Ivan, so far from being punished, were rewarded.[2]

The Tsarina Elizabeth, who reigned from 1741 to 1762, never married[3] and she adopted as her heir her nephew Peter, Duke of Holstein, who had been born in Kiel in February 1728. He was brought to St. Petersburg in 1742, made to give up his Lutheran faith to be baptised in the Orthodox Church and to relinquish his claims to the throne of Sweden.[4] Then he was married to Catherine, a princess of Anhalt-Zerbst, who had been chosen for him by Elizabeth. He was seventeen years old at the time and she was sixteen. They were second cousins, for the bride's mother also belonged to the

[2] Ivan's two brothers and two sisters were deported to Denmark in 1780, where their aunt Juliana was queen.

[3] Not officially, though possibly morganatically.

[4] Inherited from his paternal grandmother, who was a daughter of Charles XI of Sweden.

Holstein-Gottorp family and was a first cousin of Peter's father. They had in fact met once before when they were both young children. They had not liked one another much then and their mutual antipathy grew rapidly after their marriage.

Peter had had the most unfortunate upbringing. He had lost his mother at birth and his father, who neglected him, died when he was eleven years old. His early education and upbringing was entrusted to a Swedish major, who took a sadistic delight in bullying his defenceless pupil. As he was an only child Peter had no one to give him any affection or to share his hardships. So then and throughout the whole of his life he sought the company of domestics and persons of low degree. His life was rigidly regimented and, although he thereby imbibed a love for all the *minutiae* of military life, he grew up to be deceitful, lazy, cruel and cowardly. He remained an immature child, whose favourite pastime was playing with toy soldiers or even dolls. Prussian militarism attracted him and ultimately Frederick the Great became his real hero. There was little of the Romanov about him save a love of crude practical jokes and a certain ability, inherited perhaps from his grandfather, Peter the Great, to play the buffoon.

Catherine[5] was altogether different. A woman of marked intelligence and character, she was both able and ambitious. Adversity, of which she was to see quite a bit before she became Empress, so far from breaking her served to spur her on. She had an inborn capacity for rule combined with the talent necessary to place her in a position to do so.

For about nine years the marriage was not consummated—owing to psychological rather than physical difficulties on the part of Peter—but at last in 1754 a son, Paul, was born in the Summer Palace at St. Petersburg. The infant was immediately taken away by the Tsarina Elizabeth to be brought up by her. And the same fate overtook their other child, a daughter who was born in 1757.[6] Thus Catherine was deprived of the joys of motherhood and her emotional energies turned elsewhere. There has been some doubt as to the parentage of both these children and some have believed that Paul's father was

---

[5] Her baptismal names were Sophie Auguste Friederike, but these were exchanged for Catherine Alexeievna when she was received into the Orthodox Church prior to her marriage.

[6] This child died when she was fifteen months old.

Catherine's first lover, Saltykov (see page 96) and that the daughter was her child by Stanislas Poniatowski, who succeeded Saltykov in her favour.[7]

After Paul's birth Peter and Catherine more than ever went their separate ways. Peter became progressively more pro-German in his outlook, preferring to wear the uniform of Holstein to that of Russia and openly favouring Prussia with whom Russia was then at war.[8] He also took to drinking more heavily and becoming more violent, while, to humiliate his wife, he indulged in a series of trivial affairs with certain ladies at the Court. These gave him little sexual satisfaction but pandered to his perverse sense of humour.

These were also difficult years for Catherine, for she had to contend not only with the caprices of her husband but also the jealousy of the Empress who saw in her a potential rival. But they also were fruitful years as well, for she learnt all there was to learn about human nature, came to understand her adopted country and how to rule it, and made friends in important places.

In December 1761[9] the Tsarina Elizabeth, after suffering a stroke, died and Peter III became Emperor. His first act was to desert Russia's allies, Austria and France, and make peace with Prussia, thus in the nick of time saving from probable ruin his old idol Frederick the Great.[10] He withdrew the Russian troops from East Prussia and offered Frederick not only eternal friendship but a military alliance as well. His next act—and this did win him some friends— was to exempt the Russian nobility from their obligations of service, both military and civil, which Peter the Great had imposed upon them. However, the advantages of this in terms of personal popularity were cancelled out by the hostile attitude he adopted to the Church. Despite his conversion to Orthodoxy he remained a Lutheran at heart and he took every opportunity to display his contempt for the Russian Church. Not only did he himself behave outrageously at such services as he attended, but he was also responsible for a series

[7] He was elected King of Poland in 1764.

[8] The Seven Years War, 1757–63.

[9] 25 December 1761 Old Style, or 5 January 1762 New Style. Till the Revolution Russia continued to use the Julian Calendar whereas the rest of Europe had gone over to the Gregorian.

[10] His position was desperate. He was threatened on all sides and much of his country occupied by the enemy. Hitler spent his last days in the Bunker at Berlin reading Carlyle's *Life of Frederick the Great*, hoping for a repetition of some such miracle—this time from the west.

of decrees affecting their privileged position (such as planning to build a Lutheran Chapel in the palace and relaxing the measures against the Old Believers), their services (restricting the type of icons they could use) and even announcing his intention of secularising (i.e. confiscating) some of their vast wealth.

But it was the army even more than the Church that was the real pillar of Tsardom and it was here that Peter made his worst mistakes. The army did not relish being put in German uniforms, drilled in Prussian fashion and placed under the command of Holsteiners, but it was not this that brought them to the point of mutiny. What really outraged them was Peter's proposal to form a new Guards' regiment made up exclusively of Germans and other non-Russians. At one stroke this would put an end to the privileged position occupied by the four existing guards' regiments—the Preobrazhenski and Semenovski (raised by Peter the Great) and the Ismailovski and Cavalry Guards formed by Tsarina Anna. It was these regiments above all others who had decided the destiny of the Russian throne for the past fifty years.

Had Peter been a different sort of man, less unstable and less neurotic, he might have been able, like his grandfather (Peter the Great), to overcome all opposition. Instead he spent his time preparing for a war against Denmark,[11] which no one wanted, and flaunting before everyone his mistress, Elizabeth Vorontsov,[12] who became such an inseparable part of his life that many feared he intended to put Catherine away and marry her instead. Even so, there might perhaps have been no serious conspiracy against him but for the fact that in Catherine there existed an obvious practical alternative to his rule.

This was a difficult time for her, not only because of the many indignities she had to put up with at the hands of Peter and Elizabeth, who did not hesitate to insult her publicly, but also because she was pregnant by Grigori Orlov[13] and gave birth to a son in April 1762, who had to be smuggled out of the Winter Palace at birth.[14]

---

[11] The Danes had recently overrun Schleswig, which belonged to Holstein and was therefore part of Peter's patrimony.

[12] Elizabeth (1739–92) was a niece of the Chancellor, Count Michael Vorontsov. After Peter's death she married a Russian colonel and Catherine magnanimously stood godmother to her eldest child.

[13] Born in 1734 he died in 1783. Although married (in 1777) he had no legitimate issue.

[14] The son, Count Alexis Bobrinskoy (1762–1813) was so named because he was

Catherine had met Grigori Orlov some time before the death of Tsarina Elizabeth. He was a tall, well-built, handsome soldier, a war hero,[15] but a man of comparatively humble origin. He was five years younger than Catherine, and an ardent lover. Orlov had four brothers and it was they who built up between them a following in the Ismailovski Guards including the regiment's colonel, Count Cyril Razumovski.[16] Other supporters included some officers in the Preobrazhenski Guards, Elizabeth Vorontsov's younger sister, Princess Dashkov[17] and Count Nikita Panin.[18]

In June Catherine went to stay at her summer house called Mon Plaisir which stood in the grounds of the Peterhof Palace on the shores of the Gulf of Finland, fifteen miles from St. Petersburg. Five miles away at Oranienbaum Peter was keeping court with his mistress and from there he sent a message to say that he intended to come over and visit her on the 29th, his name day (St. Peter's day). On the 30th he planned to leave for Denmark. Catherine was understandably nervous as to what her husband would have to say on the eve of his departure, and she was further unnerved when on the 27th Captain Passek of the Preobrazhenski regiment, who had been outspoken in her favour, was arrested for treason. Clearly the time for action had come. The final arrangements were made in St. Petersburg and early in the morning of 28 June Grigori's brother, Alexis Orlov, appeared at Mon Plaisir, awoke the Empress and told her it was time for them to go to the capital. En route they were joined by Grigori and Prince Bariatinsky, who then went on to rouse first the Ismailovski Guards, then the Preobrazhenski and finally the Semeniovski. They swore allegiance to her and amidst scenes of tumultuous enthusiasm she entered the Kazan Cathedral to be blessed by the priests and finally

---

smuggled out in a rug of beaver skins (Bobr is the Russian word for beaver), while Peter, who loved fires, had been deliberately enticed away to watch a nearby fire, especially started for the purpose.

[15] He had been wounded three times by the Prussians during the battle of Zorndorf in 1758.

[16] He was a younger brother of the Tsarina Elizabeth's favourite, Alexis Razumovski.

[17] Catherine Vorontsov (1743–1820) played a less important part than her *Memoirs*, first published in 1840, suggest, for she was only nineteen years of age, but as a sister of Peter's mistress she was able to keep Catherine informed of the latest developments in that direction.

[18] Panin (1718–83), later Catherine's Foreign Minister, was at the time the governor of his young son, the Grand Duke Paul. He really favoured the elevation of Paul rather than Catherine.

to the Winter Palace. There they were joined by Panin and the Grand Duke Paul[19] but, forestalling any plans Panin may have had, she threw open the doors of the palace and herself appeared on the balcony with her seven-year-old son, to receive the allegiance of her subjects as Empress and Autocrat of All the Russias. Very wisely her next move was to send someone she could trust to take over the naval fortress of Kronstadt, so as to be able to cope with the invasion troops Peter had stationed at the port of Narva.

A few hours after Catherine had left Peterhof, Peter and his entourage arrived there and soon learnt what was taking place in St. Petersburg. Instead of trying to rally his forces at Narva or making his way to the capital, he suffered a nervous collapse. After some hours of indecision Peter tried to reach Kronstadt only to find it already in hostile hands, and so he tamely returned to Oranienbaum, there to await events.

At first he hoped that it would be enough to promise to amend his ways, but Catherine insisted on his signing a voluntary act of abdication in which he was made to confess that his powers were unequal to the task of ruling his country. He was then brought to Peterhof where he was stripped of his uniform and the other trappings of his exalted position. Even then he hoped to be allowed to retire to his beloved Holstein with Elizabeth Vorontsov for company. It is said that all he asked for were his mistress, his dog, his Negro servant and his violin. But Catherine had suffered enough at the hands of her rival and at Peterhof the fallen Tsar and his mistress were parted for ever. He was taken to the estate of Ropsha, the other side of St. Petersburg, which had been presented to him by his aunt, the Tsarina Elizabeth. Thus ended his six months' reign. 'He allowed himself to be deposed like a child being sent to bed,' was the comment of Frederick the Great.

At Ropsha, complete with Mopsy (the dog), Narcisse (the Negro) and his violin, which Catherine had obligingly sent him, he lived out the last week of his life. He was not left in peace because Alexis Orlov, Prince Bariatinsky and several other officers mounted guard over him. At first he appears to have kept to his apartments as nervous prostration had brought on diarrhoea, but later on his guards, notably Orlov and Prince Bariatinsky, seem to have forced themselves upon him. They were bored with their humdrum life at Rop-

[19] They had been staying in the Summer Palace in St. Petersburg.

sha, where drink and cards were the only diversions, and eventually the situation got out of hand. Peter was invited to dine with them and there was some sort of quarrel that ended in his death. The news was conveyed in two letters from Orlov to Catherine, the very writing of which betrayed the drunken condition of their author. These letters, which tell their own story, deserve to be quoted: 'Little Mother, Gracious Empress! I do not know how to begin, for I tremble before your Majesty's anger that you do not believe something awful about us, and that we are not the cause of the death of your rascal, but now the lackey Maslov has fallen ill and he himself is so sick that I do not believe that he will live until evening, and he is already quite unconscious; which the whole command knows and begs God that we shall be rid of him as soon as possible, and this Maslov and the accompanying officer can inform Your Majesty in which condition he now is, if you are pleased to doubt us. This is written by Your Faithful Servant . . .' This was unsigned. A few hours later a franker report came. 'Little Mother, Merciful Empress! How shall I explain or describe what has happened? You will not believe your devoted slave but before God I speak the truth. Little Mother! I am ready to die, but I myself do not know how the misfortune came about. We are lost if you have no mercy upon us. Little Mother! He no longer lives in this world. But no one thought that and how should we have had the idea of raising our hands against the Tsar? But, Empress, the misfortune has happened. There was a quarrel at table between him and Prince Feodor (Bariatinsky) we could not separate them and already he was no more! We ourselves cannot remember what we did, but we are all guilty to the last man and deserve death. Have mercy upon me if only for my brother's sake! I have made my confession and there is nothing more to investigate. Pardon me or make an end of me quickly. I no longer wish to see the light of day; we have angered you and our souls are bound for destruction.'

Catherine kept these letters and they were found in a drawer after her death by her son Paul, who was relieved to discover that at least his mother had not instigated what happened at Ropsha. He had his father's body exhumed and re-buried and made Alexis Orlov walk in solemn procession behind the man he had murdered.

The Orlovs need not have worried about the Empress. She owed them too much to break with them, at least at this stage. In September 1762 they were all created counts, while Bariatinsky's career suffered no set back and he lived to become a Field Marshal.

Meanwhile Catherine declared her husband had died of haemor-rhoidal colic, though it was pretty clear that the Emperor had been either strangled or suffocated. Her announcement was greeted with incredulity both in Russia and outside and the Senate suggested that it might be wiser if she did not attend the funeral. And so she con-tented herself with building him a magnificent tomb—which was later dismantled by her son Paul. Whatever part Catherine played in the events leading up to Peter's death there is no doubt that his re-moval was most convenient. There was already one ex-Tsar in cap-tivity (Ivan VI) and as long as Peter lived he would automatically act as a focal point for any opposition to her. Moreover, as he was still the reigning Duke of Holstein there would be international complications should he ever get out of Russia.

Although the ex-Tsar's body—suitably clad and treated so as not to suggest his violent end—was placed for a time on public view in the Convent of Alexander Nevski, many people, especially in the pro-vinces where they had never set eyes on their ruler, believed that he had escaped his assassins and would one day return to claim his rightful inheritance.

There was in fact a constant stream of pretenders who claimed to be Peter III. They included a shoe-maker, several deserters, a run-away serf and an escaped gaol-bird. Perhaps the most fortunate was an Austrian named Stephen who had practised surgery in Turkey, then deserted to the Russians and finally made his way to Monte-negro. There, as the reigning Prince Bishop Sava preferred the cloister to the sceptre, he was able to become the virtual ruler of the country.[20] Stephen, who persisted in saying he was Peter III, was a man of real ability and served Montenegro well. Catherine was at one time so worried about his claims that in 1769 she sent Prince Dolgoruki to Montenegro to investigate. However, Dolgoruki was so impressed by Stephen that he left him undisturbed. After all it was a long way from Montenegro to St. Petersburg.

The most long living of the Pretenders was a certain Selivanov, who belonged to the religious sect of the Skoptzy—with which

---

[20] The Russians had a special interest in Montenegro as an unconquered outpost of Orthodoxy in Turkish territory. Prince Sava had paid several visits to the Russian Court.

Rasputin was later to have some connection—who believed in self-mutilation. Although Selivanov, in accordance with these tenets castrated himself, he survived, after a long period of imprisonment, till 1830. When at the age of close on a hundred, he ended his life at the Suzdal monastery, he still maintained that he was Peter III.

But the most famous of all the pretenders was Emelian Ivanovich Pugachov. He owed his importance to his ability to organise and weld together the various sources of discontent against Catherine's government—the Cossacks who resented doing military service, the tribes round the southern reaches of the Volga and the Urals who disliked the colonising power of the central government which threatened to deprive them of their lands and their independence, the Old Believers[21] who saw in the authorities of St. Petersburg the agents of Anti-Christ, the downtrodden serfs who were little better than slaves and the workers in the mines whose plight, if anything, was worse. All these people had some sympathy with Peter III. It was thought that he had intended to follow up the Emancipation of the Nobility with an emancipation of the serfs and he had certainly relaxed the laws against the Old Believers.

Pugachov was born in the early 1740s in the Cossack village of Zimoveiskaya, on the left bank of the River Don. He spent his youth there riding and hunting, and at the age of seventeen married an orphan from a neighbouring village by whom he had several children. He saw military service in Germany, Poland and Turkey during the Seven Years War and the Russo-Turkish War of 1768, where his military ability attracted the attention of his superiors. In December 1771, however, he deserted and began to lead a wandering life in South Russia. There he came in contact with the Old Believers, [22] who were always prepared to shelter a fugitive from justice, and he also came across a runaway serf named Bogomolov who claimed to be

---

[21] They were a break-away sect whose schism began in the middle of the seventeenth century when the Patriarch Nikhon had imposed a reform of the liturgy and ritual of the Church and altered the text of the service books. This they regarded as apostasy. Anti-western and fiercely Puritanical, they regarded themselves as the sole faithful repositories of Orthodoxy. They were mainly peasants and had no hierarchy because none of the bishops had joined the secession. They were anti-Government, which persecuted them, and at times disciples of anarchism.

[22] He had taken part in a punitive expedition against them in 1764 when the whole population of the town of Vetka, near Gomel, had been transferred to Siberia.

Peter III.[23] He was several times arrested, but each time he managed to escape. In November 1772 he turned up at Iaïtsk in the Urals which was a hotbed of Cossack disaffection, and there he said he was Peter III. He said that he had escaped from Ropsha with the connivance of Maslov and made his way to Poland, then Constantinople, Egypt and finally to Iaïtsk. But here once again he was arrested and the Governor sent him in chains to Kazan. However, once again he got away and returned to Iaïtch (in September 1773) which now received him with enthusiasm. Here he reiterated his claim to be Peter III and issued a manifesto (a rather illiterate but forceful production) and announced his intention of marching on St. Petersburg, putting Catherine in a convent and reassuming the reins of government. Above all he appealed to the peasants to seize the land and murder their masters. Soon he was the head of an army of bandits numbering some thirty thousand, which by dint of skill and organisation he converted into a formidable force. He also managed to get some guns and ammunition from the workers in the Demidov mines. In no time he controlled the whole area between Orenburg and Kazan. He set up a court of his own which he conducted with a mixture of pomp and buffoonery, created his own nobility (named ironically after Catherine's favourites) and orders of chivalry, held his own ceremonial parades, minted his own coinage and married another Cossack girl, who was duly provided with ladies-in-waiting.

Actually Pugachov did not look much like Peter III. He looked older, was much stockier and more robust. With his blue-black beard and piercing eyes he was an impressive figure of a man and every inch a leader. Many people who followed him were aware of his true origin, but his programme of social reform and regional autonomy suited them and they were prepared on the surface to accept him for what he claimed to be. Moreover, he never seemed at a loss. When his original wife and children turned up he blandly explained that they were the widow and family of his old friend Pugachov, who had died in prison.[24]

At first he was not taken very seriously by Catherine, who called him a common robber and contemptuously referred to him as the

---

[23] He had his nostrils slit, was flogged, branded and condemned to forced labour after raising a Cossack revolt near Astrakhan.

[24] Another account reports him as saying: 'Take care of that woman; I knew her husband; he was very kind to me; the poor creature is at times deranged.'

Marquis Pugachov, but after he defeated each successive general she sent against him she changed her tune. She raised the price on his head to ten thousand roubles alive and five thousand dead and ruefully admitted to Voltaire that he had done more harm than anyone since Tamburlane. The whole of South Russia was aflame and it looked as though much of the country would relapse into barbarism and chaos. The nobility fled and those who could not get away were massacred. Nothing like it was to be seen till 1917.

But Pugachov, though he once got within a hundred and twenty miles of Moscow, spent too much time besieging towns like Orenburg and Kazan, which were too heavily fortified for his makeshift artillery and, as soon as the war with Turkey ended in 1774, the full force of Russia's military might was turned against him. He was gradually beaten back towards the Urals and finally only escaped by swimming across the Volga and taking refuge in a cave. There he was at last betrayed by his companions, who hoped to gain pardon as a result of their treachery. He was sent to Moscow in an iron cage as though he were a wild beast. At Simbirsk on the way to Moscow, he was interrogated by Count Peter Panin, a younger brother of Count Nikita. Panin asked him how many nobles he had killed. The reply was seven hundred and fifty and Panin was told that had he been one of them he would have been hung the highest of all.

But actually Pugachov's nerve had gone. He was put in convict's clothes, guarded day and night and brought to trial. He was questioned for ten days and confessed to his real identity. Catherine, in accordance with her 'enlightened' ideas, forbade torture, but in any case it was not necessary. Pugachov was no Stenko Razan [25] and awaited his end with apprehension. He was sentenced to be hung, drawn and quartered (alive) his hands and feet and head to be cut off and left on the scaffold, the rest of his body to be burned and his ashes scattered to the wind. Fortunately for Pugachov he was beheaded first [26] and then the rest of his sentence carried out. His wives and children were imprisoned and most of his accomplices either executed or sent to Siberia. The town of Iaïtsk and the River Iaik were changed to Uralsk and Ural, so that no one should remember the 'capital' of the rebellion by its original name.

[25] The Ukrainian Cossack leader quartered in Moscow in 1671 who met his end with superb courage.
[26] In the Red Square on 21 January 1775.

To the Bolsheviks Pugachov was a hero and they saw in him someone who had attempted to strike a resounding blow at emergent capitalism. But long before this he had been the subject of a sympathetic study by Pushkin in his two books, *The Captain's Daughter* and *The History of the Pugachov Rebellion*. Pushkin obtained special (but reluctant) permission from Nicholas I's Chief of Secret Police to tour the district between Orenburg and Kazan to interview some of the survivors of the struggle.

It was said that Pugachov was visited while in prison by Catherine (in disguise). This is highly unlikely, but if she did she must have seen someone who even in defeat had greater qualities than Peter III. Indeed it can safely be said of the many impersonators of Peter that even the most wayward and eccentric compared favourably with him. Most of them at any rate had courage.

8

The Riddle of the Temple

THE marriage of Marie Antoinette and Louis XVI, like most alliances of its kind, was purely political in origin. It was intended by the French minister Choiseul and his Austrian counterpart, Kaunitz, to set the seal on the Franco-Austrian alliance, which was one aspect of the famous Diplomatic Revolution[1] of the latter half of the eighteenth century. The marriage had been decided upon in 1766, but could not take place at once as the children concerned—Louis XVI (born in 1754) and Marie Antoinette (born in 1755)—were still too young. In 1770 it was decided that they were old enough and so they were married, first in Vienna (by proxy) on 19 April and then in person at Versailles on 16 May.

Louis, who had first set eyes on his bride two days previously at Compiègne as she and her retinue journeyed from Austria to France, was still only in his sixteenth year but, as Dauphin,[2] was heir to the French throne. He was a shy, awkward, diffident young man, reserved and rather taciturn. Marie Antoinette, on the other hand, was lively, vain and frivolous.

On their wedding night the young couple were ceremonially undressed by the courtiers and then installed in their massive bed and the curtains drawn. What happened that night is laconically recorded by Louis in his diary the next day with the one word 'Rien' (Nothing). In fact nothing happened for close on seven years despite

---

[1] So called because it was the first time the two countries were in alliance for over three hundred years.

[2] Louis XV's eldest son, the Dauphin, had died in 1765 and the latter's son, the future Louis XVI, who had originally been called Duke of Berry, then became Dauphin. The former rulers of Dauphiné had bequeathed the province to the French Crown in the fourteenth century on condition that the eldest son of the King of France should always bear the title of Dauphin.

the fact that Louis XV had died in 1774 and the Dauphin was now King of France as Louis XVI. Events took a more favourable turn in July 1777 when Marie Antoinette's brother, the Emperor Joseph II, paid an incognito visit to Versailles (as Count von Falkenstein) and managed both to persuade his sister to take her duties as wife more seriously and to convince his brother-in-law that he must assert his conjugal rights. Some historians have asserted that Louis' semi-impotence was due to a small physical defect, phimosis, which required minor surgery and that it was this operation that Joseph II persuaded him to have. But others have maintained that Louis' inhibitions were purely psychological and had no physical basis at all.[3] Whatever was the real cause, Joseph's visit certainly bore fruit, for in the December of the next year (1778) their first child, Marie Thérèse Charlotte[4] was born. Three other children were born in the following eight years—Louis Joseph Xavier François (the Dauphin) in October 1781, Louis Charles (the future Louis XVII) on 27 March 1785 and finally Sophie Hélène Beatrix in July 1786. Of these only the elder daughter was really healthy: her sister Sophie died at the age of eleven months and the elder son, the Dauphin in June 1789, at the age of seven. He died a martyr to rickets. Louis Charles, who till then had been styled Duke of Normandy, thereupon became the Dauphin.

By this time, however, the Revolution had broken out and those events which were to sweep away both the monarchy and the *ancien régime* had already begun. The first real indication of personal danger came when the mob stormed the palace at Versailles in October 1789 and brought the Royal Family—with every insult and humiliation—back to Paris. There they were accommodated in the Palace of the Tuileries which was in a state of considerable disrepair, as none of the royal family had lived there since Louis XV was a child. There they were virtually prisoners. The king's youngest brother, the Comte d'Artois (later Charles X) had already made his way abroad in July 1789 and placed himself at the head of the emigrés, and in February 1791 the king's two aunts, Madame Adelaide and Madame Victoire, managed to escape to Italy. And so in June

---

[3] Some have even advanced the theory that the charges later made by the Dauphin against his mother derived perhaps from her anxiety to see that he did not suffer from the same defect as his father had done.

[4] Mme. Royale, later Duchess of Angoulême.

1791 the rest of the family made an attempt to quit the capital. The king's younger brother, the Comte de Provence (later Louis XVIII), travelling with British papers, was successful, but not so the others. They left the Tuileries Palace the same day as the Comte de Provence left his Paris home, the Luxembourg. The party, made up of the Dauphin's governess, Mme. du Tourzel, Louis XVI, Marie Antoinette, Mme. Elisabeth (the king's sister), Madame Royale and the Dauphin, left secretly by night, armed with Russian papers. Mme du Tourzel travelled as the Baronne de Korff, Marie Antoinette as her companion (Mme. Rochet), Louis XVI (Monsieur Durand) as the family valet and Mme. Elisabeth (Rosalie) as the children's nurse with the two children both dressed as girls. Helped by Marie Antoinette's friend and admirer, Count Axel Fersen, they managed to get out of Paris. Their objective was Metz, where the Marquis de Bouillé, a strong royalist, was in command of troops still loyal to the crown. Unfortunately, however, the whole manoeuvre was badly planned, at both ends, and badly executed. When they had got two thirds of the way to Metz, the king was recognised by the postmaster at Ste. Menehoulde[5] and stopped some twenty miles farther on at the village of Varennes-en-Argonne. They were then brought back amidst scenes of unparalleled tumult and subjected to every kind of abuse and insult. And as a final humiliation they were obliged to share their coach with three deputies sent by the Assembly[6] to escort them back to Paris. It was this appalling experience that caused the queen's hair to turn white in one night.

Back in the Tuileries their life became increasingly difficult, particularly after the French had declared war on Austria (Marie Antoinette's country) and Prussia. As the Austrian bitch, l'Autrichienne, she became the special target of revolutionary hatred. On 20 June the mob invaded the Tuileries, hurled abuse at the king and made him wear a red cap and drink a toast to Liberty, Equality and Fraternity. Two months later, on 10 August, following a hot stifling night, they once again broke into the palace, this time massacring the Swiss Guard. On this occasion the king and his family were obliged to take refuge with the Assembly at the Salle du Ménage, and there, in exhausting and humiliating circumstances Louis was

[5] Jean Baptiste Drouet (1763–1824), who later became a Member of the Convention and served under Napoleon. At the Restoration in 1814 he was banished as a regicide.
[6] The National or Constituent Assembly sat from July 1789 to September 1791.

obliged to listen to a decree which deprived him of all his powers. That night the royal family spent in the nearby Convent of the Feuillants. It was then decided to place them in permanent confinement. The Luxembourg Palace was first suggested but dismissed as not sufficiently safe to prevent possible escape. So instead they were sent to the Temple—not to the royal apartments formerly tenanted by the Comte d'Artois but to one of its more gloomy and inaccessible bastions.

There, separated from all their friends at court, like Mme. du Tourzel and the Princesse de Lamballe,[7] they were to be guarded by twenty-five persons selected by the National Convention.[8] The only other persons allowed to attend them were Clery, the king's valet, and François Hue, who acted in a similar capacity to the Dauphin. A month later Hue[9] was removed, leaving only Clery.[10]

At the beginning their captivity was not too burdensome. Although they had lost all at least they were now free from the cares of state and were still together under the same roof. Like Nicholas II of Russia and his family in the early days of their captivity at Tsarskoe-Selo in 1917 they were able to achieve a certain peace and serenity. Adversity served both to deepen their religious convictions and to bring out a strong mutual devotion that was something new in their lives. Thus, despite the constant presence of guards and the lack of any real privacy, they were not unhappy. The king was able to give his son lessons every morning[11] and they had the occasional use of the garden for relaxation.

This state of affairs came to an abrupt end when, on 29 September, the king was separated from the rest of the family to tenant a room in one of the towers away from the others. They were still allowed to meet at meal times, but gradually the supervision became much more strict. Early in December the king was told to prepare himself for

[7] She was hacked to pieces by the mob during the September massacres, her head stuck on a pike and paraded in front of the windows of the Temple.

[8] The revolutionary assembly which controlled the destinies of France from September 1792 to October 1795.

[9] He published a book on the last years of Louis XVI in 1824 and became first valet de chambre to Louis XVIII. He died in 1829.

[10] Clery remained with Louis till the end and then escaped to London where, in 1798, he published a journal of what happened in this Temple during the captivity of Louis XVI. He died in Vienna in 1809.

[11] Mathematics, however, had soon to be dropped from the curriculum as the guards suspected it contained some secret code.

his public trial and thereafter the family was not allowed to see him till the day before his death. Louis, although ably defended by his advocate Malesherbes, who paid for his devotion with his life,[12] was resigned to his fate and on Christmas Day made his will in which he forgave all his enemies and exhorted his son should he ever become king not to attempt to avenge his father's death. On 20 January 1793, the day before his execution, Louis visited his family for the last time and took leave of Marie Antoinette, Madame Elisabeth and the two children, Marie Thérèse and the Dauphin. Once again he impressed upon them, particularly the Dauphin, that there must be no attempt to avenge his death. He then left, made his confession and after leaving mass the next morning went to his execution.

During the next six months the captivity of the four remaining members of the royal family grew increasingly more severe, and on 3 July the Dauphin was taken away from the others and put in a room on the second floor. He was there entrusted to the care of a Jacobin cobbler named Antoine Simon and his wife, whose task was to indoctrinate the child with revolutionary ideas and bring him up as a true child of the people, a real little *sans culotte*. His new foster parents were not the monsters that some royalist propagandists later depicted. They were coarse and vulgar, but not, as far as one can tell, intentionally unkind. The Dauphin was still allowed to play in the garden and even given some toys.

A month later, on 1 August, Marie Antoinette was transferred to the prison of the Conciergerie to await trial, and commissioners were sent to the Temple to gather evidence against her. It is doubtful if either the Dauphin or Marie Thérèse understood the purport of the document they were made to sign, in which their mother was accused of unspeakable crimes such as having obscenely corrupted her own son.[13] It was the last time the three remaining members of the family ever met together and the last time Marie Thérèse saw her brother. Next Madame Elisabeth, who had also been made to sign the infamous document, was parted from Marie Thérèse to be summarily tried and executed in May 1794.

Meanwhile the Simon régime came to an end in January 1794 when

[12] Although seventy-two years old, he was executed—on the same day as his daughter and son-in-law—in April 1794.

[13] When the charges were read out in court Marie Antoinette rose to her feet and used the memorable words: 'If I have given no answer it is because nature itself refuses to accept such an accusation brought against a mother. I appeal to all the mothers present.'

D

the shoe-maker and his wife resigned their position.[14] The Convention[15] thereupon decided not to replace them as foster parents but to confine the young prince under guard in one room (equipped with an iron grille), where he could be visited from time to time by commissioners appointed for the purpose who could make reports on him.

There is no doubt that for the unfortunate Dauphin the worst period of his life had begun. When, for instance, he was visited by Harmand de la Meuse[16] and two other emissaries from the Convention they found him silent, withdrawn and completely impassive.

According to Harmand de la Meuse he declined to answer any questions and, while appearing to listen to what the commissioners had to say, made no reply whatever. He allowed them to examine him physically without displaying emotion and they found considerable swellings on the elbow and knees and signs of rachitis and deformation in the legs. They attributed his condition as much to his obstinacy and refusal to take exercise—which they did recognise might well have been too painful for him to undertake—as to the circumstances of his imprisonment.

The day after Robespierre's fall Barras[17] paid a visit to the Temple and secured the appointment of a new warder—a member of the revolutionary committee of the Temple district named Laurent—and made provision for medical attention should it be necessary. In November 1794 Laurent was given an assistant named Gomin to help him in his duties. Laurent himself left in March 1795 because his mother had died and he was replaced by Etienne Lasne. By now the restrictions were relaxed somewhat and, although the Dauphin was still kept in the same room, at least the grille was replaced by an ordinary door to make it appear a little less like a gaol.

In May the warder became alarmed at the steady deterioration in the prince's health and the Government called in Dr. Desault, the chief surgeon of the Hôtel-Dieu, the oldest hospital in Paris, to

[14] Simon shared the fate of his protector Robespierre and went to the guillotine on the 9th Thermidor (28 July 1794). His widow died in a Paris hospital for Incurables in 1829.

[15] The revolutionary assembly which governed France from September 1792 to October 1795.

[16] He became Prefect of the Hautes Alpes in 1824, but was removed soon after.

[17] He was a renegade nobleman who was a born intriguer. He took part in the storming of the Bastille, voted for Louis XVI's execution, overthrew Robespierre and became a member of the Directory (1795–9). For a time Josephine was his mistress.

examine the Dauphin. This he did but the patient scarcely profited by it because a few days later Desault himself died—not without suspicion of poison.[18] His successor Dr. Pelletan was so disturbed by what he saw—the Dauphin had a swelling on the right knee and left wrist and was in a high fever—that he asked for a second opinion. Dr. Dumangin, the head physician of the Hôpital de la Santé, was then called in and he ordered the boy to be removed to another room where there was more light and air, but by this time the position was hopeless and at 3 p.m. in the afternoon of 8 June Louis XVII[19] died.

An autopsy performed the next day by Pelletan and Dumangin, who had seen the patient, and two doctors (Lassus and Jeanroy) who had not, established the cause of death as scrofula of long standing. That evening the corpse was put in a coffin and buried in a common grave in the churchyard of Ste. Marguerite.[20]

Marie Thérèse was allowed to leave her prison in December 1795. She was taken to Basle where on Christmas Day she was handed over to the Austrians in exchange for certain French prisoners.[21] In 1799 she married her cousin, the Duc d'Angoulême, the elder son of the Comte d'Artois. She returned to France in 1824 but again went into exile after the Revolution of 1830 which deprived her uncle and father-in-law, Charles X, of the French throne. She died, childless, at Frohsdorf in Austria in 1851. Her ultimate heirs, the Bourbon-Parmas, were descendants of her niece, the Duchess of Parma.

Louis XVI, Marie Antoinette and Madame Elisabeth had all died in public with hundreds of people looking on, but from the first there were doubts about the fate of Louis XVII. Many royalists—particularly among the Chouans in the Vendée, who in 1795 were still in open revolt against the Republic—refused to believe the official version of his death. Some asserted that he had been deliberately poisoned by his guards, while others declared that he had been smuggled out of the Temple in a clothes basket, that another child, who was probably deaf and dumb (hence his silence in face of Harmand de la Meuse's questions was not due to obstinacy but to

[18] He is said to have been taken ill the same day that he saw the boy, after having expressed some doubt as to the identity of his patient.
[19] He had been so proclaimed by the exiled royalists after they learnt of the fate of Louis XVI. In a proclamation seven days after his brother's execution the Comte de Provence acknowledged his nephew as king, but assumed the regency.
[20] It was said to have been removed to a separate unmarked grave later.
[21] Held in Austria since General Dumouriez's defection to the allies in 1793.

an inability either to hear or speak) had been substituted in his place and it was this child and not the Dauphin who had died in June 1795.

After the Restoration Louis XVIII tried to locate the exact spot of his nephew's burial ground but was unable to do so. Subsequent exhumations carried out in 1846 and 1894 turned up a coffin which corresponded to a description given by Police Commissioner Dussert, but was found to contain the skeleton of a child aged at least fourteen years.

The death certificate which bore the date of 12 June was made out in the name of Louis Charles Capet, son of last King of France and Marie Antoinette Josèphe Jeanne of Austria. He was stated to have been born in Versailles and to have died in the Tower of the Temple on the 10th. It was signed by Lasne, Robin (the Registrar) and a certain Remy Bigot who is described as a friend but of whom nothing is known beyond his address (61 rue Vieille du Temple). The original certificate has disappeared—possibly in the fire that destroyed the Hôtel de Ville during the Commune Insurrection in Paris in 1871. The certificate was witnessed by the local police commissioner Dussert who survived the Revolution to give evidence during the enquiry made by Louis XVIII.

It was not long before a succession—over forty in all—of pretenders came forward to claim that they were the rightful king of France, who had been miraculously delivered from the Temple.

The first two were of little account. Jean Marie Hervagault was a tailor's son and from childhood had led the life of a semi-vagabond. He was a good-looking, personable man and attracted the sympathy of those to whom he told his story and also the attention of Napoleon's police. He was in and out of prison several times and died in 1812.

The next claimant, Mathurin Bruneau, was a shoemaker, who in 1818 styled himself Charles de Navarre. Like Hervagault he never secured any real support and died in prison.

Somewhat more important was the self-styled Baron de Richemont, a glass manufacturer from Rouen, whose real name was Hébert. He assumed the title of Duke of Normandy and in 1828 advanced his claims with a great deal of publicity. He was brought to trial and sentenced to twelve years' imprisonment. However, the sentence was never put into effect and after a sojourn in England he was able to return to France where he died in a provincial château in 1853.

Even the New World provided its quota of false Dauphins in the persons of the famous naturalist and bird painter, John James Audubon (1785–1851) and the missionary and Iroquois chieftain, the Rev. Eleazor Williams. But by far the most persistent and plausible was Karl Wilhelm Naundorff (1785–1845).

There is no record of his birth in Germany under that name though he is supposed to have come from Weimar where the grand-ducal family were not unsympathetic to his claims. The earliest knowledge we have of him dates from 1810 when as a young man he was living at Spandau, just outside Berlin. There he married in 1828 a shopkeeper's sixteen-year-old daughter, Johanna Einert, by whom he had nine children.[22] Naundorff first came to the attention of the Prussian authorities in 1824 when he was arrested in the town of Brandenburg, where he had moved from Spandau four years pre-viously. He was accused of arson of which he was acquitted, and of trafficking in false coinage. This charge was also dropped, but he was imprisoned for three years on suspicion of false pretences. On his release he retired to Krossen in Saxony, where his claims to be Louis XVII began to attract attention. He had already written to his 'sister', the Duchesse d'Angoulême, and to her brother-in-law, the Duc de Berry,[23] but received no replies.

According to his story, published in his Memoirs, which appeared in London in November 1836, he had been drugged, a doll had been substituted in his bed and when he awoke he found himself in a fourth floor attic in the Temple. When the doll was discovered a deaf and dumb child had been substituted in his place. From this attic he had escaped in a coffin on 8 June 1795—once again after being drugged—and was taken to the royalist province of the Vendée.

From there he went to Italy and then to England. In both countries, so he says, he spent some time in prison, but in each case was re-leased through the influence of the Empress Josephine. Then he went to Germany where once again he was imprisoned in a dungeon, rather like the one tenanted by Kaspar Hauser,[24] somewhere near

[22] The first was born in 1819, the last in 1843. One died in infancy.

[23] Angoulême's younger brother, who was assassinated outside the Paris Opera House in February 1830 by a fanatic who declared that it was his mission to exterminate the Bourbon family.

[24] See Chapter 10.

Frankfurt. After his escape from there he served in the forces of the Duke of Brunswick and was wounded fighting the French. Ultimately he was able to set himself up as a watch-maker in Berlin.

Having received no response from the Duchesse d'Angoulême or the Duc de Berry—or for that matter from the Prussian Chancellor, Prince Hardenberg, to whom he had also written—he decided to go to Paris. There in May 1833 he managed to convince a number of important people, including the Dauphin's former governess, Mme. de Rambaud, Louis XVI's former private secretary (Brémond) and one of his former chamberlains (Marco de St. Hilaire) that he was the Prisoner of the Temple restored to life. Considering that his knowledge of French was distinctly poor, this was no mean achievement.

His new friends all wrote to the Duchesse d'Angoulême to support his claims. She did not reply, but she did ask the Vicomte Sosthène de La Rochefoucauld (later Duc de Doudeauville), who had been an A.D.C. to Charles X, to investigate. He interviewed Naundorff and was struck by his physical resemblance to the Bourbon family, but felt that this did not of itself constitute any proof of his identity. Meanwhile Mme de Rambaud and Morel de St. Didier, a special emissary of Naundorff's, went to Prague to see the Duchesse and beg her to receive the Pretender. The Duchesse granted an audience to Morel de St. Didier, but declined to see Mme. de Rambaud. She told Morel de St Didier that she was convinced that her brother was dead and that there was therefore no purpose in her seeing Naundorff. At a subsequent interview she repeated the same conviction. Naundorff tried then to force the issue by going to Dresden in August 1835, when the Duchesse was on a visit to the Royal Family of Saxony, but he discovered that she had left for Prague the day before his arrival.

Meanwhile in Paris in 1834 Naundorff had intervened in the trial of Richemont, not only to declare the latter to be an impostor, but also to assert his own claims. After his return from Dresden he became convinced that the Duchesse d'Angoulême never would receive him and that his only hope lay through legal action. Consequently in June, 1836, he summoned her and her husband and Charles X to appear before the civil court in Paris to answer his claims. Two days later the police arrested him, confiscated his papers[25] and expelled him from France.

[25] There were two hundred and two of these papers.

Naundorff then took up residence in England, first in London and then in Camberwell Green. His family, who had been forced to leave Saxony after his expulsion from France, joined him there and they all lived in precarious financial circumstances, Naundorff himself being several times arrested for debt. He was dogged by misfortune and, rather like Kaspar Hauser, seems not only to have spent much of his life in confinement, but also to have been the subject of inexplicable attacks. Thus, he had been stabbed in the streets of Paris in 1834, was assaulted and shot in the arm in London in 1838 and had his laboratory at Camberwell twice set on fire.

Meanwhile he continued to press his claims in the law courts of Paris and in 1840 engaged the famous French lawyer and politician, Jules Favre, as his principal advocate. But he destroyed much of his support by the publication of his extremely unorthodox religious views. In 1839 he had published and circulated privately a book couched in apocalyptic phraseology in which he affected to see in vague personal visions the real basis of religious authority. In 1841 he followed this up with a book destined for the public called *Doctrine Celeste*. It was promptly put on the Index by the Roman Curia and was later condemned by the Pope (Gregory XVI), who described its author as 'that son of perdition who usurps the title of Duke of Normandy'.

The Catholic authorities in France and elsewhere were much disturbed by the sort of religious elements who came forward to support Naundorff's claims. There was Thomas Martin of Gallardon, the peasant mystic, who claimed to have had conversations with the Archangel Raphael (in contemporary dress) while working in the fields outside his native village. He was told among other things to go and warn Louis XVIII of the dangers of his usurpation, since Louis XVII was still alive. Gallardon had died in 1833, shortly after meeting and recognising Naundorff as the son of Louis XVI. Then there had been Melanie Calvet, who at the age of fifteen claimed to have seen the Virgin Mary on the hillside at La Salette near Grenoble. She was also a partisan of Naundorff and proved so troublesome that in the end Napoleon III had her transferred to a convent in Darlington out of harm's way.

Naundorff's originality was not confined to the religious field: he was also interested in the manufacture of explosives. He spent much of his time working in his laboratory at Camberwell to produce a projectile weapon. He tried in vain to interest the government of France in the project but finally, in 1845, opened negotiations with the war office in Holland. The Dutch seemed more sympathetic and so Naundorff went to Holland early in 1845 and there managed to sell his invention. But the struggle against adversity had undermined his health and he died at Delft on 10 August (1845). His death certificate was issued in the name of Charles Louis de Bourbon,[26] Duc de Normandie, and asserted that he had been born at Versailles on 27 March 1785. His gravestone bears the inscription—'Here lies Louis XVII: Charles Louis, Duc de Normandie, Roi de France et de Navarre'. The French Government protested in vain at this quasi-recognition of his claims.

He himself had never openly used the title of Louis XVII, but had always described himself as Duke of Normandy. His descendants, however, who were naturalised in Holland, were granted the name of Bourbon in December 1863, and continued the litigation in France to secure recognition of their claims. They brought lawsuits before the courts in Paris in 1851 and again in 1874 (both times using Favre as their advocate) and when these were unsuccessful they issued a manifesto in 1883 setting out their case, and in 1910 petitioned the French Senate. In 1950 they had Naundorff's grave at Delft opened in the hope that some significant craniological or other anatomical features would help establish their cause. Their last attempt to have the death certificate of 1795 set aside as null and void came before the French court of appeal in 1954. The action was successfully opposed by the Bourbon–Parma family (as the real heirs of Louis XVI) and the court decided that the Naundorffs had neither proved that Louis XVII had ever escaped from captivity nor that he, Naundorff, was identical with him. So there—for the time being—the matter rests.

Was Naundorff really Louis XVII? On the positive side was a close physical resemblance to the Bourbon family which even struck people like La Rochefoucauld, who were in no sense his supporters. He is said to have had certain physical peculiarities—such as triangular vaccination marks, a broad mole on the thigh, prominent teeth and a scar on his upper lip—which the Dauphin was known to possess.

He also possessed an extensive knowledge of the geography of the

[26] The French royal family styled themselves as of France and not Bourbon.

Temple[27] and gave all sorts of details about the royal family, including their flight to Varennes, which seemed to indicate personal experience.[28] It was this that won him support from some of the surviving courtiers of Louis XVI. People felt that he must personally been present at some of the events he described.

There was also the fact that the body of Louis XVII could never be satisfactorily located and the evidence of people like Mme. Simon that the boy had escaped[29] and the doubts of some of the doctors as to the identity of the patient they attended. Harmand de la Meuse's report is quoted by the Naundorffists to prove that a deaf and dumb child had been substituted, as they maintain no ordinary child could have behaved in the manner described.

Then there was Naundorff's skill as a watch repairer and his inventive powers. Many thought that these had been inherited from Louis XVI who was well-known to have been a competent locksmith interested in all sorts of mechanical devices.

And finally of course his birth (or baptism) certificate has never been found and thus, unlike most pretenders, Naundorff cannot be positively identified with anyone else.

It is a great pity that the confrontation with the Duchesse d'Angoulême never took place, as she was probably the one person who might have been able to resolve the matter there and then. Her reluctance to see Naundorff has been ascribed by some of his supporters to a theory that she also had been substituted for another child and that the real duchess lived in mysterious seclusion in a castle near Hildburghausen in Germany and died there in 1837. To give him credit, Naundorff never believed this outlandish story. It was not after all unnatural that the duchess should avoid contact with anyone who served to recall the most terrible period of her life.

On the anti-Naundorff side we have to place the evidence of the warders, Gomin and Lasne, both of whom survived the Revolution. They both declared that they were present when the Dauphin died

[27] After the Restoration the Temple was handed over to the Benedictines. They left it in 1848 and it was demolished in 1854.

[28] He had named his eldest child Amelie in 1829 after the name used for the Dauphin on the flight to Varennes.

[29] She was a supporter of the clothes-basket theory. She was over seventy when she aired her views. She even declared that Naundorff had visited her in hospital and she had recognised him at once. The royalists regarded her as senile and confused, while not unnaturally the Naundorffists have been at pains to try and prove that she was in full possession of her faculties.

and both were certain no substitution had ever been made. Despite certain minor descrepancies in the evidence they both gave at the Richemont trial in 1834, it would seem they were speaking the truth.

Moreover, considering the appalling experiences the Dauphin had undergone since 1789, the circumstances of his solitary confinement, aggravated as it was by poor food, insufficient exercise and not enough fresh air, it is not surprising either that he should be silent and obstinate or that his health should have deteriorated so rapidly. It is pretty clear that he suffered from much the same sort of vitamin deficiency that had helped to terminate the life of his elder brother.

Naundorff's story, which he occasionally varied, as to how he got out of the Temple, is purely circumstantial and no one could ever be produced who could come forward and verify it, while the story of his activities between 1795 and 1820 are simply fantastic.

There is no doubt he believed what he said and died in that belief. And of course he had little to gain from the material point of view. But that does not mean the story is true. There were some mysterious and odd factors in the story of the Dauphin's last days in the Temple, but not enough to build what Naundorff built on them.

There have, of course, been other theories about Naundorff's origin. Some have supposed that he was a bastard of the royal family of Saxony (Louis XVI's mother had been a Princess of Saxony), and that this accounts for some support given him in his early days by members of that family.

Others have suggested that he was Marie Antoinette's son by Count Axel Fersen, the Swedish nobleman who had fought for France in the American War of Independence and then attached himself to the French Court. It was Fersen who had helped organise the disastrous flight to Varennes, and there is evidence that, after their incarceration in the Temple, he made efforts to extricate the royal family. On the other hand, a book written in 1926 tried to establish that he was a Prussian named Carl Benjamin Werg.

It is doubtful indeed if we shall ever know the truth. *The Times*, in a leading article on The Mystery of the Temple on 29 September 1950, concluded with the words: 'We are bound to turn all the neon lights of research upon the high road of history, but the unpenetrated twilight which seems likely for ever to envelop some of the byways adds to the charm of the study.' The Naundorff story, whatever its truth, has certainly enriched both literature and life.

9

Alexander I of Russia and Feodor Kuzmich

Most monarchs have been anxious to cling on to their power till the last possible moment and few abdications in history have been entirely voluntary. Till recent times—with the notable exceptions of the Emperor Charles V in 1556 and Christina of Sweden in 1654—the idea of retirement would never have occurred to them. Alexander I, Tsar of Russia from 1801 to 1825, was somewhat different.

He was in fact a very complex character indeed and, like most complex people, he created widely different impressions on those who encountered him. A curious blend of liberal ideas, imbibed from his Swiss republican tutor, La Harpe, and of reactionary sentiments inseparable from his exalted position, alternately swept through his mind. Thus he could at one and the same time be the patron of 'reformers' like Czartoryski[1] and Novosiltzov[2] and of the brutal and hypocritical Arakcheyev.[3] He was neither the second Agamemnon hailed by Pushkin[4] as 'the people's friend, their freedom's saviour', nor a mere 'shifty Byzantine' as Napoleon dubbed him. He was a mixture of both, with a good deal of charm and a dash of megalomania thrown in besides.

To understand the enigma of Alexander I's personality it is necessary to have some idea of his early life and the circumstances which brought him to the throne.

[1] Prince Adam Czartoryski (1770–1861), Polish patriot and statesman had spent some time in France and England. He introduced Novosiltzov to Alexander.

[2] N. N. Novosiltzov (1761–1836) had lived in England during Paul's reign and there inbibed strong liberal sympathies.

[3] Count A. A. Arakcheyev (1769–1834). One of the reasons for his remarkable ascendancy over the Tsar was his ability to play on Alexander's feelings of guilt about his father's murder.

[4] At heart Pushkin was a liberal and in 1821 Alexander banished him to his estates in the country.

He was born in the Winter Palace at St. Petersburg in December 1777, the eldest surviving child of Tsar Paul and his second wife, Marie Feodorovna, a princess of Württemberg. At that time his grandmother, Catherine II, was still ruler of Russia. She doted on her eldest grandson, supervised his education with great care and made it plain that she would prefer him to succeed her rather than his morose and unco-operative father, Paul. Rumour had it that Paul, who had been born in 1754, was her son by Saltykov,[5] the first of her long line of lovers, and there is some hint in Catherine's own *Memoirs* that this was so. But when Paul came to the throne his erratic behaviour was far more reminiscent of Catherine's husband, Peter III, than of Saltykov. So too was his slavish admiration of everything Prussian.

Whoever Paul's father was, he grew up completely estranged from his mother. Immediately after birth he had been taken away from her and he spent his early years in the palace of his great-aunt, the Tsarina Elizabeth. He was jealous of Catherine's authority and resentful of her usurpation of a throne that by right should be his, and to show his disapproval of her he set up his own opposition court at his palace at Gatchina some thirty-five miles south-west of the capital. The law governing the succession, as set forth by Peter the Great in 1722, would have allowed Catherine to nominate her successor and thus she could have passed over her son in favour of her grandson. But she did nothing about it, and so on her death in 1796 Paul became Tsar.

He suffered from the same paranoia that had afflicted Peter III, and was given to savage bouts of rage followed by equally inexplicable periods of extravagant favouritism. At home no one felt safe from his insane outbursts while abroad his policy was felt to be disastrous to the real interests of Russia. Inevitably, therefore, disaffection grew and those who could recall the splendours and glories of Catherine's reign began to look around to see if there were some way of getting rid of their new ruler.

The originator of the conspiracy against the Tsar was Paul's own Vice-Chancellor, Count Nikita Panin. Panin was a nephew of Catherine's former Minister of Foreign Affairs, while his wife was a daughter of one of the Orlov brothers who in 1762 had been responsible for removing Peter III.

[5] Serge Vassilievitch Saltykov. Born 1726. Appointed Russian Minister in Hamburg 1755 and Ambassador in Paris 1762.

However, at the end of 1800 and before the conspiracy could take real shape, Panin was disgraced and banished to his estates in the country. Fortunately, before he left the capital, he had been able to make contact with the Military Governor of St. Petersburg, Count Peter von der Pahlen, who thereafter became the real mainspring of the plot. As controller of the police in St. Petersburg he was in an unique position and able to take both effectively and safely the measures necessary for success.

His task was threefold. First—and this proved easily the most difficult—he had to get the Tsarevitch Alexander to agree to his father's removal and to agree to ascend the throne in his place. Secondly, he had to organize and assemble a band of conspirators, able and willing to do the job, and thirdly, he had to take the appropriate measures to see that the conspirators could gain entry into the palace and there remain undisturbed till they had finished their work.

Alexander was not easily convinced. He held himself bound by his oath of allegiance to his father, but eventually Pahlen, by demonstrating that this no longer applied since Paul had broken his own coronation oath, by appealing to Alexander's patriotic concern for Russia, and finally by warning him that he might soon follow the way of Peter the Great's son, the ill-fated Tsarevitch Alexis, overcame his scruples. To do this, however, he was obliged to make a solemn promise that Paul would simply be deposed and that no violence would be used against him. Whether Alexander believed this remains doubtful. Certainly Pahlen did not. They both knew how difficult it was for Russian rulers to survive their deposition.

Next Pahlen recruited a band of trustworthy conspirators. In the end there were some one hundred and eighty of them—led by the Zubovs, Prince Plato who had been Catherine the Great's last favourite, and his brother, Count Nikita. Before he had attracted the attention of Paul, Pahlen had owed his early advancement to their influence. They had been banished by the Tsar soon after his accession but so great was Paul's trust in Pahlen that he was prevailed upon to reverse this edict and allow them to return to St. Petersburg. There, in the house of the Zubov's sister, the conspirators were able to meet under the eyes of Pahlen and free from police surveillance.

By this time Paul, who was very suspicious of everybody (except

Pahlen) and who never forgot what had happened to his father, had left the Winter Palace for the newly constructed Mikhailovsky Castle. This, with its deep moat and massive towers, was more like a fortress than a palace, and here, surrounded by troops of proved loyalty, the Tsar felt safer. The Empress and her children were installed there, and so too was Paul's mistress, Princess Gagarin. She occupied an apartment immediately below his and communicating with it by a secret staircase. Another door, which Paul usually kept securely fastened so that he could not be taken by surprise, led to the Empress's apartments.

Things reached a climax in March 1801 when rumours of the plot began to filter through to the Tsar. Although he had implicit faith in Pahlen, he began to grow increasingly uneasy and suspicious. Finally he questioned the Governor-General about it but Pahlen, with calm audacity, acknowledged that there was indeed a conspiracy but that he had joined it himself so as to learn the identity of the conspirators. He promised to let his master have a list of all those involved within a few days. The Tsar asked if the names included his sons, Alexander and Constantine. Pahlen said no they did not, but he took good care to let the princes know what was in their father's mind. Not that they needed much proof of his attitude for he had placed them under virtual house-arrest.

It was clear, therefore, that the time to act had now come. On the evening of 11 March Pahlen arranged for the men of the Semenovski Guard—a regiment devoted to the Tsarevitch—to take over the guard at the Mikhailovsky Castle, and then summoned the conspirators to meet at the house of the regiment's commander, General Talytzin (who owed his appointment to Panin). There, on Pahlen's instructions, they were liberally plied with drink and there Pahlen chose Prince Zubov, General Benningsen, Prince Yashvili, Prince Wiasemsky, J. F. Skariatin and Colonels Gordanov and Tatarinov to carry out the deed. They were to depose the Emperor and take him to the Fortress of St. Peter and St. Paul.

Towards midnight these men, accompanied by some others, including Nikita Zubov, made their way to the Castle, where the guards let them in. They reached the Emperor's suite without trouble and there overcame the guards and valet on duty outside the outer door of the bedroom. They passed through the vestibule where the staircase down to Princess Gagarin's room was located (which the

Emperor had used that evening) and forced the inner door. Warned by the noise, Paul had leapt out of bed and, since the only way of escape through the door to the Empress's rooms was locked and barred, taken refuge behind a screen by the fireplace. It was only a matter of minutes before he was found and dragged out.

Exactly what happened in the course of the next half hour is not easy to establish as the accounts of those who took part are contradictory. Benningsen, accompanied by Prince Zubov, appears to have acted as chief spokesman and to have told the Tsar that he was deposed. While they were arguing Yashvili, Wiasemsky and Skariatin, who had been left behind in the castle grounds because they were so drunk, burst into the room accompanied by Gordanov and Tatarinov who had been left behind to look after them.

The situation deteriorated at once and both Zubov and Benningsen, somewhat unnerved by the turn of events, prudently withdrew, leaving Paul at the mercy of his half-drunken assassins. He asked that his life might be spared, and when he saw this was hopeless he begged that at least he might be allowed to say his prayers. By way of reply his assailants chased him round the room and when he tripped and fell behind the desk, where he was vainly attempting to take shelter, they fell upon him and strangled him. In their drunken frenzy they made his end more gruesome by first trying to squeeze the life out of him with his own scarf (picked up it is said by Skariatin from the bedpost where the Tsar usually hung it at night), and when this proved unsuccessful they seized a malachite paper weight from the writing table and pressed it hard against his throat till life was extinct. When all was over Benningsen and Zubov returned to survey the scene.

Meanwhile Pahlen, who had taken care not to be present in the death chamber, had gone to the apartments of the heir to the throne, there to await the news which would spell success or failure. Should all go well then his own future was assured: should the plot fail he could always arrest Alexander and hope for the best.

Alexander received the news of his father's death with feelings very different from those of Pahlen. He was completely overcome and suffered a nervous collapse, declaring that he would not accept a crown stained with his father's blood. It was a night he never forgot and the memory of it lived to haunt him to the grave. Confusion reigned on all sides in the Castle where an atmosphere of treason, treachery and violence produced an almost physical impact on both the innocent and the guilty. It was Alexander's wife, Elizabeth of Baden, who finally rose to the occasion and convinced her husband that the situation, however horribly brought about, now demanded firmness and resolution, if worse were not to follow. She, Benningsen (who had already performed the valuable service of calming the fears of Paul's widow and blocking any political ambitions she may have had), and the Grand Duke Constantine at last prevailed upon Alexander to go to the Winter Palace, show himself to the people and assume the reins of government. It was given out that the Emperor had died of apoplexy and cosmetics were applied to his face to conceal the discolouration. After lying in state in the Mikhailovsky Castle Paul was buried alongside his ancestors, in the Fortress of St. Peter and St. Paul on Easter Eve, 23 March.

There is little or no mystery about his death save that it is still impossible to say for certain which of the regicides were the actual murderers. None of them was ever punished (this was the same as 1762), but few benefited from it (this was different from 1762). Pahlen, whose presence was now odious to the new ruler, retired to his Baltic estates, Panin, recalled to favour, was soon banished again, the Zubovs were once again forced into retirement and only Benningsen—who at least had done something to bring comfort to the Imperial Family on the terrible night of Paul's death—survived to play a prominent part in the military struggle against Napoleon.

The story of that great struggle belongs to Russian history. It gave Alexander an undying place, not only in his own country's history but in that of Europe as a whole. He was fêted and flattered in Paris, in London, in Vienna and even in Berlin as the saviour of Europe. He enjoyed in the West a prestige that no other Tsar had ever had before.

Nevertheless, there is ample evidence that he could never divest himself of a feeling of guilt about the events of 1801. The circumstances of his father's betrayal and the awful manner of Paul's death continued to prey on his mind. His wife had written to her mother, the Princess of Baden, soon after the murder of Paul saying that her husband's soul would for ever bear the marks of what had happened at the Mikhailovsky Castle.

From 1813 onwards, after he had met the religious enthusiast and mystic, Mme. de Krüdener, to whom he described himself as a man 'crushed beneath the terrible burden of a crown', he sought deliverance in vague ideas of mystical pietism. These at first found an outlet in his schemes for a Holy Alliance of all Christian sovereigns to ensure perpetual peace—a sort of early nineteenth-century United Nations, which Metternich, the Austrian Chancellor, had managed to convert into a sort of international Gestapo whereby the monarchs of Europe could keep their subjects in perpetual servitude. Lord Castlereagh, the British Foreign Secretary, described the project as 'a piece of sublime mysticism and nonsense' and excused Great Britain from joining it on constitutional grounds. And so in the end Alexander was left with no illusions as to the failure of this dream. He could not hope to escape that way.

Thus by 1820 be began to feel that all his efforts at home and abroad were doomed to failure. The great victories over Napoleon were a thing of the past and all the bright dreams of his early years remained unfulfilled. He was a tired and disillusioned man. The revolt of the Greeks against their lawful sovereign, the Sultan of Turkey, only served to emphasise the inescapable contradictions of his position. They enjoyed his sympathies as Christians and co-religionists, but their action—if he were to support them—would involve a breach of monarchical solidarity.

The death of his favourite sister, the Queen of Württemberg, in 1819, followed in 1824 by the loss of his daughter, Sophia Narishkin, who died of tuberculosis on the eve of her marriage, made him more and more anxious to lay down his crown and find peace of mind in a life of private atonement. No Russian Tsar, as he knew only too well, had ever successfully abdicated before, and if he was to escape from his official life some other means must be found.

This was his frame of mind in September 1825 when he set out to stay in Taganrog, a small port on the Sea of Azov. There he was joined ten days later by his wife, and indeed it was ostensibly on her account that he chose it, for the Empress's doctors had advised her not to spend another winter in so cold a place at St. Petersburg.

At Taganrog, according to the official account, the Tsar died of malaria at 11.10 a.m. on the morning of 9 November 1825, and an autopsy was made by his English doctor, Sir James Wylie.[6] Six weeks later the body was taken to St. Petersburg for burial in the church of

---

[6] Dr. Tarassov says in his *Memoirs* (published in 1872) that he drew up the post-mortem report but did not sign it. Nevertheless it bears his signature with that of Wylie and eight other medical attendants.

St. Peter and St. Paul. The Tsarina stayed behind in Taganrog (though not in the same house) for the rest of the winter. She died in May 1826 in a small village in the Kaluga province, in central Russia, on her way back to the capital.

From the beginning not every one was satisfied with the official story. Taganrog was a small and distant place. There were few eye-witnesses of the closing days of Alexander's life and fewer news-papers to broadcast the events to his subjects. It took eight days in fact before the authorities in St. Petersburg learned what had hap-pened in Taganrog. People discounted Wylie's autopsy because many remembered that years before he had signed the death certificate of Alexander's father, attributing Paul's death to apoplexy, whereas he had been strangled. They also wondered why there had been such a long delay in despatching Alexander's corpse to the capital. During the journey the coffin had been sealed.[7] When it reached Tsarskoe Selo it was opened in the presence of the Dowager Empress (Alex-ander's mother), Tsar Nicholas I and his wife and Alexander's youngest brother, the Grand Duke Michael Pavlovitch. It had then been lodged in the cathedral of Our Lady of Kazan in St. Petersburg for a month and finally buried in St. Peter and St. Paul on 25 March.

The choice of Taganrog for the imperial couple to stay in struck many people as odd. It was exposed to bitter north-east winds that could do little to improve the Empress's health. Moreover, it had no suitable accommodation—merely a one storeyed villa, with a base-ment for servants, set in modest grounds.

Others recalled that before setting out for Taganrog the Tsar had put all his affairs in order and sorted out his papers as though he did not expect to come back. He had even arranged for a change in the succession, though few people were aware of this.

Both Alexander's children had died in infancy—Sophia Narishkin was an illegitimate child—and the heir to the throne, therefore, was his next brother, the Grand Duke Constantine. Constantine's first marriage, to an aunt of Queen Victoria, had ended in divorce—she left him soon after Paul's murder—and his second wife, a Polish countess, was both a commoner and a Catholic. The marriage was in fact a morganatic one and the Princess Lowicz, as she was styled,

---

[7] The body was said to be discoloured beyond recognition, and this led to the rumour, supported by a story of Tolstoy's, that the body of a man who had died from being flogged (in Taganrog) had been substituted for the Tsar's.

could never hope to be Tsarina of Russia. Constantine was his brother's Viceroy in Poland and in any event did not wish to quit his comfortable palace in Warsaw for the hazardous delights of the imperial throne. Although named in the hope that he might revive the glories of the Byzantine empire Constantine had no wish to rule. Moreover, he was childless and the succession was bound to pass ultimately to his younger brother Nicholas who was properly married to a royal princess (Charlotte of Prussia) and was already the father of a son and heir (the future Alexander II). As a result of a visit by Alexander to Warsaw and a subsequent interchange of letters between the brothers, Constantine waived his rights in favour of Nicholas. A sealed copy of this Act of Renunciation was placed in the Uspensky Cathedral in Moscow with instructions that it should be opened immediately after Alexander's death. This manoeuvre did not in fact work very smoothly in 1825. Three weeks' confusion followed the death of Alexander, in which the country was left without an effective ruler. Nicholas proclaimed Constantine while the latter flatly refused to become Tsar and messages went to and fro between Warsaw and St. Petersburg, thus providing certain disaffected aristocrats in the capital with the opportunity of staging the famous Decembrist revolt—a sort of aristocratic rehearsal of the overthrow of Tsardom in 1917.

To return to what happened at Taganrog during November 1825. For a time all went well. The imperial couple, away from the distractions and intrigues of court life and still in their forties, were able to overcome the estrangements brought by the years and recreate some of the happy atmosphere of their early married life. But the spirit of restlessness that was never far away soon re-possessed the Tsar. Most of November he spent visiting the Black Sea Coast and the Crimea. His health showed signs of strain and he was in poor spirits because on the return journey a government courier named Maskov, who was bringing confidential papers from St. Petersburg, had had a coach accident, fractured his skull and died almost immediately. In accordance with Alexander's instructions Maskov's body was brought to Taganrog.

Contradictory accounts exist of the last fortnight of the Tsar's life. These were written by the Empress (whose account is incomplete), by Prince Peter Volkonsky (who wrote up his diary some time after the events described in it) who was part of the imperial suite, by Sir

James Wylie, his English physician, by Dr. Dimitri Tarassov, his Russian doctor, and by the anonymous author of the manuscript entitled *The Official History of the Illness and Death of Emperor Alexander I*. It is not easy, therefore, to piece together the exact sequence of events.

The critical day seems to have been 11 November (23rd new style), the evening of which the Empress spent alone with her husband. The same night she sat down and wrote to her mother, the Princess of Baden, a letter, using the cryptic words: '*Où est le repose dans cette vie? Lorsqu'on croît avoir tout arrangé pour le mieux et pouvoir le goûter, il survient une épreuve inattendue*' (Where is peace to be found in this life? When one believes one has arranged everything for the best and is able to enjoy it, there intervenes an unexpected trial). Clearly this does not refer to the Emperor's approaching end for although he never left his bed again he had still ten days to live. Some writers are convinced that Elizabeth had in mind her husband's intention to abdicate when he got better, while others think that he had just disclosed to her his plans to disappear by passing off the body of the dead courier, Maskov (which had been buried in the local cemetery two days previously) [8] as his own, and his fixed resolution not merely to give up the crown but to forsake the world itself. The supporters of this theory point out that the choice of Taganrog was not really so odd: it possessed a harbour adequate, but not too frequented, from which the Tsar could hope to make his escape by sea. This they point out was the only method he had of covering his tracks, any journey by land would have been too easily traceable. And to give support to this there was in the harbour at Taganrog at this time a yacht belonging to Lord Cathcart, a former British Ambassador in St. Petersburg and a personal friend of Alexander. Moreover, this yacht left the harbour rather unexpectedly at this time.

The story then switches to Siberia, where nine years later (in September 1836) a man of about sixty years of age (Alexander had been born in 1777) arrived in the village of Krasnoufimsk, in the province of Perm. Although dressed simply, he was mounted on a fine white horse such as no peasant at that time could hope to possess. He was tall (like Alexander), had a fine and distinguished appearance,

---

[8] Maskov's body had been embalmed (why?) by Dr. Tarassov. Distance conveniently prevented any of his family being present at the funeral.

but was reserved and taciturn. After his horse had been re-shod, he spent the night at the village inn. The next morning the police, alerted by the blacksmith, asked to see his papers. He replied that he had none and refused to disclose his identity or answer any further questions. So he was arrested, charged in the local court and convicted as a vagrant. He was sentenced to six months' imprisonment, with twenty lashes of the knout, and then in April 1837 deported to Bogoyavlensk. There he adopted the name of Feodor Kuzmich although in the local police files he still figured as number 117. This was clearly a makeshift name meaning Feodor the son of Kuzmich and gives no real clue to his identity. He spent five years at Bogoyavlensk and then settled in a village near Krasnovechensk, where he lived the life of a hermit, spending the summer in solitary meditation in a hut deep in the forest and the winter lodging in the house of a rich peasant who had befriended him. From there he passed on, some years later, to Tomsk, where once again he lived with a well-to-do peasant, this time in a hut in the man's garden. And there he died on 1 February 1864, and was buried three days later in the grounds of the Bogoroditsko-Alexeyevsk monastery in Tomsk.

By this time he had established a considerable reputation as a *starets*, or holy man, for although he never belonged to any regular monastic order the austerity and simplicity of his life was apparent for all to see. His scanty possessions were said to include a beautiful icon which had engraved on it the letters A I (Alexander Imperator) surmounted by the imperial crown. He was befriended by the clergy, including the Archbishop of Irkutsk, was clearly no peasant but a man of birth and breeding. His knowledge of history and of court life impressed itself on all who met him and he bore a close physical resemblance to Alexander I. Indeed he was 'recognised' by some high ranking officials and many people believed that he was the former Tsar.

Not only did he enjoy the highest patronage in exalted circles in Church and State, but he also excited the interest of the Imperial Family. It was in fact the strong and persistent interest that they took in him that makes the mystery of his identity historically interesting. The Grand Duke, Michael Pavlovitch, Alexander's youngest brother, is said to have appeared in Krasnovechensk shortly after Kuzmich had been beaten and to have threatened the judges and others responsible with severe punishment if anything like it happened again.

It was only an interview with the prisoner that turned aside his wrath.

Nicholas I certainly took a considerable interest in Kuzmich and Alexander II, before his accession, is said to have taken his young bride to Siberia to visit him. Alexander III had his great uncle's tomb opened in the late 1880s and is said to have found it empty— something which the Soviet authorities also experienced when they opened it in 1926. Nicholas II, the last of his line, paid a special visit to Kuzmich's tomb at Tomsk and finally the Grand Duke Nicholas Michailovitch (a grandson of Nicholas I), who was shot by the Bolsheviks in 1919, published a biography of Alexander I in which he discusses the whole question. He had the advantages of having access to the family archives, although a number of these, including the vital papers of Alexander's mother, the Dowager Empress Marie Feodorovna, were missing, having been destroyed on the orders of Nicholas I. The Grand Duke confesses that he came to the conclusion that Alexander I and Kuzmich were not one and the same person, though he admits that he is frankly puzzled by the latter's identity and adds that he thinks Kuzmich was in some way closely connected with the Romanov family.

The novelist and historian, E. M. Almedingen, who shares his view, suggests as a possible solution that Kuzmich was the son of that eighteenth-century mystery figure, Princess Tarakanova. She claimed to be a daughter of the Tsarina Elizabeth, who reigned in Russia from 1741 to 1761, by her lover (and possibly morganatic husband) Count Alexis Razumovsky.

She first appeared in Paris in October 1772, where her youth and beauty attracted a good deal of attention. She was at first thought to be a Circassian princess from Persia, but later, when she went to Germany, she claimed to be heir to the Russian throne. From Germany she went to Italy to further her claims. There she so charmed the British Ambassador in Naples, Sir William Hamilton (later famous in history as the husband of Emma), that he sent her to his bankers in Leghorn to secure a loan to finance her political projects.

Her pretentions were regarded by Catherine II as sufficiently serious for the Tsarina to instruct one of the Orlov brothers, Alexis, who was commanding a contingent of the Russian fleet off Leghorn, and who was a friend of Hamilton's banker, to have the princess abducted. She was brought back to Russia—after having tried unsuccessfully to jump the boat at Southampton—and imprisoned in the fortress of St. Peter and St. Paul.

From that time (May 1775) till her death (December of the same year) she was kept in close confinement and under perpetual surveillance. In charge of the operation was Prince Alexander Golitzin (who was later Alexander I's Minister of Education). It was pretty clear that the princess died of consumption and such was Golitzin's report, but lurid reports filtered through that she had been drowned in the underground dungeons when the River Neva overflowed— this inspired a macabre painting by the nineteenth-century Russian artist Flavitzky—and some said that she had even been eaten by the rats who infested the fortress. Whoever she really was, she carried the mystery of her identity with her to the grave. Before she was caught by the agents of Catherine II she had been on friendly terms with many Polish exiles in Germany who saw in her a possible instrument for overthrowing Catherine the Great and reversing Russia's anti-Polish policy. Among them was a Prince Radziwill who is said to have married her and, when he discovered she was pregnant, to have deserted her. No one ever knew what became of this child. He could have been Feodor Kuzmich and this might explain the great interest taken in him by the Romanov family.

The weakness of this, and indeed of the whole Kuzmich story, is that it all rests on hearsay evidence. Constantly one comes across the words 'is said to have', 'is supposed to have been', etc. The identity of Kuzmich is certainly a mystery, but there is no real evidence that he was Alexander I. There are certainly some very puzzling features about the death of the Tsar and there is no doubt that he wanted to retire into private life and was probably taking measures to put this into effect. But it looks as though death anticipated his decision.

For Alexander not to have died at Taganrog, and for Maskov's body to have been substituted, would have involved, even in so remote a place at Taganrog, a fairly extensive conspiracy of silence. It is possible that Alexander's wife and the rest of the Imperial Family when they viewed the body at Tsarskoe Selo were prepared to remain silent, but what of the doctors, the courtiers and the servants? They would also have had to be sworn to secrecy and this would have been difficult. Nor is there any evidence that that is what happened.

It is easy to see how the legend grew up that Alexander had chosen the life of a monk to expiate for the events of 1801 and give peace of mind to a troubled spirit. No one can say for certain how far he was implicated in the plot against his father, but evidently it placed a great burden on his conscience and one that the years did nothing to lighten. But all the same there is no evidence that can place him as alive after November 1825. As to Kuzmich, who never specifically claimed to be Alexander, it remains an insoluble problem. And so it is likely to remain.

10

The Kaspar Hauser Story

THE Kaspar Hauser story begins on Whit-Monday in May 1828 when a young lad appeared in the deserted streets of Nuremberg and attracted the attention of a certain Georg Weichmann, a shoe-maker, who was standing in the door of his house in the Unschlitt Platz. The boy, who appeared to be tired and exhausted, asked Weichmann the way to the house of a captain of a Bavarian[1] cavalry regiment (the 6th Schmolische Regiment), who lived near by. Weichmann took the boy to be a peasant lad of about sixteen years of age and thought he was a journeyman. The captain happened to be out and his servant entertained the boy till his master returned. When the latter did come back the boy handed him a letter, or rather two letters, one inside the other—both unsigned, one in Gothic script from 'a poor day labourer' and one in Latin script from a servant woman. The handwriting and notepaper were similar and were probably written by the same person.

The first letter stated that the boy had been left in the writer's home on 7 October 1812, and wanted to be a soldier like his father. The second said that the child's name was Kaspar, that he had been born on 30 April 1812, had been baptised and that his father, a former soldier in the Sixth Cavalry Regiment[2] was dead. Apart from this, all the boy had was a rosary and a certain number of Catholic tracts, and a handkerchief.

The captain, to whom these letters were delivered, felt that this was a situation beyond him and turned the boy over to the police. They lodged him in the fortress Tower—away from the regular prisoners kept there. He stayed there about three weeks and was per-

---

[1] Nuremberg was part of the kingdom of Bavaria.
[2] Kaspar, throughout his brief life, had a great liking for horses.

suaded to give some account of himself. This he did first in June 1828 and later (February 1829) he produced his autobiography.

His story was that as long as he could remember he had been kept in confinement in a room some six or seven feet long, about four feet broad and five feet high, where he had been unable to stand upright, and that the place had two shuttered windows which were kept permanently closed. There he had lain on a straw bed. His meals consisted of black bread and water, and he said that he had never seen the face of his gaoler who apparently not only fed him in the dark but had taught him to write in the same circumstances. He professed to have no recollection of his journey to Nuremberg—which was probably effected by carriage—nor could he recall his encounter with Weichmann. Noise and light disturbed him and he appeared to be unnerved by striking clocks and terrified both of the light of the moon (which he said he had never seen before) and, more understandably, of the effects of a thunderstorm. On the other hand snow, which he had never seen before, gave him great delight.

The Burgomaster of Nuremberg appealed to anyone who had known him to come forward and help identify him. No one did so and in July (1828) the city of Nuremberg adopted him and entrusted him to a certain Professor Daumer who was, at the city's expense, to provide him with board and lodging and to educate him. He was given the surname of Hauser because his original handkerchief had the initials K.H. (worked in red) on one corner.

Although no one came forward to claim him the Burgomaster's appeal did attract the attention of Anselm von Feuerbach, Germany's leading criminologist. Feuerbach, who lived at Ansbach, some twenty-five miles away, where he was President of the High Court, came over to Nuremberg several times to make a close study of the boy.

From the first there was a difference of opinion as to Kaspar Hauser's accomplishments when he first arrived. Weichmann and others asserted that though tired and exhausted the boy could walk properly and talk normally but with a country accent. Von Feuerbach, on the other hand, claimed that both his physical and mental powers were retarded, his speech defective, his sense of colour limited, and that he had no idea of money. Neither Feuerbach nor Daumer were altogether the best judges for they both had preconceived ideas, both were interested in mesmerism, while Daumer was a homeopath and Feuerbach a keen student of hypnotism and animal magnetism.

On 17 October 1829, Kaspar Hauser, who was usually very punctual, failed to turn up for his midday meal and after the Daumer house was searched he was discovered in the cellar lying in a pool of blood. He had been cut about the forehead and although in a state of exhaustion he was not seriously wounded. His story was that earlier on in the morning he had been attacked while returning from an outside privy. His assailant was a man with a black face; at first he took him for a chimney sweep, but later decided that the man was wearing a black mask. After he had regained the house he had taken refuge in the cellar in case the man pursued him indoors and there he had lost consciousness. Feuerbach thought that the attacker was his old gaoler of pre-Nuremberg days, but Daumer was more sceptical. He had come to the conclusion that his pupil was something of a humbug if not a downright impostor.

To prevent a recurrence of any further attack the Burgomaster decided that Kaspar Hauser should now have a permanent escort of two policemen. The Daumer house could not accommodate them so Kaspar Hauser was lodged with a merchant and city councillor named Bieberbach who had larger premises. It was not an ideal arrangement because Bieberbach was away all day at his business and Kasper Hauser did not get on very well with Frau Bieberbach. Moreover, he was now sent to school, the Nuremberg Gymnasium, where pupils were prepared for the University. Kaspar Hauser found school life difficult especially as he now had to study subjects like Latin for which he had neither aptitude nor taste.

This arrangement came to an abrupt end after a few months when another curious incident occurred. After a quarrel with Frau Bieberbach Kaspar Hauser retired to his room and—according to his story —when he stood up on a chair to get a book from a high shelf he lost his balance and in grabbing at the wall to save himself he dislodged a pistol that was hanging on a nail on the wall and it went off and the bullet grazed his forehead. The two policemen who were in the next room rushed in to find him on the floor, bleeding from the head. Once again the wound was not serious and he soon recovered. So once again it was deemed wise to move him: indeed all those who now regarded him as an impostor said that he had engineered the whole business simply to achieve this.

His next mentor was Baron von Tucher, who belonged to one of Nuremberg's oldest and most distinguished families. He now took Kaspar and the two policemen into his house. But a new protector now appeared in the person of Philip Henry Stanhope, 4th Earl Stanhope. He was considerably older than either Daumer or von Tucher and had been born in 1781. He first met Kaspar Hauser in May 1831 at the Burgomaster's where Kaspar had his lunch every Saturday morning. Stanhope was an eccentric peer,[3] who had received part of his education at the University of Erlangen in Bavaria and could speak fluent German. He had even brought a lawsuit against his own father, who contemptuously referred to him as 'Citizen Stanhope'. As a disciple of Rousseau, he was attracted by the idea of the noble savage and as a Whig he was equally interested in Locke's theory of the mind as a *tabula rasa*. Thus he was considerably intrigued by the whole Kaspar Hauser story. He spent five days in Nuremberg in the company of his new protégé, whose wardrobe and pocket money he lavishly replenished. Von Tucher, who was anxious to give Kaspar a normal life, did not relish Stanhope's interference and took a poor view of his excessive prodigality.[4] When Stanhope returned to Nuremberg in September—having kept up a brisk correspondence with Kaspar in the interval—to stay for two months, von Tucher suggested bluntly that Stanhope either took over complete charge or ceased to interfere.

As the city of Nuremberg was growing tired of paying for the upkeep of their famous prodigy, they were quite glad when Stanhope offered to take over the burden.[5] He spoke of taking his new charge to his English home at Chevening[6] near Sevenoaks and even perhaps of adopting him.

There had been for some time a vague idea that Kaspar Hauser's original language was Hungarian and not German and that he was in fact the son of a Hungarian landowner. In July 1831, at Stanhope's

[3] He had been a Whig M.P. till he succeeded to his father's peerage in 1816. According to the *Complete Peerage*, Vol. XII, Part I, page 236 he voted in the most erratic fashion. For Queen Caroline (1820), against Catholic Emancipation (1829), for the Reform Bill (1831–2), against Peel (1841 and 1846 (Repeal of Corn Laws)) and for censure on Palmerston's conduct of foreign policy (1850).

[4] Five days after he met him for the first time Stanhope gave him 500 florins.

[5] To do him credit Stanhope paid all the expenses connected with Kaspar Hauser till the latter's death in 1833.

[6] When his great grandson, the 7th Earl, died childless in 1967 the peerage became extinct, and he left Chevening to the nation as a residence for the Prince of Wales.

instigation von Tucher took the lad to Hungary, but it proved a fruitless visit and no progress was made in the matter of the secret of his birth.

In November 1831 Stanhope took Kaspar Hauser away from Nuremberg to Ansbach where von Feuerbach lived. He tried to persuade Feuerbach to take Kaspar in, but Feuerbach's health prevented this.[7] Instead he lodged him with a Protestant pastor named Meyer and employed a Lieutenant Hickel to act as his bodyguard. In February 1832 Hickel, this time alone, again went to Hungary, but again no evidence was found to connect Kaspar Hauser with that country.

Kaspar did not take much to either Meyer or Hickel and matters were made no better when it became increasingly apparent that Stanhope was losing interest and wished to wash his hands of the whole affair. Kaspar and Hickel were constantly at loggerheads and both threatened to go to Stanhope with their grievances. But by this time Stanhope had ceased to write to Kaspar, whom he now regarded as a liar and an impostor, although he still kept in touch with Hickel. In December 1832 he wrote to Hickel expressing complete disbelief in Kaspar's claims and suggested that as the lad was now twenty years of age it might be a good thing if he were apprenticed to some trade and began to earn his own living. It was ultimately decided that he should become a copying clerk in the law courts at Ansbach and that Meyer should continue to look after him and act as his tutor. Stanhope had not altogether given up hope of finding out Kaspar's parentage and he and Hickel were sent to Gotha in January 1833, where they met the Duke and Duchess of Saxe-Gotha[8] but nothing came of this visit. In September 1833 Kaspar and Hickel paid a brief visit to Switzerland and then went to stay for a few days in Nuremberg. There Kaspar not only renewed his old friendships with the Burgomaster, Daumer and von Tucher, but was also presented to the King and Queen of Bavaria.[9]

After his return to Ansbach Kaspar seemed somewhat out of sorts.

[7] He died on 29 May 1833, seven months before Kaspar Hauser, having written a book suggesting that the secret of Kaspar's origin was to be found in high quarters. His son, Ludwig, wrote several books in favour of Kaspar.

[8] The Duke was the father of the Prince Consort.

[9] The famous Ludwig I of Bavaria and his consort, Theresa of Saxe-Hildburghausen. In 1829 the king had offered a reward of 500 florins for the discovery of the identity of the man who had attacked Kaspar.

Feuerbach was dead and Stanhope, although he came to Germany in the autumn of 1833, avoided all contact with Kaspar. His only real friend was Pastor Fuhrmann, who had prepared him for confirmation.[10]

The end came that December when on the 14th, in the early afternoon, Kaspar staggered back to Meyer's house mortally wounded. His story was that he had gone to the Hofgarten (the Court Park) because a man, a stranger, whom he had previously seen in the town and who had then spoken to him, told him that the Court gardener wanted him to go and have a look at a new artesian well that was being sunk there. He had found no one in the park and had gone to sit on a bench by the monument erected to one of Ansbach's most distinguished citizens, the German lyric poet Johann Peter Uz (1720–96). While he was resting there he was accosted by a man who gave him a small silk bag (which he later dropped), stabbed him in the breast and then fled. Meyer, understandably enough, was so suspicious of this far-fetched story that he insisted on accompanying Kaspar back to the park to investigate for himself. But on the way Kaspar collapsed and doctors had to be sent for. Although once again the wound did not appear to be serious and although he was attended by three physicians, fever set in and he died three days later. He was conscious almost to the end[11] and according to Pastor Fuhrmann made a Christian end, forgiving all his enemies and commending his soul to God. But he also maintained to the end the truth of his account of what had happened.

The mystery of his death was never cleared up and is never likely to be. No trace of the unknown assailant was ever discovered,[12] nor was the knife that dealt the fatal blow. But the bag was found. It contained a note which was difficult to decipher and which appeared to be only a collection of vague phrases about the Bavarian frontier.[13] According to one of the doctors attending him the wound had been struck by a left-handed man and Kaspar Hauser was said to be left-

[10] He had been confirmed in May 1833.
[11] He was visited in his last days by a number of people including Hickel, who had returned, and his old friend the Burgomaster of Nuremberg.
[12] There appeared to be only one set of footprints in the snow although it is fair to say that the 'other side' produced seven witnesses (all workmen) who declared that they had either seen Kaspar in the company of an unknown individual or had seen the unknown man by himself.
[13] According to Frau Meyer it had to be held up to a mirror to read anything. It was signed with the letters M.L.O.

handed. This and the two previous attacks on him might well have been self-inflicted, but it is impossible to say. All Kaspar's many supporters have thought they were not, while all those critical of him believed that whenever he seemed to lose the limelight he chose this method of regaining it. It certainly did not look at first as if this wound was going to be any worse than the previous ones, but on the other hand we have to balance the fact that when Kaspar knew he was dying and accepted the ministrations of a pastor he still stuck to his story.

If his death is a mystery his birth remains a still greater one. The most persistent theory about his origin is the one that affirms he was a prince of the south German State of Baden. Almost from the first moment of his appearance in Nuremberg gossip had connected him with certain strange events in the royal family there. These events if they are true sound even more far-fetched than the story of his 'imprisonment' first told by Kaspar.

Towards the end of the eighteenth century Charles Frederick then Margrave of Baden, finding himself a widower, decided in his sixtieth year to marry again. His choice fell upon a Fraulein Louisa Geyer von Geyersberg who was nineteen years of age and a maid of honour to his daughter-in-law, Amalia. On the day of her marriage—24 November 1787—Louisa was duly created a baroness, but as the marriage was a morganatic one, since Louisa was not of royal birth, there was little prospect of her children ever succeeding to the throne of Baden. In fact as the Margrave had three grown-up sons by his first wife the succession seemed quite safe. Louisa bore her elderly husband[14] three sons and a daughter and managed to improve her position in 1796 by becoming a countess of the Holy Roman Empire under the title of Hochberg.[15] She was an ambitious women who was determined if possible to get her children recognised as princes and princess,[16] and ultimately capable, should the occasion arise, of succeeding.

In 1801 the situation changed slightly in her favour, for Charles

[14] Court gossip attributed their parentage not to the Margrave but to his youngest son, Prince Louis, who was five years older than his stepmother and on friendly terms with her.

[15] This was a territory in South Baden held by the margraves since the twelfth century.

[16] Children of a morganatic marriage, though quite legitimate, can only inherit titles from their mother and not their father. Thus they were styled Hochberg and not Baden.

Ludwig, her eldest stepson (see Table No. 12), who had visited one of his daughters, the Tsarina of Russia (wife of Alexander I who had just succeeded to his murdered father's throne), and was on the way to see another, the Queen of Sweden, was thrown from his sledge—it was night and he was asleep—and killed instantly. He left six daughters but only one son, Charles (born in 1786), who now became heir to his grandfather's throne. Of his two brothers Prince Frederick (1756–1817), though married, had no children and Prince Ludwig (1763–1830) was not married and not likely to do so. Thus only Charles now stood between the Hochbergs and the possibility of their ultimate succession.

Meanwhile the fortunes of Baden, because of its close proximity to France, prospered. With the advent to power of Napoleon the old Margrave[17] switched his allegiance from Vienna to Paris. As a reward the French Emperor allowed him to exchange his modest title of Margrave first for Elector and then Grand Duke. And in return the young Charles was married to Napoleon's adopted daughter Stephanie de Beauharnais. Between 1800 and Charles Frederick's death in 1811 Baden quadrupled her territory and became one of the leading powers in south Germany.

Charles and Stephanie had a daughter in 1811 and then a son who was born on 10 September 1812. Six days later the child, though apparently healthy, suddenly died, so suddenly in fact that the French Minister in Karlsruhe (Baden's capital) demanded an autopsy. This was performed by eight doctors, only one of whom (Dr. Kramer, the Grand Duchess's personal physician) had ever seen the child before. The Grand Duchess never saw her son after his birth, because the confinement had been a difficult one and she was still unwell, and a wet nurse had been brought in. Moreover, the doctor who had actually delivered the child was a specialist from Mainz and had gone back there. The verdict was meningitis. Although the Grand Duke did see the corpse, it was by then almost unrecognisable.

The legend soon grew up that the real baby had not died but instead one substituted by the Countess Hochberg. According to this story she had gone to a certain Christopher Blochmann,[18] who lived

[17] He lived on till June 1811 when Charles succeeded.
[18] Not the least confusing in this remarkable story is that most writers refer to this man as Blechner. E. Bapst in his *A la conquête du trône de Bade* (1930) and *Une mère et son fils* (1933) gives the name as Blochmann.

in Karlsruhe, was employed by her, and whose wife had recently given birth to a son. Blochmann, who was not only poor but already had three children, was easily persuaded to surrender the new infant, Johann Ernst Jakob and take instead the new Hereditary Grand Duke.

Then—if we are to believe it—the countess, dressed up as 'The White Lady', a ghost traditionally said to appear at the Court of Baden just before a death in the family and who consequently was not likely to be challenged by any terrified onlooker, effected the substitution. She had previously taken the precaution of drugging the two nurses who were the only persons present in the infant's bedroom and thus was able to take him away and leave the Blochmann child in his place. The prince was then hastily taken to a waiting carriage to be driven away to the Blochmann residence.

This sounds a pretty tall story, as the risks of detection must have been enormous, quite apart from the number of accomplices both inside and outside the palace who would have to be let into the secret. Nevertheless it was successful.

Such a dangerous undertaking could only be prompted by some very powerful motive. The motive usually put forward is that the countess hoped that her possession of the heir to the throne of Baden would enable her later on to produce him as a pawn in her unending struggle to secure further advancement for her children. If this were so the plot failed almost immediately because the substituted child became so ill the same night that he woke everyone up (including apparently the drugged nurses), had hastily to be baptised and died the next day.

The countess was now left in the difficult position of having to dispose of the real prince, as she could scarcely come forward and confess what she had done. So the unwanted young prince became Kaspar Hauser.

Another variant of this theme affirms that on the other hand the countess had deliberately substituted an ailing child hoping that it would die and that she had even helped to do this by poisoning it. The post-mortem on the child revealed no trace of poisoning and this motive is even less plausible than the other.

In fact it is difficult to give much credence to either version, for both seem pointless. The Grand Duchess Stephanie was only twenty-three years old in 1812 and was clearly capable of having many more children. It is true that the Grand Duke, who was only three years older than his wife, was leading a rather dissipated life and in consequence his health was uncertain,[19] but he was not exactly at death's door and still had six more years to live. There were in fact three more children born to them before he died in 1818, two daughters and a son. The son, named Alexander after his uncle, the Tsar of Russia, although very carefully looked after and guarded, died when he was one year old. This happened in May 1817 and so in 1818 the succession passed to Prince Ludwig. He had always been friendly with his stepmother and according to some accounts had known about the substitution she had engineered in 1812. He was content to live with his mistress, a former actress, whom he created Countess of Langenstein and their children and had no intention of marrying and providing for the succession in a regular manner. Thus after all, the Hochbergs became his heirs and the countess could have let destiny do its work without interference. There had been talk at the end of the Napoleonic Wars of dividing Baden between Austria and Bavaria should the royal line die out, but the opposition of Alexander I of Russia, whose wife was a princess of Baden, put an end to any such plans. The countess was raised to the status of a princess of Baden in October 1817 and in 1830 her eldest son, Leopold, duly succeeded as Grand Duke.[20] The countess did not live to see this as she died in 1820, estranged, as it happened, from her children who complained that her prodigal spending had reduced the family to beggary.

Meanwhile the infant prince was left in the care of the Blochmanns (Blechners) till Frau Blochmann died in July 1815. Blochmann was then pensioned off and Kaspar Hauser was transferred to Beuggen near Lauffenburg to a fortress that had been used in the Napoleonic Wars as a typhus hospital. There were still a few Hungarian prisoners there and it is supposed to have been from them that Kaspar learnt a few Hungarian words that led people like Stanhope to believe he was connected with that country.

It was while Kaspar was here that in November 1816 a fisherman came across a bottle in the River Rhine which contained a note written in mediaeval Latin and signed S. Hanes Sprancio. The note

[19] It was said that the Hochberg partisans encouraged the Grand Duke in his way of life in the hope that he would die prematurely.

[20] His great great grandson, a nephew of the Duke of Edinburgh, is the present Margrave of Baden.

said that the writer was being kept under close and cruel custody in an underground prison near Lauffenburg. The Kasparites—as the partisans of Kaspar Hauser were later called—said that S. Hanes Sprancio, which made no sense, should have been Hares Spranka and was probably badly copied. Then it would have been an anagram of Kaspar Hauser! Although the Paris paper *Moniteur Universel* published the letter nothing further came of it. However, it was now decided that Beuggen was no longer safe and so the child was removed to Pilsach, an estate belonging to a Baron von Griesenbeck. Griesenbeck, who was serving in the Bavarian army, rarely if ever went to Pilsach. The castle, although not many miles from Ansbach, lay well off the beaten track. Kaspar's new gaoler was a certain Franz Richter, an old soldier, who acted as caretaker at Pilsach. He was suitably bribed (not of course told the identity of his charge) and Kaspar stayed with him till 1828.

In February of that year Frau Richter died and Richter found it difficult to continue alone especially as the boy was rapidly growing up and becoming less manageable. So he decided that the best solution was to let the boy join the army and as Nuremberg was the nearest garrison town he took him there on Whit-Monday (23 May), set him free and gave him a letter to take to a cavalry officer there.

The three principal villains, according to the Kasparites, were the Countess Hochberg who had planned the exchange, a certain Major von Hennenhofer who took the baby prince away from the palace and moved him first to Beuggen then Pilsach and, according to some writers, even to the gates of Nuremberg, and Lord Stanhope who was later said to have been won over by the Baden faction.

Stanhope certainly knew various members of the royal family of Baden, including the Grand Duchess Stephanie. She had read a book on Kaspar written by Anselm von Feuerbach shortly before his death and was naturally somewhat curious. She had two interviews with Stanhope at Mannheim in February 1832 and expressed a desire to see Kaspar Hauser. Stanhope, however, felt that if she really was Kaspar's mother he might lose his charge and so, without proceeding any further in the matter, he returned to England. According to the Kasparites Stephanie went incognito to Ansbach to see for herself and was struck by Kaspar's physical resemblance to her late husband, but her cousin Napoleon III told Ludwig I of Bavaria that it was a crazy fairy story (*'une fable insensée'*). [21] Stephanie's daughter, the Duchess of Hamilton, held similar views.

Stanhope's rather equivocal part in the whole affair led to a lot of criticism and soon after Kaspar's death he defended his actions in a book published first in German and then in English.[22] His daughter, the Duchess of Cleveland, reproduced the same arguments in a book in 1893.

The affair continued to trouble the House of Baden for years and in 1875 the German Emperor William I, whose only daughter was married to the Grand Duke of Baden, took the unusual course of publishing in the *Augsburg Allgemeine Zeitung* the official record of the post-mortem of 1812 and full details of the young Hereditary Prince's death and burial.

The whole affair is said to fill close on fifty folio volumes in the public record office at Munich and it is still a subject that exercises a permanent fascination for many writers. Among others it inspired a play by Anicet Bourgeois and Dennery in 1838, Verlaine's famous poem Sagesse (1881) and a novel by Jacob Wassermann in 1908. As late as 1950 it was still receiving fictional treatment from the German writer Otto Flake.

For all this it is doubtful if anyone will ever know where Kaspar Hauser came from or who he really was.

On his tombstone in Ansbach cemetery are carved the following lines:

Hic jacet
CASPARUS HAUSER
Aenigma
Sui Temporis
Ignota Nativitas
Occulta Mors
MDCCCXXXIII.

and an enigma he must ever remain.

[21] Probably the strangest incident in this very strange story is the seance held in Paris by the medium Daniel Hume, when Kaspar was summoned before his distinguished audience and promptly announced himself as Karl Friedrich Ludwig, Hereditary Prince of Baden.

[22] Tracts relating to Caspar Hauser 1836.

11

Stella Chiappini: A Princess of Orleans?

THE riddle of the Temple was not the only question to agitate French royalists in the early nineteenth century. The Chiappini mystery proved equally piquant if less baffling.

The story opens in April 1773 in the small village of Modigliana in North Italy—in the Grand Duchy of Tuscany—when two French travellers calling themselves the Comte and the Comtesse de Joinville arrived exhausted at the local inn. The comtesse was well advanced in pregnancy and in fact gave birth to a daughter that evening. This was a bitter disappointment to her husband who was hoping for a son and heir who would have an unchallenged right to his extensive but entailed estates. It so happened that another birth took place in Modigliana that day, when the wife of the village gaoler, a certain Lorenzo Chiappini, gave birth to a son. The count thereupon proposed, for a consideration,[1] that the infants be exchanged and that he should take away the boy and leave his daughter instead. As the Chiappinis were poor and already had several children,[2] they were not averse to the idea. The exchange was therefore effected and the Comte de Joinville drove off with his new son and heir and his daughter, Mlle. de Joinville, was left to be brought up as Signorina Chiappini.

Her certificate of baptism, issued the next day and preserved in the register of the Church of St. Stephen at Modigliana, gives her name as Maria Stella Petronilla and affirms that she had been born the previous day to Lorenzo Ferdinando Chiappini, public constable of Modigliana, and Vincenzia Viligenti, his wife.

There is some evidence that from the beginning Stella was treated

---

[1] Said to be fifteen million francs, a monthly allowance and a house at Fiesole.
[2] Their final quota was seven.

rather differently from the other Chiappini children. Her 'mother' disliked her—perhaps not unnaturally in view of what had happened —but she was befriended by a local noble family, the Countess Camilla Borghi and her son, Count Pompeio.

When she was four years old the family moved to Florence as her father Lorenzo had been appointed squadron officer of gendarmes. This promotion was said to have been engineered by the Joinvilles. Certainly since 1773 his circumstances had become much easier and the family unexpectedly affluent. Stella seems to have received an education above her station although this did not prevent her, at an early age, trying her fortune on the stage.

There she attracted the attention of a rich but eccentric Englishman. Thomas Wynn, 1st Lord Newborough, was certainly an odd character and not greatly esteemed by his contemporaries. He had been born in 1736 and, because of his ability to raise a great number of volunteers and militia forces in North Wales,[3] where he had built at his own expense a large fort to defend the entrance of the Menai Straits against any possible invasion by the French, and because of his unfailing support of the government of Lord North, he had been given an Irish peerage.[4]

He was a wealthy landowner with extensive estates in Caernarvonshire (where his principal seat, Glynllifon Park, was situated), in Denbighshire, Anglesey and Merioneth. At the time he met Stella he was a widower[5] with one son. According to gossip, Newborough bought her—which, when one considers the early career of her contemporaries Lady Hamilton and Lady Blessington, is certainly possible.[6]

But he certainly married her, for there is a copy of the marriage certificate in the archiepiscopal archives at Florence. The wedding took place in the church of Santa Maria Novella on 10 October 1786. He was fifty years old and his bride thirteen and a half.

[3] The Glynllivon Volunteers, the Lord Newborough Volunteer Infantry and the loyal Newborough Association of Volunteers.

[4] In 1776, on eighteen consecutive days, eighteen new Irish peerages were created. Newborough was number six. As Irish peerages did not prevent their holders from sitting in the House of Commons, Newborough was thus able to retain his seat at St. Ives (which he held till 1780). He subsequently sat for Beaumaris from 1796 to 1807.

[5] His first wife, a daughter of the 2nd Earl of Egmont, had died in 1782.

[6] In 1804, at the age of fifteen, Margaret Power had been sold by her father to Maurice Farmer (her first husband) and then by a certain Captain Jenkins, with whom she was then living, to her second husband, Lord Blessington, for ten thousand pounds.

After his first wife's death Lord Newborough seems to have spent the next ten years in North Italy. He was cordially disliked by most Englishmen there including the British Envoy in Florence, the veteran Sir Horace Mann, and his successor Hervey. Mann described Stella as 'a singing girl', daughter of a policeman, and both he and Hervey disapproved of Newborough's extravagant and dissolute way of life. In 1791, for instance, Newborough spent some days in prison for debt till his agent could come out from England and bring him the necessary funds. He quarrelled both with his wife and her relations who appear to have occupied different floors in the same house. Indeed his brief imprisonment was supposed to be due to financial disagreements with his father-in-law.

In 1792 the Newboroughs quitted Italy for England. On the way they stayed in Holland where they were received by the Prince and Princess of Orange. Lord Auckland, the British Minister at the Hague, was a little more reserved in his attitude. He was not able to forget Lady Newborough's modest origins and her early stage career.

Thus when they arrived in London Lord Newborough gave out that his wife had previously been the 'Marchesina' of Modigliana and that she was the niece of a General Chiappini who was in the Imperial service. She was naturalised in 1798 and duly presented at court. In fact their whole manner of life was a distinct improvement on Florence, for Lord Newborough, besides his estates in North Wales, had a commodious house in Portland Place where they were able to entertain lavishly.

In 1800 his only son by his first wife died at the age of twenty-eight. Although he had been married seven years he had no other children and thus unless Lady Newborough could now be persuaded to take a more conjugal view of her position the peerage was threatened with extinction. In her *Memoirs* Stella insists that up till then her relationship with her husband had been purely Platonic but that she now agreed that the new circumstances called for some modification or this. So in quick succession she had two sons—Thomas (later 2nd Lord Newborough),[7] born in April 1802 and Spencer (afterwards 3rd Lord),[8] born in May 1803. The famous Corsican patriot, General Paoli, then in exile in England, was Thomas's godfather.

[7] He died unmarried at Glynllivon in November 1832.
[8] He married his first cousin whose mother was one of Chiappini's daughters. The present Lord Newborough is his grandson.

Lord Newborough, who had again become a Member of Parliament,[9] died in 1807 and three years later his widow married a Russian baron, Edward von Ungern-Sternberg, who had estates in Esthonia. She lived with him partly in Russia and partly in England. But in 1818, at his request, she went back to Italy to see her father. They had kept in touch throughout her married life and Lorenzo and other members of her family had visited her both in London and North Wales after she and Lord Newborough had returned to England in 1792.[10]

When Chiappini died in December 1821 he left Stella a letter which (in translation) reads as follows:

'Milady

'I have come to the end of my days without having ever revealed to anyone a secret which directly concerns you and me.

'This is the secret

'The day you were born of a person I must not name, and who has already passed into the next world, a boy was also born to me. I was requested to make an exchange, and, in view of my circumstances at that time, I consented after reiterated and advantageous proposals; and it was then that I adopted you as my daughter, as in the same way my son was adopted by the other party.

'I see that Heaven has made up for my fault, since you have been placed in a better position than your father's, although he was of almost similar rank; and it is this that enables me to end my life in something of peace.

'Keep this in your possession, so that I may not be held totally guilty. Yes, while begging your forgiveness for my sin, I ask you, if you please, to keep it hidden, so that the world may not be set talking over a matter that cannot be remedied.

'Even this letter will not be sent to you till after my death.

LORENZO CHIAPPINI.'

Stella was at Siena when she received this letter and she hastened to Modigliana, looked up all who could remember anything about what had happened there at the time of her birth. From them she

[9] For Beaumaris in Anglesey 1796 to 1807.
[10] Chiappini is said to have told Lord Newborough the secret of Stella's birth on one of these visits.

gathered that she was really the child of a Comte de Joinville. He was clearly a Frenchman and so she went to France to investigate further.

Her first objective was Joinville, a small village in Champagne with the ruins of a feudal castle originally belonging to the mediaeval family of that name.[11] There she discovered that the Joinville family had long been extinct, but that their heirs were the Orleans branch of the French royal family, who from time to time still used Joinville as one of their subsidiary titles.[12] So in July 1823 she moved to Paris and advertised for information about any Comte de Joinville who had been travelling in North Italy in 1773 and was at Modigliana at the time of her birth.

She is next said to have received a visit from the Abbé de St. Fare, who asked if it was a question of any money owing to the Comte de Joinville. What gave special interest to this visit was that the Abbé was an illegitimate son of that Duke of Orleans who was the father of Egalité [13] and grandfather of the then head of the family, Louis-Philippe. He was then a man of sixty-four and not impecunious. On being told that the advertisement had nothing to do with money he passed rapidly out of Stella's life and had no further contact with her.[14] Stella next paid a visit to the Palais Royal, then the Paris residence of Louis-Philippe, and later said that all the servants had recognised her and saluted her as Mlle. d'Orléans because of her obvious physical resemblance to the family. During her tour of the palace her twelve-year old Russian son—for she had had a further son by Ungern-Sternberg[15]—pointed out the likeness between a portrait of Louis-Philippe and grandfather Chiappini. To the end Stella always maintained that Louis-Philippe looked like an Italian peasant, coarse and swarthy, whereas she looked every inch a Bourbon.

Lady Bute had furnished her with a letter of introduction to the French Court, but she never presented it because she abruptly returned to Italy on learning that at the Convent of St. Bernard at Brisinghella, there had been detained for a few days in 1773 on the

[11] The most famous of them was the Sire de Joinville who accompanied St. Louis on his crusade and then wrote his memoirs.

[12] Louis-Philippe's third son was entitled Prince de Joinville, but the family had sold out their property in Joinville during the French Revolution.

[13] So called because of his 'egalitarian' attitude in the French Revolution. He is the supposed father of Stella. Born in 1747 he was guillotined in November 1793.

[14] Born in 1759, he died in Paris in July 1825.

[15] His descendants are now scattered all over the world—in England, France, Germany, Sweden, Romania, Egypt, Argentina and South Africa.

orders of the Cardinal Legate, a certain Comte de Joinville. This she felt was enough to justify an application to the ecclesiastical court at Faenza—Modigliana, though in Tuscany, happened to come under the ecclesiastical jurisdiction of the Bishop of Faenza in the Papal States—to have her baptism certificate altered to show that she was Maria Stella de Joinville, a daughter of the Comte Louis de Joinville.

Cardinal Consalvi, the Papal Secretary of State, allowed the Vatican archives to be searched and as a result the Faenza tribunal gave as its verdict in May 1824 that a substitution had taken place at Modigliana and that the prime mover in the exchange was the man detained at Brisinghella and that he was a Frenchman called Comte Louis de Joinville.

So Stella Chiappini was transformed into Stella de Joinville. But this no longer satisfied her and she began to describe herself as Marie Etoile d'Orléans.[16] Her case was that she was the daughter of Louis-Philippe Joseph, Duke of Orleans (1747–93) and his wife Adelaide de Bourbon-Penthièvre (1753–1821),[17] whom he had married in 1769 and that she was born in the spring of 1773 while her parents were travelling *incognito* in North Italy as the Comte and Comtesse de Joinville. His actual title at the time was Duke of Chartres.[18]

The Duchess of Chartres was one of the richest heiresses in France and she brought her husband a vast dowry, including such fine estates as Amboise, Aumale, Anet, Blois, Rambouillet, Dreux, Eu, etc., and one can understand the desire of the Orleans family to retain so vast a heritage. Among other titles set out in their marriage contract the duke was described as Comte de Joinville.

Stella now spent the rest of her days, either in France, Switzerland or Germany promoting her claims as a princess of Orleans. She became friendly with a number of well-known personalities such as Alexander Dumas. As a novelist he was intrigued by her story although he was politically wise enough not to give it any credence. The whole affair became such a mania with Stella that her Russian husband and son left her to go back to their estates on the Baltic and enjoy a little peace.

[16] The French form of the Latin word *Stella*, meaning star.
[17] She was a daughter of the Duke of Penthièvre whose father, the Comte de Toulouse, had been an illegitimate son of Louis XIV by Mme. de Montespan.
[18] The eldest son of the Duke of Orleans usually bore the title of Chartres till he became Duke of Orleans. Thus Louis-Philippe Joseph was known as Duke of Chartres from 1752 till his father's death in 1785.

She wrote to the aged Mme. de Genlis, who had been governess to the Orleans children[19] (and the duke's mistress into the bargain), but got no reply. Then in 1830 she published a book setting out her claims.[20] This was little better than one long sustained attack on the Orleans family, and, as the Revolution of July 1830 had brought Louis-Philippe to power as king of the French, it did not command much official sympathy. Louis-Philippe did not relish being described as of the lowliest origin, and his father stigmatised as a bad son, a bad husband, a bad father and a bad friend.

Her claims, however, did command support among some of the Legitimists. They stood for the legitimate or lawful line of Bourbons deposed in 1830. They remained strong partisans of the ex-king Charles X, and, after his death, of his grandson, the Comte de Chambord—or Henri V as they preferred to call him. The Legitimists detested the Orleans line as usurpers and regicides.[21] As late as 1889 a group of them from the city of Lyons put on a play (for private viewing) called *Maria Stella ou le dernier des Orleans*, but the police intervened to stop it after its first performance.

Despite Stella's persistent efforts to secure legal recognition the Paris courts refused to endorse the verdict of the ecclesiastical court at Faenza. Because she was a wealthy woman Stella was able to continue the struggle. But gradually she became the dupe of unscrupulous lawyers who saw in her a bird ripe for the plucking. Once she complained to the British Ambassador in Paris, Lord Stuart de Rothesay, who was a distant connection of her old friend, Lady Bute, about one of them, an Englishman named Henry Driver Cooper,[22] but he wisely refused to involve himself in so dubious a matter.

The end came in December 1843 when she died in her apartment in the Rue de Rivoli. The police promptly sealed the room and confiscated all her papers. Three days later she was buried in the Montmartre cemetery, where she still lies.

[19] She was born in 1746 and died in December 1830. She had been appointed in 1770.

[20] *Maria Stella, ou échange d'une demoiselle du plus haut rang contre un garçon de la condition la plus vile.*

[21] In the National Convention in 1793 Egalité had voted for the death of his cousin, Louis XVI. As the verdict was only reached by a majority of one the Legitimists regard the Orleans vote as the casting vote.

[22] According to Stella he had been an unsuccessful hop-merchant in England and was obliged to live abroad to escape his creditors. In France he set himself up as a lawyer and swindled his clients (including Stella) out of most of their property. The whole affair occupies much space in her *Memoirs*.

Who was Stella Chiappini? She certainly was not, as she imagined she was, a princess of Orleans. We have the French historian, André Castelot, to thank for proving this. He has traced in detail the movements of the Duc de Chartres and his wife in the critical years 1772–3 to prove that neither of them could have been out of France at the time.

He has constructed a complete timetable in the Orleans family to prove this. He shows decisively that neither the duke nor the duchess could have been in Italy at the time of Stella's birth.

They had been married at Versailles in 1769 and the duchess had given birth to a stillborn daughter in October 1771. To recuperate from this she had gone to Forges-les-Eaux in Normandy, a spa whose waters were supposed to assist fecundity. She arrived there on 1 July 1772 and remained there till 24 August when she went directly to Chantilly and then back to the Palais Royal in Paris. She appeared at the Opera for the performance of a new ballet on 25 August and then in September retired to Saint Cloud, the Orleans château on the outskirts of Paris and from there in October back to Chantilly. There was no suggestion at any time during this itinerary that she was pregnant: indeed it was not known in Paris till April 1773 that she was three months with child. She never left Paris in April 1773 and on the 24th of that month she was present at a service in the church of Saint Eustache. It therefore seems impossible to place her at Modigliana on the 16th.

Moreover, when she gave birth to a son—Louis-Philippe—that self-same year, in October, the birth took place not merely in the presence of the accoucheur, Millot, but also, as was the custom, with a cohort of princes and princesses in the room. Present at the birth were the Prince de Condé, the Duc de Bourbon, the Duc de Penthièvre (her father), and the Duc de Chartres (her husband). It was 3.45 a.m. and soon after came the Duc d'Orléans (her father-in-law), the Duchesse de Bourbon and the Prince de Conti. The child was baptised straight away by the Abbé Gautier, Doctor of the Sorbonne, in the presence of the Comte d'Hunolstein and the Comte de Schomberg.

It is pretty clear therefore that the duchess could scarcely have given birth clandestinely in North Italy to one child in April and then publicly—in the presence of so many witnesses—to yet another in Paris in October.

But of course it could be argued that while the duchess was in France the duke might have gone roaming with one of his mistresses and that Stella was the result of an illicit connection of this nature. But once again Monsieur Castelot makes this an impossibility. Just as he has traced the day-to-day movements of the duchess at critical moments so he has those of the duke. Thus on 8 April Chartres was present at a mass in the chapel of Versailles attended by the whole royal family, while on 13 May he attended a review of the Swiss Guards held by the king and during the vital period from 7 to 14 April he presided each evening over the meetings of the Grand Orient Lodge, of which he was the Grand Master.[23]

It is therefore quite clear that at the time Stella was born neither the duke nor his wife was absent from France. In any case they would have had to obtain the royal permission to go away and this would have been recorded.

Moreover the duchess was still a young woman (born in 1753) and because she had had one stillborn daughter in 1771 there was no reason to believe that she could not have any more children. And in fact she had four children after the birth of Louis-Philippe, namely Antoine (1775–1807), Louise (1777–82), Adelaide (1777–1847) and Alphonse (1779–1808). Much as the duke might have wanted to retain the Penthièvre inheritance there was no desperate need as early as 1773 to practise the kind of deception staged at Modigliana.

Monsieur Castelot's researches do not of course solve the question of Stella's birth. Considering Lorenzo Chiappini's deathbed confession and her superior education it is quite possible that the Faenza tribunal were right in supposing that she was the daughter of some French nobleman who was passing through Modigliana at the time.

It is possible—though this is mere conjecture—that her father belonged to another family (not the Bourbon-Orleans) who used the title of Joinville. There was for instance a family named Chaillon, who had been ennobled in 1694 with the style of de Joinville and who were ultimately created counts under that name in 1825.[24] And there was yet another family of Joinville whom Napoleon created barons of

[23] The masonic movement had a political significance as one of the liberal forces out to fight despotism. With the duke it was a passion.

[24] They were originally enobled not by letters patent but by a charge—i.e. through holding some official office that carried enoblement. Such families often used a variety of titles.

the Empire in 1813 and who later (in 1826) became barons under the Restoration. French noblemen were notoriously careless in the way they used titles and the rank they often assumed. It is possible that a member of one of these families fathered Stella. Another possible alternative is that her father was the Grand Duke of Tuscany, a brother of Marie Antoinette, in whose domains all this took place. He later became the Emperor Leopold II but was dead (1792) long before Stella set out on the treasure trail.

12

The Mystery of Lake Starnberg

To understand the events leading up to the death of Ludwig II of Bavaria in Lake Starnberg in 1886 it is necessary to have some idea of the family and kingdom into which he was born. The kingdom of Bavaria was created by Napoleon in 1805, but the reigning family, the Wittelsbachs, were among the most ancient in Europe, and had ruled over the country since the eleventh century. In the thirteenth century they divided into two main branches, the elder ruling in the Palatinate and the younger in Bavaria. In the course of time the rulers of both branches became Electors—the name given to those dignitaries responsible for the election of Holy Roman emperors—and they themselves had provided the Empire with three of its sovereigns. They had also supplied a king to Denmark, four monarchs to Sweden and in the nineteenth century the first king of Greece. They had also come within an ace of founding a dynasty in Spain to succeed the last Habsburg king there, Charles II, for the First Partition Treaty of 1698 had assigned the Spanish throne to Joseph Ferdinand (1692–9), the Electoral Prince of Bavaria. Unfortunately for Wittelsbach hopes in this direction the Electoral Prince had died of smallpox a year before Charles II. The Wittelsbachs had even crossed the path of English history, for one of them, the 'Winter' King of Bohemia had married James I's daughter, Elizabeth[1] while two of her sons, Prince Rupert and Prince Maurice, had fought in the Civil War for their uncle, Charles I.

They could trace their descent back to the ninth century and so could look upon not only families like the Hohenzollerns and the Bonapartes as *parvenus* but could by descent and continuity claim to be much older than either the Habsburgs or the Romanovs. Only

[1] From her the present Queen Elizabeth II of England is eleventh in descent.

the House of Capet in France could claim an older and more illustrious past.

At the end of the eighteenth century the Bavarian branch had become extinct and the Palatinate line had succeeded as sole rulers of the united patrimony. In 1805 they were represented by Maximilian I who had become Elector in 1799 and was now made king. Fortunately for Bavaria the real control lay in the hands of Maximilian's chief minister, Count Montgelas. By first opposing France and then, in 1801, changing sides to support Napoleon, and then once again going over to the other side in 1813, Bavaria was able to emerge from the Napoleonic Wars, not only as an independent kingdom, but with such additions of territory and population to make her, after Austria and Prussia, easily the most important German state.

Maximilian I died in 1825 and his son and successor, Ludwig I, who reigned till 1848, added much to the prestige and distinction of his country. He was eccentric to the point of mild lunacy but he transformed Munich from a drab provincial city into a capital that was universally admired. He had all the genius of a town planner, united with a taste for the bizarre in architecture. Greece, Rome and Palladian Italy were his models. Much of his work was destroyed by allied bombing during the Second World War, but scattered over his domains are the remnants of his fantastic activity. Outside Ratisbon, for instance, there stands the Temple of Valhalla which looks like the Parthenon and at Aschaffenburg on the River Mein (some twenty miles from Frankfurt) is the Pompejanum which is an imitation of the House of Castor and Pollux at Pompeii. What time he had left over from building he spent writing bad verse and relaxing with a bevy of mistresses.

The most favoured of these was Lola Montez, who came as a dancer to Munich in 1846. Her real name was Maria Dolores Eliza Rosanna Gilbert. She had been born in Ireland in 1818 and spent her childhood in India. There she eloped with a penniless lieutenant, then deserted him to embark on a career as a dancer. She claimed— quite falsely, for she was a pathological liar—that she was of noble Spanish descent and connected with the Bourbons, but her exotic and sultry beauty, combined with immense vitality and tempestuous manners, had enabled her to become an international adventuress. She travelled over most of Europe and a good deal of Asia (and later America) and had at one time been the mistress of Dumas and of

Liszt. Although her ascendancy over Ludwig was comparatively short-lived—he had to abdicate in the course of the revolutions which swept over Central Europe in 1848—it was an eventful and passionate association. She was created a countess, loaded with riches and jewels and virtually governed the kingdom. Not since the days of Pompadour and Dubarry had Europe seen so colourful or powerful a royal mistress. She ousted the government of the conservative ultramontanes and installed the liberals in their place and her slightest whim became law.

After his abdication Ludwig retired to a villa at Nice to enjoy his old age.[2] Lola departed for England where she married again and then to the United States where she contracted another union. She died in poverty and obscurity in New York in 1861.

The next king of Bavaria, Ludwig's son, Maximilian II, who reigned till 1864, was a more conventional figure, but he inherited the same streak of extravagance that marked the whole family. In 1832 he had bought the old ruined castle of Hohenstaufenburg, picturesquely situated in the Bavarian Alps and looking down on the two mountain lakes of Alp See and Schwan See. The site was connected with the legend of Tannhaüser. Maximilian had it rebuilt in the style of the original castle and renamed after the Swan Lake, Hohenschwangau.

Maximilian's son and successor, Ludwig II, was born at Nymphenburg, the summer palace just outside Munich, in August 1845. He grew up a wayward and eccentric personality and from childhood showed signs of being mentally unbalanced. There was in fact a history of insanity in the family. There had been a great deal of intermarriage among the Wittelsbachs and one of his aunts, Princess Alexandra (1826–75) was mentally unstable and had to spend her life in confinement. And Ludwig's own younger brother, Otto (1848–1916), who was to succeed him and of whom he was very fond, developed pronounced signs of incurable insanity and had to be put under restraint. One of the tragedies of Ludwig's life was to see Alexandra's symptoms appear and become worse in Otto. He wondered how long it would be before he in turn was affected. Their mother, Maximilian II's widow, Marie of Prussia, also came of a family where there was insanity. Her cousin, Frederick William IV, who was one of Ludwig's godparents, had been obliged as a result of

[2] Born in 1786, he did not die till 1868.

mental incapacity to hand over the government of his kingdom to his brother who was installed as Regent.[3]

In Ludwig's case he was able to hold out for the next twenty-two years but in the end heredity caught up with him. It is possible of course that environment as well had something to do with his mental condition. He had lost his wet nurse when he was only a few months old and there was never any real affection in his early life save from his governess. There was never much understanding between him and his mother who was too retiring and self-effacing to be of much help,[4] while he found his father rather a martinet.

But in 1864 the future still looked bright. Ludwig was only eighteen when he became king and although somewhat delicate he appeared to have many advantages. He was tall—over six foot three inches—and handsome (in a rather epicene way), and till he put on weight in later years had an impressive bearing. But he had not the temperament necessary for day-to-day rule. Like his cousin, the Empress Elizabeth of Austria, he disliked responsibility, felt weighed down by the pomp and circumstance of orthodox court life and bored by etiquette and ceremony. He was by nature a solitary man with something of the hermit in his make-up. He came to dislike Munich and the officialdom it stood for and increasingly he loved to escape to the mountains of Bavaria where he could lead an untrammelled existence and feel really free. Abdication (like Christina of Sweden), emigration (as John Orth was to choose) and even suicide (as Crown Prince Rudolf was to choose) all passed through his mind. It is not difficult to penetrate his thoughts for from the end of 1869 he began to keep a secret diary in which he recorded his feelings. The references in the diary are often fragmentary, some cryptic and obscure, but they do reveal the real man. After Ludwig's death the diary was placed in the Royal Archives at Munich and only came to light in recent times.[5] Also, most of Ludwig's letters have survived, as not long before his death he asked the recipients to return them.

Like so many lonely people Ludwig attempted repeatedly to achieve close relationships with a select few. A series of passionate male friendships swept through and at times controlled his life.

[3] Later the German Emperor, William I.

[4] She found strength and consolation in the Catholic religion to which she was converted in 1874. As a Prussian princess she had been brought up a Protestant.

[5] It was first used by Major Desmond Chapman-Huston in his excellent biography, first published in 1955. *Bavarian Fantasy: The Story of Ludwig II*, published by Murray.

Some of these friendships were innocent enough but it is quite clear from his diary that some were not.

Prince Paul of Thurn and Taxis was one of the first of these.[6] His eldest brother was married to Helena of Bavaria, Ludwig's cousin and a sister of the Empress Elizabeth of Austria.[7] He served Ludwig as his A.D.C., during the early years of his reign. He was 'succeeded' by Richard Horning, who was of middle-class origin and who became Ludwig's equerry. Their friendship, perhaps the most satisfying Ludwig ever found, went on—off and on—till within a few months of the king's death. Then came Baron von Varicourt, who also served as A.D.C.; then a poor actor named Josef Kainz who lasted two years. And many others much lower in the social scale— peasants, woodcutters, soldiers, grooms, etc. They were the recipients of Ludwig's closest confidences, often taken on holidays, expeditions and even walking tours. They were isolated and at times almost kidnapped. They had to be ready to dance attendance whenever he wished and as his demands on them were too concentrated and intense—he was always a jealous master—they were usually unequal to the relationship thus thrust upon them. Although no doubt most Bavarians were ignorant of this aspect of their monarch's life, gradually gossip seeped down from court circles and from the king's servants.

Of his friendships the most important (for posterity) was that with Wagner, whom he sent for within a few days of his accession. There was nothing overtly homosexual in their relationship, for the composer was then fifty-one years old and in love with Liszt's daughter, Cosima von Bülow, whom he later married. Wagner was the Great Friend and this friendship had to be played out in the limelight of publicity. Their close relationship was apparent for all to see, whereas many others of Ludwig's friendships few people knew anything about at all. Their intimacy lasted till Ludwig learnt of the real relationship between Wagner and Cosima von Bülow, but the friendship persisted to the end and a few days after Wagner's funeral Ludwig went incognito to Bayreuth to pay his last respects to his old friend. Though it cost the Bavarian treasury a good deal of money— Wagner's debts were paid off and money was lavished on him and his musical productions—both the world of music and Bavaria in many

---

[6] Prince Paul died in 1879 having renounced his rank and made a morganatic marriage.
[7] Helena (1834–90) was originally intended as the wife of Francis Joseph, but he preferred and married her younger sister.

ways profited from their mutual connection. The first production of *The Meistersingers* took place in Munich in 1868 with Wagner in the royal box calmly acknowledging the applause of the audience while the king was almost elbowed into the background. They were both supreme egotists, but between them the world became a richer place.

In 1867 Ludwig made one half-hearted attempt to break out of the bondage forced upon him by the habits of his personal life by getting himself engaged to his cousin, Sophie of Bavaria (1847–97). She belonged to another branch of the Wittelsbach family, the ducal line,[8] which had split off from the main stem in the seventeenth century, but which by marriage had remained closely connected with the royal line. This had been reinforced in the early nineteenth century when King Maximilian I's daughter Ludovica (1808–92) married Duke Maximilian. Their children included Duke Ludwig (1831–1920), known as Gackl (or Cock) in the family and who, after a morganatic marriage became the father of Countess Marie Larisch who played a somewhat sinister part in the drama of Mayerling (see next Chapter), the Princess of Thurn and Taxis, the Empress Elizabeth of Austria, Duke Karl Theodor (1839–1909), the distinguished oculist,[9] Marie, the last Queen of Naples (1841–1925), who distinguished herself against the troops of Garibaldi at the siege of Gaeta in 1860, the Countess of Trani (1843–1925), who had married a brother of the King of Naples, Sophie of whom we speak, and Duke Maximilian (1849–93).

They lived at Possenhofen, the opposite side of Lake Starnberg where the king often stayed in the castle of Berg. Duke Maximilian had purchased the house in 1834. It was used as a country house, was pleasant but unpretentious and affectionately referred to by the family as 'Possi'.

The engagement of Ludwig and Sophie lasted just over eight months and, after the marriage had been twice postponed, came to an end in October 1867, when Ludwig wrote to his fiancée to tell her that everything was over. He blamed her mother, who was a very ambitious woman, anxious to see her daughters seated on as many

[8] They were styled dukes and duchesses *in* Bavaria and in 1845 had been granted the style of Royal Highnesses.

[9] And father of Queen Elizabeth of the Belgians (1876–1965) who during the First World War showed the courage of her family and, after the Second World War as the first royal personage to penetrate the Iron Curtain, some of their eccentricity.

thrones of Europe as possible, for trying to force the issue. He told Sophie that he would always regard her as a 'dear sister' and even suggested that if she had not managed to find a husband in a year's time and if he was also still free they might review the position! But he had already become emotionally entangled with Richard Horning whom he met about this time and it is clear from the entries in his diary that he was distinctly relieved at not having to share his life with her and rejoiced in the recovery of what he thought mistakenly was his freedom.[10]

A year later Sophie married the handsome Duc d'Alençon who was a year older than Ludwig and who was a grandson of the French king Louis-Philippe, and found security, if not peace and fulfilment, in a normal married life.[11] The end of the Duchesse d'Alençon was in its way to be no less tragic than that of Ludwig. She perished in May 1897 in a fire at the Charité Bazaar in the Rue Jean Goujon in Paris, which cost the lives of many of the French aristocracy. It was said she died trying to save others and her body was so charred that identification was only made possible by the records of her dentist.

Ludwig had inherited the Wittelsbach mania for building and each time personal relationships collapsed he threw himself into it with renewed vigour. He was responsible for the building of Neuschwanstein (begun in 1868 and completed after his death), Schloss Linderhof, built between 1869 and 1878 and Herrenchiemsee begun in 1878 but left incomplete and Schloss Falkenstein which never got off the drawing boards.

Neuschwanstein is a fairy castle built on a mountain summit opposite Schloss Hohenschwangau. It is a mixture of styles, principally Romanesque and Gothic, and was inspired by Wagnerian ideas. Its foundations had to be blasted out of solid rock and despite its theatrical appearance it has an undeniable grandeur and majesty. Schloss Linderhof on the other hand was inspired by the *grand siècle* in France. Ludwig visited the Paris Exhibition in 1867 and came away with a consuming admiration for Louis XIV. This was

---

[10] 'Now I live again after this torturing nightmare . . .' 'Thanks be to God the fearful thing was not realised' are two typical entries in his diary. See Chapman-Huston, page 137.

[11] On the eve of her marriage Ludwig paid an unexpected and secret visit to her at Possenhofen. In 1887 her nervous condition necessitated a consultation with Krafft-Ebing. Her descendants now live quietly in France, Bavaria and Scotland.

to be another Trianon with other features added. The famous Blue Grotto, for instance, was modelled on Capri. Herrenchiemsee, on the other hand, was an attempt to build another Versailles, this time on an island. It was given a Hall of Mirrors to copy Versailles and certainly remains a most remarkable building. Schloss Falkenstein, on the other hand, which never got built, was to be constructed in Chinese style.

By the spring of 1886 Ludwig had become a total recluse, living in a dream world of his own, and the business of governing the country which had never occupied much of his attention[12] was virtually at a standstill. When he did meet his ministers it was only to upbraid and revile them. His habit of taking midnight drives by sleigh and usually in the moonlight, aimlessly round the countryside struck people as odd, while his habit of prancing round his castles at the dead of night clothed in white like Lohengrin seemed to suggest positive mental derangement. On top of this his habit of consorting with low company and the enormous debts piling up because of his mania for building more and more castles made official circles feel that some radical solution must be found and found quickly if the Bavarian monarchy and the Bavarian treasury were to survive. Early in June a delegation of four doctors led by Dr. von Gudden, a well-known alienist who had been in charge of his brother Otto since 1872, managed to interview the elusive king by pretending to be lawyers and on 8 June they drew up a report to the effect that Ludwig was suffering from hopeless paranoia.

Two days later, by proclamation, the king was deposed as unfit to rule and his uncle Prince Luitpold was installed as Regent. On 9 June a commission made up of ministers and court officials set off for Hohenschwangau where they thought the king was to inform him officially of what had happened in Munich and to apprehend him and take him to Schloss Linderhof, there to place him in confinement. At Hohenschwangau they discovered that the king was at nearby Schloss Neuschwanstein. There, where they arrived early (5.30 a.m.) on the morning of the 10th they were refused admission, and on the king's orders they were disarmed, sent back to Hohenschwangau

[12] For instance at the critical times of the Seven Weeks War in which Bavaria sided with Austria against Prussia in 1867, Ludwig was found to have gone on a visit to Wagner in his villa on Lake Lucerne, and during the Franco-Prussian War of 1870–1 he was occupied with his own domestic affairs.

and there placed under house arrest. Here they contrived to persuade their captives to let them return to Munich and report to the Government.

The next day it was decided that the castle of Berg on Lake Starnberg, twenty miles from Neuschwanstein, would be a better place of confinement and a fresh commission, this time made up almost exclusively of doctors and keepers with a military escort, set off to take the deposed king there. This time they managed to reach Ludwig —partly because the king's valet feared that Ludwig would commit suicide by throwing himself off the castle turrets—and they seized the king and the next morning (the 12th) started off for Berg, which had hastily had some bars put in the windows and been converted into a sort of private lunatic asylum. The journey in three coaches with the king locked in the central coach took almost eight hours and they arrived about midday.

Ludwig knew Berg very well as he had often stayed there and in happier days had entertained Wagner there. He also knew every inch of the countryside around the lake.

The first day at Berg passed quietly enough, for Ludwig, who had not gone to bed at all for the previous twenty-four hours, was exhausted and was only too glad to retire. He also seems to have been successful in gaining the confidence of Dr. von Gudden who sent a reassuring telegram to Munich reporting reasonable progress.

The next day, Whit-Sunday, 13 June, the king got up at 2 a.m. as usual,[13] but was persuaded to go back to bed. When he got up again Ludwig was much put out that he had no valet and still more that he was refused permission to go to mass.[14] But he recovered his good spirits in the morning and he and von Gudden (with two keepers walking behind them) took a walk together by the lakeside. It is possible that Ludwig wanted to reconnoitre the grounds for the scene that was to take place later in the day. At 6.30 p.m. in the evening he proposed a second walk, before supper. Dr. von Gudden agreed but for some reason told the keepers that they need not come. So, unaccompanied, the two set off—the sixty-two-year-old doctor and the forty-year-old monarch. Ludwig was wearing a light over-

---

[13] Increasingly he preferred the night, which assured him better privacy and which he often spent in nocturnal drives around the countryside.

[14] Von Gudden was a Protestant and was not very sympathetic to this request. Moreover, he feared a public appearance of the king might cause popular demonstrations.

coat and carrying an umbrella, for it was overcast and later came on to rain.

At 8 o'clock when they had not returned the occupants of the castle grew alarmed and had the grounds searched. Not till 10.30 p.m. was any trace of them found and then they came across the king's hat, his coat and jacket and umbrella, together with von Gudden's rather badly battered hat. These were by the shore of the lake. A boat was then procured and there in the lake, in fairly shallow water not far from the shore, the bodies of both the missing men were found. Von Gudden's feet were embedded in the mud and he was face downwards in the water: Ludwig's body was a little farther out.

Artificial respiration was tried, but by midnight they were both pronounced dead. An enquiry held almost at once revealed that there were some puzzling features, for the doctor's face had bruises and scratches as well as some tell-tale marks round the throat, while the king's body was completely unmarked. An open verdict was returned, for suicide would raise religious problems about burial that were unthinkable, but most people from that day to this have been inclined to believe that Ludwig had done away with himself, rather than face growing old in asylum like his brother. No autopsy was performed on von Gudden.

What really happened? It is of course quite impossible to say for certain, as the only two eye-witnesses were both dead. Whatever happened must have happened fairly soon as Ludwig's watch (which was inside his waistcoat pocket) had been stopped by immersion at 6.54 p.m. Equally clearly it was no accident and there had obviously been a struggle between the king and his medical attendant on the shores, and probably in the lake.

After that it is a matter of conjecture. It may have been a simple case of suicide which the doctor tried to prevent and which cost them both their life. Although the fact that Ludwig took off both his overcoat and jacket and was apparently able to do so without being interrupted suggests that his opponent was already out of action, and raises the possibility that the king may have hoped to escape.

He knew that the land routes through the forest were being patrolled by his keepers, whereas the lake at this point was not much more than two or three miles wide and fairly shallow: and he was a good swimmer. Moreover, on the other side lay Possenhofen and a chance of salvation. He may even have thought that it was possible that the Empress Elizabeth was actually staying there at the moment.[15]

Against the suicide theory is the fact that he had taken off his coat and jacket. This seems an odd procedure, to say the least of it. It would have been easier and quicker to drown with them on and easier to swim with them off. It is true that Ludwig had often spoken of suicide, but the moment to have taken his life was at Neuschwanstein when he could have thrown himself off the battlements as he had threatened to do and even on the way to Berg when the party stopped to have refreshments.

The most probable reconstruction is that Ludwig suddenly struck von Gudden (perhaps with his umbrella), took off his coat and jacket, waded into the lake (whether to escape or to commit suicide can never be established) and was there overtaken by the doctor who by that time had recovered from a blow that possibly had only stunned him. A further struggle occurred in which both men were drowned.

Yet another theory has been suggested that one or both of them were attacked by cramp or had a seizure. But there is no evidence to support this though it is true that the king (though not von Gudden) had eaten a heavy meal just before starting out.

It has also been suggested that Ludwig was determined to take his revenge on his captors and deliberately murdered von Gudden. He certainly resented the way his 'abdication' had been forced upon him and the fact that before action was taken against him he had had no proper medical examination but was just assumed to be insane on the basis of a casual encounter. The Empress Elizabeth was not the only person who felt that for all his obvious eccentricities Ludwig was not actually out of his mind. Bismarck appears to have thought so too. But if murder was in the king's heart it seems a strange way of accomplishing it. We shall never know, for the secret of what happened on that June night lies for ever buried in the waters of Lake Starnberg.

The king's body was taken to the Residenz Palace in Munich to lie in state and, on 17 June, he was buried with his ancestors. The

[15] She was not, in point of fact. She was, as Ludwig knew, in Bavaria at the time, but at Feldafing. She had just visited her mother not at Possenhofen but at nearby Garatshausen, another Wittelsbach property. Even if there was no help at Possenhofen the Austrian frontier was not too far away.

chief mourner was the Empress's son, Crown Prince Rudolf of Austria, himself already a doomed figure.

The Bavarian monarchy had just over thirty years more to live. Otto automatically succeeded his brother, but he was a figurehead and remained in captivity in Schloss Fürstenried, on the road between Munich and Berg, till at last death released him in October 1916. Prince Luitpold remained Regent and after his death in December 1912 his son, Prince Ludwig, assumed control. However, in November 1913, as it was clear there was no prospect whatever of King Otto's recovering his reason, the throne was declared vacant by decree and the prince—who in any event was the heir apparent—ascended the throne. He was the last King of Bavaria. A revolution in November 1918 deprived him of his throne and he died in Hungary in 1921.

13

Mayerling

On 21 November 1916 the Emperor Francis Joseph of Austria died in the Schönbrunn Palace at Vienna, where he had lived in his latter years in Spartan simplicity. After lying in state in St. Stephen's Cathedral he was buried in the vault of the Capuchin Church where all the Habsburgs since 1633 had been interred. He was the last Emperor to be buried there[1] and was the last great ruler of his House. The Dual Monarchy still had two more years of life to run under his great nephew and successor, the Emperor Karl, but that reign was little more than an epilogue: the main drama was over.

Francis Joseph had come to the throne in 1848 and his long reign—the longest in modern history since that of Louis XIV—was one long series of disasters, both political and personal. Politically Austria lost her Italian possessions, found herself excluded for ever from German affairs, was obliged to share with Hungary dual control, and finally plunged into a war in 1914, which led to her disintegration and ruin. On the domestic side Francis Joseph had suffered successive personal blows by the execution of his brother Maximilian at the hands of a firing squad in Mexico (1867), the suicide of his only son, Crown Prince Rudolf (1889), the estrangement and assassination of his wife at the hands of an Italian anarchist in Geneva (1898) and finally the murder of his nephew and heir, Francis Ferdinand, in Serajevo in 1914. But in many ways the death of Rudolf was the hardest blow to bear, for on him the best hopes of the dynasty had rested.

The Crown Prince Rudolf, the only son of Francis Joseph and

[1] His successor died in exile in 1922 at Funchal, where his body still lies in the church of Our Lady of Mount Madeira.

143

Elizabeth of Bavaria, had been born in the summer palace of Laxenburg, just outside Vienna, in August 1858. He was a highly intelligent, but at the same time a highly strung child. He suffered, as so many royal children have done, in that in his early years he saw little of his parents, and was handed over to be brought up by strangers. Francis Joseph and Elizabeth had been much in love with one another when they were first married (1854), but partly because of Elizabeth's difficult temperament and partly because of the jealous interference of her mother-in-law the Archduchess Sophie,[2] there grew up a barrier between them, which was never completely to come down. Already in 1860, Elizabeth had taken herself off to Madeira,[3] the first of her many journeys of escape which only came to an end with her death in Switzerland.

Thus Rudolf was deprived of the day-to-day love of his parents, and soon became aware how incompatible their temperaments really were. The first person placed in control of his upbringing was Count Gondrecourt,[4] one of those soldiers with the outlook of a drill sergeant who believe in toughening up their charges, and, although he was superseded at the end of three years, when the Empress realised what sort of man he was, the damage to a delicate, sensitive and highly nervous child had already been done.[5]

Gondrecourt's successor, Joseph Latour, was also a general, but at the same time a conscientious and reasonable man of liberal tastes. He remained in charge till Rudolf came of age, and whatever there was in Rudolf's character that was sane and sensible was probably due to his influence.

On the intellectual side, Rudolf had a whole host of tutors, many of them quite brilliant men. He was well taught and had a wide knowledge of subjects ranging from history and politics to geography and zoology. Among his teachers were Professors Brehm (Zoology) and Menger (Economics), both from Vienna University, and it is a pity that Rudolf, who had the capacity, was not allowed to attend the university in the ordinary way, but of course Habsburg tradition put that out of the question. As it was, only two other Habsburgs can

[2] She lived on till 1872.

[3] One half of her married life was spent out of Austria.

[4] He owed his position to the Archduchess Sophie, who warmly approved of his strict religious views.

[5] Part of Gondrecourt's discipline was to foster the child's courage by having pistols discharged unexpectedly in the boy's room at night!

claim to have had a better education and been intellectually superior, namely the Emperor Joseph II and the present head of the House, the Archduke Otto.

As a result of this good grounding and because of an inherent ability to express himself well, Rudolf was able to become the author of many pamphlets and articles on politics, economics and military affairs—for he had imbibed a sound knowledge of the art of war as well. Most of his writings, though not all of them, were published anonymously and his friendship with Moritz Szeps, the editor of the liberal *Neues Wiener Tagblatt*, [6] not only permitted him to contribute to that influential newspaper, but ensured the widest publicity for his views. Most of the articles had a distinctly critical outlook and encouraged the belief that the Crown Prince was both a liberal and a free thinker. For despite Gondrecourt, or perhaps because of him, Rudolf showed little interest in formal religion. He had of course been duly instructed in the Catholic faith and outwardly accepted it, but his attitude was cool and detached.

In 1877 Rudolf came of age, was given separate apartments in the Hofburg Palace and allowed his own 'court'. The comptroller assigned to him was Count Bombelles, who has been blamed, not without reason, with encouraging the Crown Prince to indulge in heavy drinking and to seek out amorous adventures. But it may well be that the tensions already obvious in his life compelled him to seek this sort of outlet. Meanwhile he did his military service, at first in Prague and then in Vienna. And here again, like his cousin, the Archduke John Salvator (see next Chapter), his progressive outlook brought him into collision with the conservative establishment and notably the Archduke Albert (see page 157 *et seq*). Like John Salvator he was no friend of Prussia, was apt to poke fun at the posturings of William II whose bragadaccio he despised. He was critical of the Dual Alliance of 1878, which tied Austria to the apron strings of Germany, and preferred to dwell instead on the great services France had rendered to the cause of progress and civilisation.

As heir to the throne, it was Rudolf's duty to marry young and produce an heir. His choice was restricted to the few Catholic dynasties still left in Europe, and after inspecting a Saxon princess, who was rather plump and never did get married, and a Spanish infanta, who was later to try and divorce her (Bourbon) husband and

---

[6] This paper had the biggest circulation in Vienna.

cause much embarrassment to her family, he selected Stephanie, the daughter of King Leopold II of the Belgians. Though the Coburgs were a bit parvenu, her mother had been an Austrian archduchess. She was not unpleasant to look at, though rather gauche, but she had been brought up in a court where there was no affection, and she had none to give. Moreover, although she was not unintelligent, she could be small-minded, and was apt to be spiteful. The Empress, who opposed the connection and who by now had achieved a much greater understanding of her son, who was in so many ways more obviously a Wittelsbach than a Habsburg, saw from the beginning that Stephanie would not know how to handle Rudolf.

However, the marriage duly took place—in Vienna in May 1881—and although Stephanie was later in her *Memoirs* [7] to complain of the shocks awaiting her on her wedding night, [8] the couple settled down as well as could be expected. A daughter was born to them in September 1883. But the birth was a difficult one, and necessitated an operation soon after that ended any chance of further children. Thereafter neither of them had much time for the other. Appearances were preserved, but nothing else.

Rudolf tried to forget the disappointments of his family life by throwing himself with renewed, and even fervent abandon, both into politics and into a life of casual promiscuity. Apart from the police, who kept meticulous reports on his visits to Sacher's café and to various night resorts, the only two men who must have known most about this side of his life were Loschek, his personal valet, who conducted his visitors in and out of his master's apartments at the Hofburg, and Bratfisch [9] who drove the coach or cab which took Rudolf out on his various expeditions. Both of them were absolutely loyal and, though some attempt was made by the government to exile Bratfisch after Mayerling, they had to give way before his blank refusal to move from Vienna; while Loschek, though he lived to be eighty-five and did not die till 1930, refused to open his mouth. Rudolf does not seem to have been a man of strong sexual tastes but liked

[7] *I was to be an Empress*, published by Ivor Nicholson and Watson, 1937. The very title betrays its author's essential vulgarity.

[8] This seems to have been endemic in her family. Her mother complained of hers and so did her sister, Princess Louise of Coburg. They were probably no worse than many a nineteenth-century bride had to put up with.

[9] Bratfisch was a cab driver used by Rudolf when he did not wish to turn out his own coach which was too conspicuous.

variety. Had he had a stable domestic background, he might have satisfied himself with a few casual affairs and left it at that. By temperament he was not really a libertine.

Meanwhile he still kept up his literary activities. He had already written a book on his travels to Egypt and Palestine, but his major work was to launch and organise a study, entitled *Austria-Hungary in Pen and Picture*. This, like the Victoria County History in England, was to cover in considerable detail every aspect of life in the Monarchy. The first volume appeared in 1885. He himself was a major contributor and got many other gifted writers to help. He also kept up his spate of articles in the *Neues Wiener Tagblatt*, and often Szeps, its editor, was smuggled into the Hofburg by the back stairs to receive his latest ideas. These were often quite radical—such as articles on the pernicious nature of the German alliance, the evils of Prussianism, the right of the French to possess Alsace-Lorraine, the intrigues of the Jesuits and the iniquity of anti-Semitism—and Szeps had to tone them down to avoid press censorship.

Although denied any real share in the government of the country, Rudolf was allowed to see some Foreign Office documents, and for a time he enjoyed a close relationship with Count Kalnoky, who was Foreign Minister from 1881–95. Through him, he did try to influence national policy, but he found Kalnoky too subservient both to Germany and Russia. He would have preferred a much more independent Balkan policy for Austria instead of one trimmed to please Berlin and St. Petersburg. With certain Hungarian politicians too he kept in close touch, for he had inherited something of his mother's regard for the Magyars.

With his mounting frustrations, however, his temper grew worse and so did his drinking. His father's health was excellent and there was little prospect of his succeeding for years. He had taken to using drugs and was in debt. By the end of 1888 he had come to the end of his tether. The stage was now set for the final act of his life, the drama of Mayerling. For about this time he met Marie Vetsera.

She was only seventeen years old but already had promise of great beauty. She had not long left the convent, where she had been educated, and had all the charm and bloom of early youth. She was of Hungarian extraction and her family, though of modest origin by the standards of the Viennese nobility—her father who was dead had received his title as late as 1870—they were rich and, in the case of her mother[10] ambitious.

Somehow or other Rudolf became aware of her existence and became interested in her, while on her side Marie had seen him riding in the Prater (Vienna's Hyde Park) and in the Imperial box at the Opera, and had formed a strong romantic attachment to him. He wrote to her and took steps to meet her, but found himself hedged in by his position, while she found it difficult to dispense with a chaperone. A go-between was found in the person of Countess Marie Larisch, who was a cousin of Rudolf and also a friend of the Vetsera family. She was a daughter of the Empress's eldest brother, Duke Ludwig in Bavaria, by a morganatic marriage with a German actress, and had been befriended by her aunt who had found a husband for her among the Austrian aristocracy. She was ambitious and had a taste for intrigue, but was also superficial, irresponsible and an inveterate liar. After Rudolf's death the Empress refused to have anything more to do with her.[11] She lived in the Grand Hotel and sometimes the two lovers met there, sometimes in Rudolf's apartments in the Hofburg and sometimes in some quiet spot in the Prater. Usually the countess collected Marie from the Vetsera house and on the pretext of taking her shopping took her to see Rudolf. Their first meeting appears to have taken place sometime in October or November 1888. Very few of their letters to one another survive, and what we know of their feelings for one another come mainly from Marie's letters to her old governess. Thus we know that by mid-January 1889 she was not only his mistress but they had pledged eternal love to one another in life and in death. Marie gave Rudolf a gold cigarette case engraved with the words *Dank dem glucklichen Geschicke* (Thanks to a happy Fate), while he presented her with a polished iron ring bearing the slightly more sinister letters I.L.V.B.I.D.T., which stood for *In liebe vereint bis in dem tode* (In love united until death).

[10] Baroness Helene Vetsera belonged to a family of Levantine merchants who were well known in international circles—two of her brothers had owned the horse that won the English Derby in 1876—and it is possibly from her Greek antecedents that Marie owed her good looks. Helene Vetsera survived the fall of the Habsburgs and died in Vienna in 1925.

[11] Count Larisch divorced her in 1896 and she married twice again, both times to obscure commoners, and finally died in New York in July 1940. Her account of events published in 1913 under the title of *My Past* is completely unreliable.

1 Edward IV (1441–83), portrait by an unknown artist

National Portrait Gallery

2 Engraving of Elizabeth Woodville (1437–92)

3 Richard III (1450–85), portrait by an unknown artist

National Portrait Gallery

4 Engraving of the meeting of the Princes in the Tower, 1483

5 Edward V (1470–83)

Engraving from an MS book in the Library at Lambeth

6 Engraving of Lambert Simnel (*c.*1471–1535) as a turnspit in the royal kitchen

7 Perkin Warbeck (*c.* 1475–99)
From a drawing in the Library at Arras

8 Henry VII (1457–1509), portrait by an unknown artist
National Portrait Gallery

9 Engraving of Philip II of Spain (1527–98)

10 Isabelle de Valois, Queen of Spain (1545–68), portrait by J. Pantoja de la Cruz
Prado Museum, Madrid

11 Don Carlos of Spain (1545–68), portrait by Alonso Sanchez Coello
Prado Museum, Madrid

12 Engraving of Don John of Austria (1547–78)

13 The Palace of the Escurial outside Madrid, engraving by Rennaldson

14 Mary, Queen of Scots (1542–87), portrait after J. Clouet

National Portrait Gallery

15 Lord Darnley (1545–67) and his brother, Charles, 6th Earl of Lennox (1555–76), portrait formerly attributed to Hans Eworth

Reproduced by gracious permission of H.M. the Queen

16 James VI of Scotland and I of England (1566–1625), portrait attributed to Arnold Van Bronkhorst
National Portrait Gallery of Scotland

17 James Hepburn, 4th Earl of Bothwell (1536–78), portrait by an unknown artist
National Portrait Gallery of Scotland

18 James Stewart, Earl of Moray (1511–70), copy by H. Munro from an unknown original
National Portrait Gallery of Scotland

19 James Douglas, 4th Earl of Morton (1516–81), portrait attributed to Arnold Van Bronkhorst
National Portrait Gallery of Scotland

20 Dimitry, Tsar of Russia 1605–6 (1583–1606), contemporary portrait

Hessische Landes- und Hochschulbibliothek, Darmstadt

21 Engraving of Ivan IV (the Great), Tsar of Muscovy (1530–84)

22 Peter the Great (1672–1725), Tsar of Russia, portrait by Sir Godfrey Kneller

Reproduced by gracious permission of H.M. the Queen

23 Engraving of Alexis, Tsarevich of Russia (1690–1718)

24 Peter III, Tsar of Russia (1728–62), engraving by Anthony Walker, 1752, from a portrait by G. C. Grooth, 1749

25 Catharine the Great, Empress of Russia, (1729–96), engraving by W. H. Mote from a drawing by G. Staal

26 Ivan VI, Tsar of Russia, (1740–64), visited by Peter III in prison in the fortress of Schlüsselburg

27 Portrait of Grigori G. Orlov (1734–83)

28 Louis XVI, King of France (1754–93), portrait by Duplessis
Château de Versailles

29 Marie Antoinette, Queen of France (1755–94), portrait by Vigée Lebrun
Château de Versailles

30 The Dauphin (Charles Louis of France), Louis XVII (1785–95), portrait by Kucharski
Château de Versailles

31 Karl Wilhelm Naundorff (1785–1845), who claimed to be the Dauphin rescued from the Temple in 1795, engraving by E. Scriver from a portrait by Lecourt

32 The Tower of the Temple, from a painting by an unknown artist
Carnavalet Museum, Paris

33 Alexander I, Tsar of Russia (1777–1825), engraving by J. M. Fontain from a portrait by Gerard

34 Engraving of Elizabeth of Baden (1779–1826), wife of Tsar Alexander I

35 The death of Alexander I at Taganrog, 1825, a facsimile of the engraving by T. Koulakov, 1827

36 The tomb of Feodor Kuzmich at Tomsk in Siberia

Kaspar Hauser—the foundling of Nuremberg (1812–33), a facsimile from one of the earliest signatures after Hauser's arrival at Nuremberg

38 Engraving of Kaspar Hauser at the home of his tutor, admiring a wooden model of a horse

39 Kaspar Hauser, after a painting by Kreal, 1830

40 Engraving of the family of Philippe Egalité, Duke of Orleans (1747–93) with Mme. de Genlis, the children's governess

41 Maria Stella Chiappini (1773–1843), who claimed to be the daughter of Philippe Egalité, Duke of Orleans (*below*), lithograph by Delaunois

42 Engraving of Louis-Joseph Philippe, Duke of Orleans (1747–93), nicknamed Egalité

43 Louis-Philippe, King of the French (1773–1850), the eldest son of Egalité, lithograph by Delpeche. Stella Chiappini claimed he had been substituted in her place

44 Ludwig II, King of Bavaria (1845–86)

45 Schloss Neuschwanstein, where Ludwig II was arrested

46 Lake Starnberg in Bavaria, where Ludwig II and Dr. von Gudden were drowned on Whitsunday, 1886. The cross marks the place where Ludwig's body was found

47 Crown Prince Rudolf of Austria (1858–
89), only son and heir of the Emperor
Francis Joseph

48 Rudolf with his wife, Stephanie of
Belgium (1864–1945)

49 Baroness Marie Vetsera (1871–89)

50 Engraving of the hunting lodge at Mayerling where Rudolf and Marie Vetsera were found dead on 30 January 1889

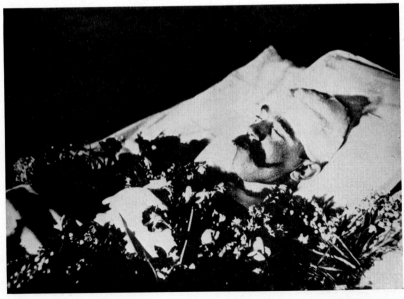

51 Rudolf on his deathbed

52 Engraving of the arrival of Rudolf's body in Vienna by night

54 John Orth and his crew on board the *Santa Margherita* before leaving for their last voyage, 1890

53 The Archduke John Salvator (1852–90)

55 Schloss Orth near Gmunden-on-the-Traunsee, John Orth's last home before leaving Austria

56 Nicholas II, Tsar of Russia, (1868–1918) with his guards, a photograph taken in the grounds of Tsarskoe-Selo in 1917

57 The last Tsarina of Russia, Alexandra Feodorovna (1872–1918)

58 The children of the Tsar, from a family group taken about 1910. *l-r*, the Grand Duchesses Marie (1899–1918), Tatiana (1897–1918), Anastasia (1901–18), Olga (1895–1918) and the Tsarevich Alexis (1904–18)

59 Nicholas II and his family at Tobolsk in Siberia, where they were interned from September 1917 to April 1918

60 Anna Anderson, who claims to be the Grand Duchess Anastasia, a photograph of her as a patient in the Mommsen Sanatorium in Berlin, taken in 1926

61 The burial place of the Romanovs, a photograph of the opening of the mine-shaft in a clearing in the forest of Koptiaki, where the bodies were buried

A fortnight later, on 27 January, a stormy interview took place between the Emperor and his son. No one knows for certain what the subject of their quarrel was, but the presence of the Cardinal Archbishop of Vienna has led people to suppose that it concerned a possible dissolution of Rudolf's marriage to Stephanie, which rumour declared him to be anxious to secure.[12] But later the same day, all four—Francis Joseph, Rudolf, Stephanie and the archbishop—were present at a reception at the German Embassy given by the ambassador Prince Reuss to celebrate the birthday of the new German Emperor, William II. This was the last time father and son met and, as they shook hands, it was assumed that they must have patched up some of their differences. Present also at the reception was Marie Vetsera,[13] with whom Rudolf exchanged a few words. That night Rudolf spent with another of his mistresses Marie ('Mizzi') Kaspar, whom he had known for many years. She seems to have filled much the same function, though with less discretion, in his life that Frau Schratt did for his father's.

Rudolf had arranged a shooting party for the 29th at Mayerling, a hunting lodge belonging to the imperial family in the Wiener Wald, just over twenty miles from Vienna. But the day after the reception at the German Embassy, namely the 28th, he altered his plans and, postponing an interview arranged to take place that day with the archbishop, departed for Mayerling just before midday. Meanwhile Countess Larisch had been sent to collect Marie Vetsera, whom Bratfisch drove to Mayerling, to join the Crown Prince. There they spent the night together. No one, except the servants (and of course the police), seems to have been aware that he was not alone.

On the morning of the 29th Rudolf had breakfast alone with Count Hoyos, one of the Emperor's chamberlains, and Prince Philip of Coburg, his brother-in-law,[14] whom he had invited to

[12] He is said to have made enquiries to the Vatican about this without consulting the Emperor.

[13] Everyone seems to have been there including Rudolf's most hostile critics in the family, the Archduke Albert and his brother, the Archduke William.

[14] He was married to Stephanie's sister, Louise, who succeeded in making relations between the imperial couple worse by repeating to her sister all the gossip she heard about Rudolf's life. She later ran off with a Croatian count, whom she had met casually while riding in the Prater. She was disowned by her family, who for a time confined her to a lunatic asylum, and divorced by her husband. She died in Wiesbaden in 1924, having written a book of memoirs which for pretentious nonsense rivals Stephanie's work.

F

shoot with him that day and who arrived by the early train from Vienna.

After breakfast Rudolf excused himself from accompanying his guests on the shoot on the grounds that he was suffering from a chill, and they went alone. That afternoon, however, Coburg returned to Vienna to be present at a family dinner at the Hofburg, to celebrate the engagement of Rudolf's youngest sister to the Archduke Francis Salvator. Rudolf had also been invited, but he again pleaded his cold and asked his brother-in-law to make his excuses to the Emperor. Hoyos stayed and dined alone with Rudolf and at 9.0 p.m. retired to his own quarters in a separate lodge in the grounds. Rudolf, having arranged once again to breakfast with Hoyos and Philip of Coburg (who had promised to return from Vienna next morning by the early train), then also went to bed.

At 6.30 the next morning, the 30th, Rudolf, fully dressed, came out of his bedroom into the adjoining room where his valet Loschek always slept, and told him that he wanted a further hour's rest but was to be awakened at 7.30. Just before eight o'clock, the valet sent a message to Hoyos to say that he was worried because he could get no answer from the Crown Prince's bedroom, which was locked on the inside. Ten minutes later, Philip of Coburg arrived back from Vienna and it was decided to break into the apartment. There, on the bed, were the dead bodies of the Crown Prince (still dressed), and of Marie Vetsera, almost naked, both shot through the head. But, in the confusion of the moment and because of the blood round Rudolf's mouth and the presence of a glass of liquid by his bedside, they thought, at first, that he had been poisoned. From later medical evidence it became clear that they both had been shot: the liquid was brandy, which Rudolf had drunk steadily throughout the night to steel himself for his final act of self-destruction.[15] Medical evidence also showed that Marie had died some hours before Rudolf and that he must have shot her,[16] and then, ultimately, after agonising hours, put an end to himself. Further examination revealed that they were both suffering from gonorrhoea[17] and that Marie Vetsera was pregnant.

[15] Done with the help of a hand mirror, also by the bedside.
[16] This was made abundantly clear in that Marie was shot from the left-hand side, although she was lying on the right-hand side of the bed and was known to be right-handed.
[17] Rudolf had been infected even before his marriage.

They both left a collection of farewell letters—though none to the Emperor—which made their intentions clear.

Count Hoyos—Philip of Coburg was too prostrated to act—hurried back to Vienna (in Bratfisch's cab) to give the appalling news. No court official could be found who had the courage to tell the Emperor, so it was finally decided to tackle the Empress. Through her secretary, Elizabeth learned what had happened[18] and agreed to tell her husband. She told him and then sent Frau Schratt[19] to him to mitigate the blow. Stephanie was told and Hoyos was made to give a full account of what had happened at Mayerling.

Actually the Court was overwhelmed. In any ordinary family what had happened would have been bad enough, but for the Habsburgs it was little short of a disaster. For the heir to the throne of the principal Catholic power in Europe to die in such circumstances was appalling. So the first news given to the public and to the courts of Europe was that he had died of heart failure. A more guarded telegram, merely specifying sudden death, had to be sent to the Pope.

As the truth began to leak out, the Austrian Court changed its story. They admitted the Crown Prince's suicide but attributed it to mental derangement,[20] and still inferred that he had died alone.

In fact the treatment meted out to the Vetsera family was both heartless and disgraceful. Marie's mother may have been something of a social climber but at least she genuinely loved her daughter and was distracted by her disappearance. Her agony began when, on the 28th, Countess Larisch returned to the Vetsera house and told the Baroness that her daughter had given her the slip while she was in a jeweller's shop and so must be considered missing. When Marie did not return that night Helene Vetsera went to the police and the next

[18] Typically enough she was having a Greek lesson at the time, as by now her favourite place of retreat outside Austria was Corfu.

[19] She was originally an actress from the Burgtheater, who came to Francis Joseph's notice in the 1880s. With the Empress's approval she gave the Emperor that domestic relaxation that Elizabeth could not provide. A loyal, discreet and kind woman, she died in Vienna in 1940, having steadfastly refused lucrative offers to write her memoirs.

[20] The report signed by Drs. Hofmann, Kundrat and Widerhofer, after a post-mortem held at the Hofburg on 31 January spoke of:

'The premature cohesion of the fontanelles, the remarkable depth of the skull cavity and the so-called fingerlike impressions on the inner surface of the skull-bones the evident subsidence of the brain-passages, and the enlargement of the brain-chamber are pathological circumstances which experience has proved appurtenant to abnormal mental conditions, and which therefore justify the supposition that the deed was committed in a state of mental derangement.'

day (the 30th), because she knew something of Marie's liaison with the Crown Prince, turned up at the palace. To her surprise she was admitted almost at once, for by that time the Empress had received the news from Mayerling. Elizabeth, without attempting to soften the blow, told her outright that her daughter was dead and warned her to say nothing, but if questioned closely to reply that the Crown Prince had died of heart failure. Soon after this she was told to leave Austria for a time and went to Venice.

Meanwhile Marie's body had been removed to an outhouse and two of her uncles, Alexander Baltazzi (one of the Derby winners of 1877) and Count Stockau were told to come and collect it. This they were made to do by night to avoid undesirable publicity. Rudolf and Marie in their farewell letters had expressed a wish to share a common grave (at Alland) but this was out of the question. Francis Joseph not only overruled this but chose the near-by burial ground of the Heiligenkreuz (Holy Cross) monastery as Marie's last resting place and there she was to be interred under police supervision. They had to identify the body, provide a coat and hat (to conceal her head wounds), and then drive with her in an upright position, as if she were still alive, till they reached their destination some five miles away. They were also made to sign a paper before they were given the body that Marie had committed suicide. It was a difficult journey over the mountain roads in wintry conditions, and it was past dawn by the time the whole operation was over.

Rudolf's body, of course, was laid to rest, after the usual pomp and circumstance, in the crypt of the Capuchin Church in Vienna. Most of the Habsburg family—this was the last official function attended by the Archduke John Salvator—were there, except the Empress, and there was the usual sprinkling of foreign royalty.

There was some criticism from a few strict Catholics, led by Cardinal Rampolla, about such a burial being given to someone who had committed suicide. This was to have repercussions later on, in 1903, when Francis Joseph imposed a veto on Rampolla's candidature at the conclave held to elect a new Pope after the death of Leo XIII. The right to veto one Cardinal at a papal election, which was enjoyed by the monarchs of Austria, France, Spain and the Two Sicilies had not been used since the seventeenth century and was promptly abolished by the new Pope six months after he was elected.

Despite certain puzzling features it is possible to reconstruct what probably happened at Mayerling that night. Obviously Rudolf shot Marie Vetsera and—from the position of her wound and from the absence of any kind of struggle—with her consent. Then after a time he killed himself. This is clear from the notes left by Rudolf to his mother and Marie's letters to her family:[21] in his case they indicated that he had no choice, in hers a desire to be with him come what may. The real mystery is not so much what happened that night as what led him to do what he did. And there have been very divergent opinions as to the pressures that drove him to his death.

There is plenty of evidence that death, particularly in the form of suicide, had a morbid fascination for him and many people who knew him testified to this. There is also evidence that death in the form of a suicide pact—a Liebestod (Love-Death)—had occupied his thoughts for some time and Mizzi Kaspar had felt bound to inform the police some time before that this was what he had proposed to her. But no notice was taken of her because the police did not deem her to be a very responsible person. Marie Vetsera, who was much younger and much more impressionable and who was clearly head over heels in love with him, may well have struck him as a much more pliable instrument in this way. In one of her valedictory letters she spoke of Rudolf and herself as being curious to know what life was like the other side of the grave. Rudolf was clearly fond of her but did not regard her as the great love of his life. He would scarcely have spent his final night in Vienna with Mizzi Kaspar had he looked upon her in this way.

Was he really mentally deranged? There was some insanity in the Habsburg family, for Rudolf's great uncle, the Emperor Ferdinand reigned (1835–48) only nominally and there had to be a Council of Regency to rule in his name. But the real mental instability came from the Wittelsbach, his mother's family. Three out of Rudolf's four grandparents had been Wittelsbachs and thus there was a heavy concentration of their blood in his veins. One look at Table No. 15

---

[21] They must have spent a good deal of time letter writing. Rudolf wrote to his mother, his wife (a brief note asking her to look after their daughter), his sister Valerie, to Szogenyi-Marich, a Hungarian Foreign Office official whom he appointed his executor, to Bombelles and Loschek. The longest and most affectionate was to Mizzi Kaspar to whom he left a handsome bequest. The omission of any communication to his father is most pointed. Marie, on her side, wrote to her mother, sister, brother and uncles, and also to the Duke of Braganza, a former admirer. To this last letter Rudolf added a friendly postscript.

will show how much a product of inbreeding Rudolf was. Elizabeth's own branch of the family were notoriously unstable while two of Rudolf's cousins, Ludwig II and King Otto, had both been mentally afflicted. Ludwig had committed suicide eighteen months previously and King Otto was at that very time under restraint with a regent ruling for him. Rudolf knew them both well and had attended Ludwig's funeral. The dice was certainly loaded against him as far as heredity was concerned.

But those who knew him best could not see any signs of insanity. They saw much to cause them grave disquiet, but nothing approaching mental disease. It is true that he was depressed and frustrated, but this alone should not have led to suicide.

It is also true that he found his domestic situation intolerable. He was unable to get on with his wife, but at the same time unable to get rid of her, but here again some *modus vivendi* could have been found. Like most royal personages he was able to have a separate life of his own. This life of his own he found increasingly unsatisfactory. A dissolute way of life was a poor substitute for a happy family life. It was the symptom and not the cure of his condition, and he was intelligent enough to see that. His addiction to drugs and his debts must have been an additional worry. Perhaps this all built up into a crisis that he was at last unable to control and for which his *damnosa hereditas* could suggest only one final solution.

The last theory, advanced by Countess Larisch in her sensational *Memoirs*, was that the real cause lay in political affairs and that Rudolf was not only in touch with Hungarian separatists like Count Stephen Karolyi but intended to make himself king of a breakaway Hungary. And this was about to come out. It is true that Rudolf was—like his mother—deeply interested in Hungarian affairs and had a warm admiration for the Magyar people. He was in touch with Karolyi, who was a deputy in the Hungarian Parliament and who was pressing for Hungary to have its own army, and Hoyos says that while they were at Mayerling Rudolf produced three recent telegrams from Karolyi and spoke a good deal about events in Budapest. But it is highly doubtful if he was prepared to carry any ideas he may have had to the length of treason against his own father. Not so long before he had roundly condemned his cousin, the Archduke John Salvator for going behind the Emperor's back to further his own political ambitions.[22]

[22] See Rudolf's letter of 22 December 1888 to Kalnoky (pages 160-1).

Thus there is no satisfactory 'solution' to Rudolf's conduct. It may well be that, as often in the case of humbler people, it was the combination of many circumstances that led him to take his life. We are never likely to know. It had been hoped that when the Imperial archives were opened after the First World War the truth might then be revealed. But it was then discovered that the papers concerning the Crown Prince's death (and the Hungarian file) were not there. It is said that an important dossier on the whole subject had been handed over by the Emperor to his friend and Prime Minister, Count Taafe[23] and that these were accidentally destroyed in a fire in the Count's castle in Bohemia some years later.

The secret may possibly be found in the Vatican archives, for during the delicate negotiations to secure Rudolf a Christian burial Francis Joseph is said to have addressed to Leo XIII a telegram of some three thousand lines setting out the whole story.

Following the Emperor's wish that Mayerling should become a place of prayer and expiation, a memorial chapel was built there and the old hunting lodge converted into a monastery for Carmelite nuns. They still occupy it and the place where the bedroom door, forced by Coburg on that terrible morning, was can still be seen (blocked up) on the chapel wall. Marie Vetsera's grave at Heiligen-kreuz is marked by a simple cross with a text from Job: 'Man cometh forth like a flower and is cut down.'

Stephanie found happiness of a sort in a second marriage (in 1900) with a Hungarian count, though both her father and her hus-band's family blamed her to some extent for what had happened and they had little more to do with her. She and her husband both died shortly after the end of the Second World War. Rudolf's only child, the Archduchess Elizabeth lived to be eighty and died in 1963. She also married twice, first to an Austrian prince and then, after divorce, to a Socialist politician.

---

[23] Taafe, who was also an Irish peer, was Prime Minister of Austria from 1877 to 1893. He had known Francis Joseph since childhood.

14

The Disappearance of John Orth

JOHN ORTH was the name later taken by the Archduke John Salvator of Tuscany, who belonged to a branch of the Austrian Habsburgs who had ruled in Tuscany since 1791. He himself was born in Florence, in the Pitti Palace (now the famous art gallery) in November 1852, and his parents were the Grand Duke Leopold II and his second wife Maria Antonia of Bourbon-Sicily.

When he was still a young child his family lost their throne as the result of a series of events that culminated in the unification of Italy under the House of Savoy. In July 1859, soon after the Austrian defeats at Magenta and Solferino which precipitated these events, his father abdicated, and after a brief reign of nine months his eldest brother, Ferdinand IV, the last Grand Duke, was driven into exile.

As the Grand Ducal family were Habsburgs they naturally sought refuge in Austria, where the Emperor Francis Joseph made over to them the large but rather gloomy Residenz at Salzburg, once the palace of the Prince-Archbishops. As John Salvator was not quite eight years old when all this happened he was brought up virtually as an Austrian prince. In his early youth he showed himself to be a person of precocious ability and marked intellectual originality. He was interested in the arts and in science, but above all in music. When he grew up he became friendly with Johann Strauss and himself composed a waltz and later on produced a ballet.

But as a member of the Imperial Family there was little scope for talent of this kind and the only profession open to him was a military one and so perforce he had to choose the Austrian army. Nevertheless he soon made a name for himself in his army career. As a young Colonel he commanded a brigade during the Austrian occupation of the Turkish provinces of Bosnia and Herzegovina following the

Treaty of Berlin in 1878. Before he was thirty years old he had become a full-blown general. Such promotion was rapid even for an archduke, but it was based on genuine ability, for some of John Salvator's ideas won praise from the German Commander-in-Chief, the veteran Count von Moltke, still the most brilliant soldier of the day. In fact in any country less hidebound by tradition than Austria the archduke might have made still further progress.

Unfortunately, however, although he had a bold and critical intelligence the archduke possessed neither tact nor discretion. In 1875, at the age of twenty-three, he had published a pamphlet entitled *Observations concerning the Austrian Army*, in which he designated Germany as Austria's hereditary enemy and suggested among other things that the long frontier between the two countries should be properly fortified. This cut across all the ideas then in favour in Austrian military and political circles, ideas which a few years later were to reach fruition in the formation of the Dual Alliance between Austria and Germany, the alliance which was ultimately in 1914 to bring Germany into the First World War on the Austrian side.

Both the Emperor and his Foreign Minister, Count Andrássy (who was a firm ally of Bismarck's Germany), took a serious view of John Salvator's action. He was summoned to an interview at the Hofburg Palace and in the presence of the Archduke Albert and the latter's brother, the Archduke William, was given a severe reprimand.

The latter were both Field Marshals; Albert was Inspector-General of the Army and William Inspector-General of Artillery. Their father had been that Archduke Charles who had been one of the few allied generals able to defeat Napoleon at a time when the Emperor was at the height of his powers.[1] They were both inordinately proud of the military achievements of their branch of the family. Albert had defeated the Italians at the battle of Custozza in June 1866 with forces less than half of those of the enemy, and as the only Habsburg to win a battle since the Napoleonic Wars he regarded himself as the sole repository of military wisdom in the family. He himself had published a military pamphlet in 1869, *Responsibility in War*, in which he had shown himself the champion of conventional, if not positively outdated, ideas, and his approach to all army problems was primarily bureaucratic. Unlike John Salvator, who had liberal

---

[1] Battle of Aspern, May 1809, followed in July by the crushing Austrian defeat at Wagram.

and progressive views and was credited with being a free thinker, Albert was deeply conservative, was a friend of the Jesuits and moved in circles that were exclusively reactionary.

It is difficult to assess his military capacity. The test would have been what, if anything, he could have done against the Prussians in 1866. But on the outbreak of war he was sent, not to the Bohemian front, a theatre of operations of which he had made a special study, but to deal with the much less serious threat from the Italians in the South. The Emperor was frightened that Albert might be defeated by Moltke with a consequent disastrous loss of prestige to the dynasty, and so he was assigned to the Italian front where he could be expected to win.

In his place, General Benedek, who wanted the Italian command as he was familiar with the terrain there and where he felt he could cope successfully, was sent, much against his will, to deal with the Prussian invasion of Bohemia. After his inevitable defeat at Moltke's hands at the battle of Sadowa, Benedek had been superseded as Commander-in-Chief by Albert. Albert was then astute enough to extract from the man he had replaced a written promise that the general would never speak or write about the Bohemian campaign and was thus able to set the stage for a court of enquiry into the Austrian defeat which was able to dismiss Benedek with impunity since the 'scapegoat' had already been silenced and would never be able to defend himself.[2]

Having thus dealt with a man of the calibre of Benedek, Albert felt quite capable of disciplining John Salvator. By way of punishment the latter was transferred from his artillery regiment (the 13th) to an infantry regiment (William No. 12) belonging to the Archduke William and relegated to the Galician border fortress of Cracow, as being the army post farthest away from Vienna. There John Salvator settled down to study the fortifications and produced a brochure on them. Later on this 'banishment' was mitigated and he was transferred to Linz. There he spent four restless but happy years and there he published a study of architecture and painting dealing with the surrounding province of Upper Austria.

But for all that John Salvator remained unrepentant in his unorthodox views. Already in a history of the Twelfth Infantry Regiment —which it will be remembered belonged to the Archduke William—

[2] Benedek kept his word but on his death in 1881 he left instructions that he was not to be buried in the Emperor's uniform.

he had somehow managed to speak favourably of the 1848 Revolutions in Austria and Hungary which had very nearly brought the Habsburgs down in ruin, and in 1883 he gave vent to further unusual and unpalatable ideas in an article in a military paper entitled *Drill or Education?* This caused a *furore* in army circles in Vienna. The very title was expressive of the author's point of view. He accused the military authorities of slavishly copying Prussian models and pointed out that the net result of their formal and inflexible approach was to stifle all freedom and initiative. He also criticised the confusion caused by the practice in the Austrian army whereby each army corps had its own drill book and its own separate interpretation of army rules and regulations. This he maintained led to needless confusion when a soldier from one corps got posted to another.

The military authorities were not best pleased to discover that the article proved so popular that it was translated into three different languages and that it was taken seriously outside the Empire, if not within. John Salvator was once again summoned to the Hofburg for another painful interview with Francis Joseph and another apology to the Archduke Albert.

Still not learning discretion, the culprit next meddled in international politics. In August 1886 Prince Alexander of Battenberg, as a result of persistent Russian intrigues, had been obliged to abdicate his throne and leave Bulgaria. Various princes were suggested as possible replacements and for a time the Bulgarian crown was hawked around Europe. The favourite, and ultimately successful, candidate was Ferdinand of Saxe-Coburg who was then a junior officer in the Austro-Hungarian army. The Austrian authorities did not look with much favour on his political ambitions and were not averse to placing obstacles in the way of their realisation. The Court of Vienna was therefore scandalised to learn that John Salvator, who was in correspondence with both Alexander and Ferdinand, had taken it upon himself to receive envoys from Bulgaria, first in Venice and then (in June 1887) at Linz. It became clear that he was even toying with the idea of accepting the throne itself. This was too much for Francis Joseph, particularly as the town of Linz chose this moment to offer their distinguished resident the freedom of the city. It was one thing for a Habsburg prince to become Emperor of Mexico—though that had turned out tragically—but quite another to become a Balkan princeling. Moreover, Maximilian of Mexico had had the

Emperor's blessing while John Salvator had neglected even to consult Francis Joseph. The indignant Emperor therefore sent for the archduke to come once again to the Hofburg.

Having made it plain that members of the Imperial Family did not accept from their subjects the kind of honour the people of Linz were offering, he then used the plainest language on John Salvator's ambitions either in Bulgaria or anywhere else. This meeting, the stormiest that had so far taken place between the two men, ended in a complete rupture between them. The Emperor relieved John Salvator of all his posts, deprived him of his own regiment—the Second Artillery of Upper and Lower Austria—and made it clear that his career in Austria was over for good and all.

The unfortunate archduke retired to the family property at Orth on Lake Traunsee in the province of Upper Austria to consider how best he could retrieve his position.

First of all he made an appeal to Crown Prince Rudolf with whom he had for a brief time enjoyed friendly relations. The two princes had a lot in common. They were both of an age, both possessed ambition and ability and both were 'angry young men' who were disquieted by the stupidity and inertia of the establishment. But they were not really in sympathy with one another and there was an inevitable gulf between the heir to the imperial throne and a junior archduke.[3] There may also have been some element of jealousy between them and there was certainly a touch of malice in Rudolf's character that made any genuine friendship difficult. He preferred the company of his brother-in-law, Philip of Coburg and of the Duke of Braganza to any Habsburg prince.

His attitude can best be seen in a letter he wrote on 22 December 1888 to Count Kalnoky, the Foreign Minister:

'Bombelles (Comptroller of Rudolf's household) has just given me, in your name, the extremely strange information concerning Archduke John's rôle as negotiator. I have already witnessed much incorrect behaviour on the part of that gentleman, but negotiation of external affairs with a foreign deputation, at this critical time, without permission, and behind the back of the Emperor and the Minister for Foreign Affairs, is, particularly for an Archduke and a General, con-

---

[3] John Salvator was actually the most junior of all the thirty Habsburg archdukes then living.

duct which must be most severely punished. What are we coming to when such things are possible within the Imperial Family and the Army, and the Emperor can no longer rely on those elements, who should know no other principles than those of unconditional obedience and perfect loyalty? If I make a suggestion to you it is this: after complete investigation of the occurrence to go to the Emperor, report it to him, and implore him to take vigorous steps against such happenings, for how can anyone be Minister for Foreign Affairs when Archdukes can calmly follow their own foreign policy behind his back?'

The tone, as well as the content, of this letter makes it clear that Rudolf was implacably hostile to John Salvator's ambitions.

The story later put around that this archduke had acted as an intermediary between Rudolf and certain Hungarian politicians with separatist ambitions has no foundation. They were never on sufficiently intimate terms for this to be possible. Nor is there any truth in the persistent and sensational stories that connect John Salvator with the drama of Mayerling (see Chapter 13). The fact that the career of the one and the life of the other came to an end at much the same time has led some people to attempt to find a connection between them. There was none. John Salvator was not present when Rudolf died and played no part in the events that led up to it.

Ironically enough, Rudolf's funeral was the last official function that John Salvator attended as an Austrian archduke. Thereafter he retired from court life and after taking a sea voyage he returned, and in October 1889 renounced his rank and his rights of succession and became a commoner. He took the surname of Orth from the castle near Gmunden where his mother lived. In the same month he married Milly Stubel, a dancer at the Viennese Opera, and left Austria for ever. They had known one another since the archduke was in his early twenties and had met rather romantically in the forest of Semmering, outside Vienna, when John Salvator was in a hunting party. They were devoted to one another and she shared to the full her husband's musical interests.

Before his renunciation John Orth, as he must now be called, had transferred his affection from the land to the sea and soon after his departure from Austria he secured his Master's Certificate and purchased a three-masted schooner, the *Santa Margherita*. In this ship, with a Croat captain named Sodich and a crew made up mainly of Croats and Italians, John Orth and his wife set sail from Chatham on 26 March 1890, bound for South America. When they reached La Plata in Argentina the former archduke, who did not see eye to eye with Sodich, took over command of the ship, signed on a new crew and with a cargo of saltpetre set sail for Valparaiso.

The *Santa Margherita* never reached Chile and in fact was never heard of again. An intensive search of the course she must have taken yielded no result and no trace of her was ever found. It is generally supposed that she foundered while rounding Cape Horn and that there were no survivors. These were still the days of the sailing ship and few voyages in the world presented greater hazards. Moreover, John Orth was not an experienced navigator—this was his first command—and there is plenty of evidence that the summer of 1890 (the *Santa Margherita* left La Plata in July) was marked by exceptionally severe gales and storms.

Some of his family, notably his mother, who was greatly attached to him as the youngest and most gifted of her children, refused to believe that he was dead. Till her own death in 1898 she refused to wear mourning and kept a room at Schloss Orth in readiness for him against the day of his return. His favourite niece, the Crown Princess of Saxony—who by running away with her children's Belgian tutor was to cause a much greater scandal among the Habsburgs than ever John Orth made—was emphatic that when the archduke had visited his family on the eve of his departure from Austria he had made a solemn promise to return when things were better. In her *Memoirs* she says that his final words were: 'Never, never believe that I am dead; for I will return one day, and we shall meet again and talk of this.'

Not only his family, but many outsiders believed that he had not gone down with the *Santa Margherita*. Rumour had it that he was still alive and well and that, as Alexander I of Russia was reputed to have done, he had staged a successful disappearance so that he could enjoy his private life in peace. One or two pretenders turned up at Schloss Orth in the hopes of converting their fraud to pecuniary advantage, but they proved obvious adventurers and unconvincing liars. The most plausible of them was discovered to have a considerable criminal record and was at the time being sought by the police.

Some people said that John Orth had retired to Spain as a monk, which accords neither with his temperament nor his recent status as a married man; some maintained that he had become a polar explorer, which sounds ever more outlandish; while others claimed to have seen him either in the streets of Buenos-Aires, or sitting in a cafe in Berlin, or enjoying life on the French Riviera.

Some support for the idea that he was still alive came from Captain Sodich, the former commander of the *Santa Margherita*, who as a Croat was therefore at that time an Austrian subject. On his return to Europe he declared that John Orth and his wife had left the ship at La Plata and that it was someone else impersonating him who sailed for Valparaiso. Instead he said that the former archduke had settled down as a gentleman farmer somewhere in South America.

Count Polzer-Hoditz, who was secretary to and later biographer of the last Austrian Emperor Karl says that in 1907 his master (then still the Archduke Karl) told him that John Orth was still alive and living in South America. Karl is quoted as using the words: 'He is as much alive as you or I. Papa corresponded with him to the last.' 'Papa' was Francis Joseph's nephew, the Archduke Otto, who died in 1906. He was also something of a rebel but in a purely personal and not a political sense. His quarrel was with decorum. He was a handsome playboy who is best remembered for his unconventional pranks. The two best known of these were the halting of a funeral in Vienna one day when he was riding in the Kärnterstrasse so that he could jump over the bier and the other was to appear naked, except for a shako (or as others said, the Austrian Order of the Golden Fleece), in Sacher's, the capital's most fashionable restaurant—an incident which led to diplomatic repercussions as the British Ambassador and his wife happened to be dining there that night. Temperamentally the Archduke Otto and John Orth were poles apart, and it is very strange that they should have corresponded at all, especially as Otto was only twelve years old when John Orth left Austria.

In support of his contention that Orth did not go down with the *Santa Margherita*, Count Polzer-Hoditz quotes a letter from a certain José Boglich, Chief of Police in the town of Concordia in the province of Entre Rios in Argentina. In a letter to a friend in Paris, a former Uruguayan senator, Boglich states that an Austrian named Johann Orth stayed for a time in Concordia in 1899 before going to Uruguay to work on a lumber estate at Chaco belonging to an Italian, Signor Villa Rey. There he was joined by a woman: but according to the same informant he left for Japan shortly before the outbreak of the

Russo-Japanese War in 1904. No one seems to have taken the trouble to follow this up and Villa Rey, when questioned, maintained that the only Austrian employed by him had been a certain former merchant named Hirsch.

What then did happen to John Orth? It seems pretty clear that the *Santa Margherita* sank on its last voyage. The only question is whether John Orth was on board or not. No one can say for certain that he was, but for the following reasons it seems a reasonable assumption.

First, if John Orth wished to stage a disappearance he could have done so at any time after he landed at La Plata. It would not have been a difficult operation in those days: he only needed to go far enough inland and no one would ever have found him in the dense tropical jungles of the interior. South America has proved a haven for those wishing to conceal their identity, and even with the modern hazard of good communications certain Nazi war criminals (including, it is said, Hitler's deputy, Martin Bormann) have been able to find safe hiding places off the beaten track. While farther inland still the fate of Colonel Fawcett shows that involuntary disappearance was far from unknown.

But if getting away was uppermost in his mind, to allow the *Santa Margherita* (which he still owned) to sail was folly. He could not possibly tell that it was going to founder and for the ship to arrive in Valparaiso without him would have been to invite enquiries as to where he was and what had happened to him. It would have been simpler to sell the *Santa Margherita* and for he and his wife to make their way to wherever they wanted to go.

Secondly, there was no real need for him to 'disappear'. He was not after all a criminal and he was not in fear of his life. He was far away from Europe and was in a continent no longer interested in monarchy or its trappings. He was free to come and go as he liked and he was not likely to be pursued by newspapermen. He could have lived as a private citizen in the suburbs of Buenos Aires for that matter without anybody taking much interest in him.

Thirdly, if he were still alive during the First World War why did he not return to Austria either after the death of Francis Joseph in 1916 or after the collapse of the Habsburg Empire two years later? He would then have been in his middle sixties and his memoirs, if not his reappearance, would have brought him a fortune.

One of his nephews, the Archduke Leopold Salvator, who also renounced his rank—in his case to marry a commoner—recalled in his memoirs the promise to return that John Orth had made to his family at Salzburg just before his departure. He quotes the identical words used by his sister, the Crown Princess of Saxony, but, writing nineteen years later, he adds that although till 1918 he still believed his uncle to be alive he became convinced after that that he was dead: 'I had to reconcile myself to the certainty,' he writes, 'that he must have died. Death alone would have prevented so gallant a patriot from returning to his beloved native land in that dark hour of need.' Leopold himself returned and for a time ran a grocer's shop in Vienna.

Despite all rumours his family never saw him again and never heard from him again. Devoted as he was to his mother it is surely odd that he should have made no attempt to communicate with her but left her a prey to uncertainty and to any adventurer who cared to batten on her. Count Polzer-Hoditz does say that Count Franz Harrach, who was one of the Court Chamberlains, told him that John Orth did on one occasion visit his niece, the Countess of Caserta, in her villa at Cannes. But there is no proof of this.

All the evidence of his continued existence after 1890 is second-hand. It is never the writer himself who can personally vouch for having seen or corresponded with him, but always someone else who has told him, or someone else who knows yet a third party who has been in touch with him.

John Orth's tragedy was that of a man who, though born with position and endowed with talent, had not enough of either to secure him a life of fulfilment. His birth gave him certain advantages, but it also hedged him in and restricted his activities. He had not wealth to give him independence and his character was unable to support his ability. His mind, like his life, lacked discipline, while his tempera-ment—wayward and erratic—would have militated against him in any walk of life. If he had not been driven on by the demon of ambi-tion he might have been able to come to terms with himself and found an outlet for his energies in a harmless pursuit of the arts and sciences. This is after all what his brother, the Archduke Ludwig Salvator (1847–1915)[4] was able to do. He escaped the tedium of

[4] The Tuscan Habsburgs were easily the most colourful, if wayward, branch of the family. Possibly their years in Italy had done this for them.

court life by living part of the time in his remote estate on the Elbe in Bohemia and part of the time in the Balearic Islands. There in his villa on Majorca he was able to lead a reasonably simple life and achieve a reputation as a botanist and student of natural history. But for John Orth the life of the dilletante was not enough. Perhaps, if he had become Prince of Bulgaria with his own independent sphere of action, life might have been different, but it is doubtful whether he really possessed the stability necessary for the exercise of power. Indeed in character he much more closely resembles the successful Alexander of Battenberg than the successful Ferdinand of Coburg.

The last echo of the mystery of his disappearance came in May 1945 when a ninety-three-year-old Norwegian, Hugo Koehler, died at Kristiansand. Soon after this his widow declared that she thought her husband was the missing archduke, who would have been the same age had he still been alive. Fru Koehler maintained that till his death she had known nothing about her husband's family or his past, despite the fact that he had lived in Norway for over forty years. It was only when she came across certain documents he had kept locked away—among others a highly coloured version of what had happened at Mayerling—that she became convinced that her husband was John Orth. Nothing has been heard of this claim since.

It does in fact seem almost certain that the key to the mystery of what happened to John Orth lies buried in those stormy waters that separate the South Atlantic from the South Pacific.

15

Anastasia

OF all the Pretenders considered in this book the 'Grand Duchess' Anastasia of Russia remains the sole existing survivor. She was the fourth and youngest daughter of Nicholas II and was born at Peterhof on 5 June 1901, but her story really begins with the murder of the Imperial Family in July 1918.

This happened when Russia was disrupted by civil war and still cut off from the rest of Europe by the struggle between the Entente and the Central Powers, which was then entering its final and most crucial phase. Moreover, it took place in a provincial city in a comparatively remote part of Russia, away from all the news facilities of the capital.

Although the Russian Revolution bore some resemblances to its famous French prototype, as far as the fate of the Royal Family was concerned it pursued an entirely different course. Nicholas II and his wife were never put in one of Russia's famous prisons like the fortress of St. Peter and St. Paul—or the Lubianka prison in Moscow—were never brought to trial and never mounted the scaffold to die in public. Instead they were done to death in a way that was surrounded by mystery and which both invited and produced every kind of rumour. It was some time before everyone, either in Russia or the rest of Europe, learned what had happened, and it was inevitable that it should produce its quota of pretenders. Anastasia is the most famous of these, but by no means the only one.[1]

To understand what happened it is necessary to take a look at the Romanov family and then trace the events from the time of the outbreak of the Revolution in March 1917 to the time of their death at Ekaterinburg in July 1918.

---

[1] Someone claiming to be the Tsarevich (equipped with a wife named Irmgard and a daughter Tatiana) was pressing his claims in New York in July 1967.

The Romanovs, who had celebrated the tercentenary of their dynasty in 1913, were a numerous family and in 1917 numbered over fifty princes and princesses.[2] Among them, however, the family of the Tsar formed a unit apart. It consisted of Nicholas II (born in 1868), the Tsarina Alexandra Feodorovna (born a princess of Hesse-Darmstadt in 1872) and their five children, Olga (born 1895), Tatiana (born 1897), Marie (born 1899), Anastasia (born 1901) and the Tsarevich, Alexis (born 1904). Nicholas, through his mother, a princess of Denmark, was a first cousin of George V of England, to whom he bore the most striking physical resemblance, and the Tsarina was a granddaughter of Queen Victoria: on the Hesse side they were second cousins. They had been married since 1894, the year of Nicholas II's accession, and were a happy and devoted couple: but there was a personal tragedy in their married life in that their only son and heir was a victim of haemophilia, a rare but crippling blood condition for which there was no cure.[3]

Moreover, the fact that the heir to the throne was a haemophiliac had political as well as personal repercussions. Not only did it make Alexis's ultimate succession distinctly problematical but it also provided the means whereby the unfrocked monk Rasputin—through his faith healing powers, his knowledge of herbal medicine and his hypnotic gifts—was able to gain such an extraordinary ascendancy over the Tsarina. He seemed to be the only person able to stay the disease, alleviate the child's agonies and help him lead a quasi-normal life. It became the Tsarina's mission to see that her son lived to succeed to all the absolute powers wielded by previous Tsars of Russia.

She was a far more dominant personality than her husband and the comparison between them and Louis XVI and Marie Antoinette struck not only professional historians but also men like Trotsky and other onlookers. The Tsar, like Louis XVI, would have made an admirable country gentleman at any time and a good constitutional monarch in times of political stability, but again like Louis XVI he was quite unequal to the destiny that history had thrust upon him.

[2] Of these eighteen were shot or murdered in the Revolution.

[3] This disease appears only in males and is usually transmitted only through females. It came from the Saxe-Coburgs and affected many of Queen Victoria's descendants including not only the Tsarevich but two of the sons of Alfonso XIII of Spain and various princes of the royal families of Prussia and Hesse.

The Tsarina had none of the frivolity of Marie Antoinette (nor her charm or beauty) and was religious to the point of hysteria, but like the French Queen she was the real driving force behind her husband and like Marie Antoinette her reactionary sympathies and foreign origin made her the object of universal dislike. She was suspected of being pro-German but although the German Emperor (William II) was her first cousin she had in fact inherited the dislike that many of the Hesse family had for the Hohenzollerns.

Most of the other Romanovs disliked her[4] and this helped to isolate her and her husband. There was not even a Madame Elisabeth in the family to keep Nicholas II and Alexandra company in their darkest hours: the Tsarina's sister, the saintly Grand Duchess Serge, was away in Moscow in the convent she had founded there.[5] So they had to rely on themselves alone. They had never liked court life very much and the outbreak of war in 1914 gave them an excuse to put an end to what little there was. The Tsar spent much of his time with the army of which he took over supreme command in 1915, and the Tsarina and her elder daughters took up nursing.

Thus when the March Revolution broke out in Petrograd[6] in 1917 the Tsarina and her children were at the Alexander Palace at Tsarskoe-Selo, fifteen miles away, but Nicholas II was five hundred miles away at the General Army Headquarters at Moghilev. On the last day of February, the Military Governor of Petrograd sent a telegram to the Tsar stating that he was no longer able to preserve order in the city. Two telegrams from the President of the Duma (Parliament) and one from his brother, the Grand Duke Michael, both reported a steady deterioration of the situation and urged the appointment of a government that could command popular support. Till then Nicholas had not paid much attention to the disturbances in Petrograd. He had weathered the revolutionary movement of 1905 after the Russian defeat by the Japanese, he had held his throne for twenty-

[4] Rather as the French Bourbons in 1789 had disliked Marie Antoinette, and in 1917 the conduct of the Grand Duke Cyril reminded some people of the behaviour of the Duke of Orleans.

[5] She was arrested in the spring of 1918 and taken to Alapaevsk (near Ekaterinburg), where with five other members of the Romanov family she was thrown down a disused mine shaft and two hand grenades dropped in. The victims died, some from wounds, some from exposure and some from starvation.

[6] The name given to St. Petersburg in 1914 to rid its name of any associations with Germany. In 1924 it was re-named Leningrad. The Bolsheviks transferred the capital to Moscow in March 1918 to emphasise their complete break with the imperial past.

five years and was not unduly worried.[7] But as the news grew worse he decided he had better return to Tsarskoe-Selo and investigate the situation for himself.

So he left Moghilev on 13 March. However, his special train had to be diverted, to Pskov, headquarters of the northern command, because the revolutionaries now controlled the direct line with Petrograd. At Pskov, he received most unfavourable reports from the commander there, General Ruzky, who placed before him the opinions of the commanders on the other fronts including the Grand Duke Nicholas (then commanding in the Caucasus) and the admiral commanding the Baltic Fleet. Nicholas then for the first time realised that the loyalty of the armed forces could no longer be guaranteed and after a telephone conversation with Rodzianko (President of the Duma) he consented to receive two emissaries from that body. They gave him an account of the situation in Petrograd and told him that there was no alternative but abdication. It was not so much their words as Ruzky's report that determined him to follow their advice.

First he thought of abdicating in favour of his son, but the boy's youth and precarious health made this impracticable, and so Nicholas signed a document on 15 March passing his heritage to his thirty-nine-year-old brother, the Grand Duke Michael,[8] 'not wishing', as he put it, 'to be parted from our beloved son'. He also signed the necessary decrees appointing Prince Lvov Prime Minister (with Kerensky as Minister of Justice) and reinstating the Grand Duke Nicholas (whom he had dismissed from the post in 1915) as Commander in Chief. Prince Lvov's ministry lasted four months,[9] but the other two appointments proved empty gestures, for the next day the Grand Duke Michael declined to accept the throne unless called to it by a Constituent Assembly duly elected by universal suffrage; the Grand Duke Nicholas was asked to resign and he retired to his estates in the Crimea.

Having abdicated, Nicholas returned to Moghilev and there drafted a farewell message to his army, but this was suppressed by the

[7] The trivia recorded in the Tsar's diary have led Trotsky and others to complain of his 'inner indifference, a poverty of spiritual forces', but the same charge could easily be levelled against others—George V, for example.

[8] He was shot by the Bolsheviks on the outskirts of Perm some time between 5 and 15 July 1918. He left a son by his morganatic marriage, who was killed in a car accident in France in 1931.

[9] Lvov resigned in July 1917 and Kerensky then became Prime Minister.

authorities in Petrograd. Nicholas II was the first Russian ruler ever to abdicate. Several of his ancestors had been deposed, assassinated or murdered, but he was the first to go of his own accord.[10] He rather hoped now that he was simply Colonel Romanov he might be able to retire to his summer palace at Livadia in the Crimea, where the mild climate might help the delicate Tsarevich. But this was out of the question as it was much too close both to Russia's enemies and her former allies, and much too accessible to British warships.[11] His other idea—that he might be allowed to go to England—was equally hopeless.

At Moghilev Nicholas received a visit from the Dowager Empress, who came from Kiev. Theirs was a sorrowful meeting and three days later she left to return to the south. This was the last time mother and son were to see one another, for the day she left delegates arrived from Petrograd to arrest the ex-Tsar and take him to captivity at Tsarskoe-Selo.

Meanwhile at Tsarskoe-Selo the Tsarina had her own problems, for two of her daughters, Olga and Tatiana (and later a third, Anastasia) and the Tsarevich contracted measles. In the midst of this domestic crisis mutinous soldiers from Petrograd seized the village of Tsarskoe-Selo and penetrated the palace grounds. In face of opposition they withdrew, but their advent unsettled the palace guard, most of whom now deserted. On 21 March General Kornilov, as commander of the Petrograd garrison, came to Tsarskoe-Selo to place the Tsarina under house arrest and reorganise the guard, who were told that their masters were now the authorities in Petrograd and not the Imperial Family. Thus the next day, when the Tsar arrived under escort from Moghilev, he found his family prisoners in the Alexander Palace and the old imperial guards replaced by enthusiastic supporters of the new régime.

The captivity at Tsarskoe-Selo lasted five months. At first the

[10] And the first monarch of any country to abdicate in a train.

[11] In April 1919 *H.M.S. Marlborough* evacuated from Yalta (not far from Livadia) not only the Dowager Empress, but the Grand Duchess Xenia (whose husband and eldest son were in Paris on a political mission), her remaining children, her son-in-law Prince Yussopov (one of the murderers of Rasputin), the Grand Duke Nicholas and his wife, the Grand Duke Peter, his wife and children. With attendants and servants the refugees numbered over eighty and included, oddly enough, Count Fersen, who was on the staff of the Grand Duke Nicholas. He belonged to the same family as Marie Antoinette's admirer who had planned the disastrous flight of the French Royal Family to Varennes in 1791.

Provisional Government still hoped that the detention of the Imperial Family would be short-lived and that arrangements to get them to England (via Murmansk) would soon be completed. Lvov was a monarchist at heart and Kerensky, who paid several visits to the prisoners, ultimately came to have some regard for them, but the Petrograd Soviet was inflexibly opposed to their deliverance and hoped to be able to incarcerate them in the fortress of St. Peter and St. Paul, where they could be conveniently disposed of at will. Unfortunately negotiations with the British Government, for a variety of reasons, broke down and from that moment the Imperial Family were doomed.

At first, however, their position did not seem too bad. Although cut off completely from the outside world, they still had a few devoted courtiers (despite the fact that some, like Anna Vyrubova, who had acted as a go-between for the Empress and Rasputin, were removed in custody), a handful of loyal servants, two doctors and two tutors. Relieved of all state responsibilities they were able to settle down to a routine of lessons for the children, reading and a number of quiet domestic diversions: they also had the use of a limited section of the park for exercise.

They were of course subject to a number of petty vexations from some of the guards which served constantly to remind them of their plight, and from time to time eruptions from Petrograd, such as when a band of soldiers desecrated Rasputin's tomb which was in a chapel in the park and burned the monk's body. But in May, Kornilov appointed Colonel Kobylinsky to be in charge of the guard and as he was a regular soldier and a fair-minded man he did his best to protect his captives from insult and humiliation.

However, the arrival of Lenin in Russia in April from his exile in Switzerland led to a revival of revolutionary fervour in Petrograd. Lvov resigned in July and Kerensky decided that it would be in the interest of the Tsar and his family if they were removed farther away from the capital. After considering various alternatives he decided upon the town of Tobolsk in Western Siberia. The day before their departure, on 13 August, they were allowed to receive a farewell visit from the Grand Duke Michael.

The journey to Tobolsk took six days by train and two days by boat. It was a moderately comfortable affair, for they were allowed to take a few attendants and servants with them, some valuables and even a few small articles of furniture. And although the blinds were drawn at each station they passed through, the train was halted in open country from time to time to allow the Tsar to take exercise.

At Tobolsk they were installed in the Governor's house and although the grounds were minute compared with Tsarskoe-Selo the Tsar and his family were allowed to walk about them freely and the former ruler was still able to pursue his two favourite hobbies of felling trees[12] and amateur photography.

At first they were allowed to attend services in the near-by church and food and other delicacies were often sent in by well-wishers in the town. Some of the guards were hostile but others were friendly and they still had Kobylinsky with them.[13] Despite the rigours of a Siberian winter the six months at Tobolsk were not without their compensations. The children still had their lessons, there were books to read and amateur dramatics helped to pass the time. Even the Empress, who felt the turn of events more keenly than the others, had her sewing and her embroidery.

But after the October Revolution, which swept away Kerensky and the Provisional Government and placed the Bolsheviks in power, began to make itself felt even in places as remote as Tobolsk, the visits to church were stopped, the friendly guards replaced by hostile ones, the household expenses cut down and the number of domestics reduced.

In April 1918, at the prompting of the regional Soviet at the mining town of Ekaterinburg in the Urals, the authorities in the Kremlin decided to move the Imperial Family from Tobolsk and an order to this effect by Sverdlov, a high ranking official in the Kremlin[14] was made. The health of the Tsarevich, who was in bed recovering from an attack of haemophilia, made it impossible to remove him and so, after consultations with Moscow and agonised discussions among themselves, it was decided that the Tsar and Tsarina accompanied by the Grand Duchess Marie should go, leaving the two elder daughters, Olga and Tatiana (who was also unwell) and the youngest daughter, Anastasia, to look after the Tsarevich.

---

[12] Ex-monarchs seem to have enjoyed sawing wood. It was later one of the favourite pastimes of William II when in exile at Doorn.

[13] He was dismissed soon after the Tsar left for Ekaterinburg, while the Tsarevich and his sisters were still at Tobolsk.

[14] He was an important member of the Central Committee of the Bolshevik Party. The city of Ekaterinburg was renamed Sverdlovsk in his honour.

They started out on 26 April and proceeded by road to Tyumen, past Rasputin's old home at Pokrovskoe, and then by rail to Ekaterinburg where they arrived on 30 April. Throughout the journey they were closely guarded and at Ekaterinburg, where a villa belonging to a merchant named Ipatiev had been hastily fenced around and converted into a prison with barracks for the guards, their confinement was much the most severe they had so far had to endure. Three weeks later Alexis was pronounced fit to travel and he and his three sisters joined their parents in the Villa Ipatiev. By this time the household consisted solely of the Tsar, his wife and children, Dr. Botkin, his personal physician, the Tsarina's maid, Demidova, a valet named Trupp and a cook named Kharitonov. There was also a young kitchen boy, but he was not present when the rest met their death.

At Ekaterinburg the guards were veteran Bolsheviks and out and out partisans of the new order. They took delight in humiliating and insulting their prisoners, allowing them no privacy (even when they went to the lavatory), spicing their remarks with coarse jokes, decorating the house with obscene drawings and passing the time by singing ribald songs and holding drunken orgies. But in Moscow even they were thought to be too lenient and early in July they were replaced by members of the Cheka or secret police, who were trained executioners. For by this time the Kremlin was worried by the military situation in the Urals where the counter-revolutionary forces, led by Admiral Kolchak, were rapidly approaching Ekaterinburg. In the middle of July they sent orders to Yurovsky, who was in charge of the guards at the Villa Ipatiev, to execute the Tsar and his family.

On the night of 16 July the Imperial Family and their 'household', who had gone to bed in the normal way, were awakened about midnight, told to dress and go to the basement of the house. There they were summarily executed. Most of them died at once from shots fired at point blank range, but Demidova and Anastasia, who survived the first volley, were finished off with bayonet thrusts. The bodies were taken by lorry to a disused mine in the woods some ten miles from the town. There they were stripped, dismembered and burnt by fire and acid. Someone—probably the Austro-Hungarian prisoner Rudolf Lacher, who was an orderly to Yurovsky—scribbled on the walls of the Ipatiev House a quotation from the German poet Heine which translated reads: 'On the self-same night Belshazzar was slain by his slaves.'[15]

A few days later Kolchak's forces captured Ekaterinburg and the Admiral immediately instituted a full enquiry into the fate of the Imperial Family. In February 1919 this enquiry was entrusted to Nicholas Sokolov, the White Army's examining magistrate. He made an exhaustive enquiry into what had happened and published his findings. These established that the Tsar and Tsarina and all their children, Dr. Botkin, Demidova, Trupp and Kharitonov all perished in the cellar of the Villa Ipatiev. Sokolov died in France in 1924. This remains the official version of what happened on the night of 16–17 July 1918.

The Anastasia story begins in February 1920, when a police sergeant rescued from the Landwehrkanal in Berlin a young woman of about twenty years of age who had no papers or other clues of identity. After a short stay in hospital she was transferred to a psychiatric clinic. There her claim to be the Grand Duchess Anastasia attracted attention and in March 1922 Baron Kleist, a Russian emigré, took her into his own home. From that time until 1948 when she came to live at her present address—a modest villa, at Unterlengenhardt in the Black Forest, replacing an old army hut, bought for her by Prince Frederick Ernest of Saxe-Altenburg, a nephew of the late Grand Duchess Constantine—she has been befriended by a succession of people, some of high rank and some not.

Most of her life has been spent in Germany, but she did go to America for two and a half years and it was there that she was first called Anna Anderson. It was not a very happy time in her eventful life, for a stay with her 'second cousin', Mrs. Leeds (Princess Xenia of Russia) proved a disappointment, while for a year she was confined to a mental home.

Briefly, her story, told in her own book *I, Anastasia* (published in German in 1957 and translated into English in 1958) is that she had only been wounded in the cellar at Ekaterinburg and that when she regained consciousness she was in a farm cart, having been rescued by

[15] In the original language it has a more dramatic ring:

'*Belsatzar ward in selbiger Nacht,
Von seiner knechten umgebracht*'

I am indebted for this information to Victor Alexandrov in his interesting book *The End of the Romanovs* (Hutchinson, 1966).

a Red Guard named Alexander Tchaikovski. They made their way—close on two thousand miles—to Romania where she bore Tchaikovski a son who was apparently placed in an orphanage. She then married Tchaikovski—apparently in a Catholic church, for he appears to have been of Polish extraction. Soon after Tchaikovski was killed in Bucharest and she decided that she must go to Germany and get help from her 'aunt', Princess Henry of Prussia (the late Tsarina's sister) whom she had last seen in 1912. Accompanied by Tchaikovski's brother, Serge, she made her way to Berlin, only to be deserted by him soon after their arrival. It was then that in a fit of desperation she threw herself into the canal.

At the beginning the survivors of the Romanov family were divided in their attitude towards her.

Contrary to the plays and films about her (the revenues from which have incidentally helped to maintain her), she never met her 'grandmother', the Dowager Empress Marie Feodorovna who perhaps might have been able to settle the whole question. Princess Henry of Prussia, who did see her, rejected her claims outright and so, after some initial hesitations, did the Grand Duchess Olga, Nicholas II's sister. The other sister, the Grand Duchess Xenia, who never met her, regarded her as an impostor, and so too did the head of the family, the Grand Duke Cyril. On the other hand, Cyril's younger brother Andrew met her and recognised her. Mrs. Leeds was at first impressed but later changed her mind and became hostile. In fact there is now no Romanov left who is prepared to believe her story.

In September 1967 Anna Anderson, who was in Paris to supervise certain films concerning her life story, had a two-hour interview with the ninety-five year old widow of the Grand Duke Andrew, the former ballerina Mathilde Kschessinska. The Princess Romanovsky-Krassinsky—to give the Grand Duke's morganatic wife her present title—said that she thought that she saw in Frau Anderson the former Grand Duchess Anastasia. But she was also obliged to confess that she had never been presented to the former Grand Duchess and had only ever seen her in a crowd in the distance. Consequently this *coup de théatre*, as the French press described it, really does not advance the matter.

Even more divided have been those Russians who escaped the Revolution and who had known the Imperial Family well. Some like

Gillard, the Swiss tutor, whose wife had been nurse to the Grand Duchess Anastasia, and Baroness Buxhoeveden, a former lady in waiting, declared her to be a fraud, while on the other hand Dr. Botkin's son and daughter have been among her most enthusiastic supporters.

Matters came to a head in 1933 when the Berlin Civil Court issued a certificate of inheritance relating to Nicholas II's property in Germany, naming the late Tsar's heirs. These did not include Anastasia. In the view of the Court the whole family had perished at Ekaterinburg. Anna Anderson's lawyers felt obliged to challenge this decision, and in 1938 they began the proceedings which off and on have gone on ever since.

On 28 February 1967 the Court of Appeal in Hamburg rejected Frau Anna Anderson's claim to be recognised as the Grand Duchess Anastasia and this ends yet another chapter in the long litigation. It is not, however, the end of the story, for Frau Anderson has already declared her intention of appealing to the Federal Supreme Court in Karlsruhe.

The spokesman for the Romanov heirs is Barbara, Duchess of Mecklenburg (born in 1920) who also represents the interests of the House of Hesse. She is a granddaughter of Princess Henry of Prussia, who died in 1953. Her lawyers have tried to establish that the claimant, so far from being Anastasia, is in fact a certain Franziska Schankowska, the daughter of a Polish landworker who had emigrated to Germany. The Courts, while rejecting Anna Anderson's claim to be Anastasia (thus maintaining the terms of the certificate of inheritance first issued in 1933), have declined so far to identify her with Franziska Schankowska—this despite the fact that at least one of the Schankowski family has declared Anna Anderson to be her sister.

From the beginning this litigation has had a distinctly financial significance, for Anna Anderson has affirmed that Nicholas II deposited twenty million roubles in a bank of England. The Bank of England has denied that it holds any such money and several Romanov princes have declared that no such treasure exists.[16] To be fair to Anna Anderson she has never been much interested in the

[16] It would appear that the Tsar withdrew his deposits from Baring's Bank in 1912, but the Imperial Government had some money in the Bank of England to buy armaments.

money. She is now in her middle sixties, in poor health, and not likely to be tempted by thoughts of future affluence.

The evidence of anthropologists, doctors (Frau Anderson has some significant scars) and graphologists has been inconclusive. Perhaps the three factors that have weighed most in her favour are first her obvious physical resemblance to Anastasia, secondly her persistence in her claim in the face of ill-health, misfortune and without much hope of reward, and thirdly her intimate knowledge of Russian court life (including a supposed visit of the Grand Duke of Hesse in 1916 to sound out his sister and brother-in-law about the prospects of a separate peace between Germany and Russia).

But all these three points have been countered by the other side who declare that the scars come from a bottle factory where the claimant (as Franziska Schankowska) worked for a time: that her persistence is due to delusions of grandeur resulting from her mental instability: and that memoirs and even gossip could provide a fair knowledge of Russian court life. Finally they quote from the Hesse archives to show that the Grand Duke (who died in 1938) could not have been in Russia at the time mentioned. Moreover, they point out that in the early days of her 'reappearance' she either would not or could not speak Russian—it was this that one of the earlier judges, Herr Backen described as 'the great puzzle of this case'. They also affirm that her English was spoken with a strong Slav accent and even her German with Polish undertones.

What then are we to believe? One is constantly reminded of the famous Tichborne Case in the 1870s where there was the same complexity of issues, the same sort of conflicting testimony and where there was a sharp division of opinion both in the family and among the general public. But here, of course, the claimant was ultimately— and it was the longest lawsuit in English history—identified as Arthur Orton, the son of a butcher from Wapping. So far Anna Anderson, although she has failed in her claims, has not been definitely identified as someone else.

It is, of course, possible that she could have escaped. One of her witnesses, an Austro-Hungarian prisoner of war named Rudolf Lacher, who was present at the Villa Ipatiev, has agreed on this point and another prisoner of war (Frank Svoboda, now dead) maintained on oath that Anastasia was carried from the Villa Ipatiev to the house where he was billeted and there looked after. But in his case he was obliged to confess that he was relying on the word of his landlady as to the identity of the person brought into the house. Since 1945 we have had evidence of Jews who miraculously survived the mass shootings in concentration camps, though here no doubt the numbers of those executed helped to produce confusion. But the Tsar's murder was premeditated and carefully planned in advance. It seems most unlikely that the bodies (after all there were only eleven of them) were not checked. It was too important an occasion for careless-ness.

In the absence of any real evidence, let alone documentary proof, Anna Anderson's story has no objective reality. It is purely circum-stantial. One might at least have expected something from Romania, but an intensive search of records there instigated by Queen Marie has yielded nothing. Not till the German police records place her in Berlin in February 1920 has Anna Anderson any legal existence.

Yet when all is said and done she remains a personality in her own right and has managed to command over the years the respect and even devotion of a wide variety of people.

The Anastasia affair has a certain legal interest in England, for there appear to be people who still use the legal device of tying up their estate until ten years after the death of all the surviving descen-dants of Queen Victoria (Anastasia, of course, is one of them) who were alive at the time of the making of the will. From time to time there have been efforts to have these wills set aside on the grounds of uncertainty—i.e. that the fate of Queen Victoria's descendants cannot after several wars and revolutions any longer be established with complete certainty. The most famous of such cases was Cooper *v.* Leverhulme in 1943, but there had been a previous one (Public Trustee *v.* Villar) in 1927 and I myself was called upon to give evi-dence in the High Court of Justice in a similar case in 1961.

In conclusion it is difficult to foresee the end of the Anastasia litigation. The costs must now be so great that it could easily bank-rupt either side. Perhaps the death of Anna Anderson will settle it. On the other hand the Paris Court of Appeal was still concerning itself as late as 1954 over the claim of Karl Naundorff, the Dutch watch repairer, to be the Dauphin (Louis XVII) who died in the Temple prison in 1795, although Naundorff had died in 1845.[17] It is true that he left descendants to continue his claims, but it is always

[17] See Chapter 8.

possible that Alexis Tchaikovski may emerge from obscurity in Romania and claim to be Nicholas II's only grandson.

Postscript

Anastasia's case came before the Supreme Court at Karlsruhe in July 1967, when her principal advocate, Baron von Stackelberg— himself belonging to a distinguished family of Baltic barons (one of them married a sister of Julia Hauke, Princess of Battenberg, the Duke of Edinburgh's great grandmother)—asked for the judgment of 28 February 1967, made by the Court of Hamburg, to be set aside. Owing to the backlog of cases already before the Court and to the complexity of the issues involved, no final judgment from Karlsruhe is expected before 1969.

Stackelberg criticised the Hamburg Court for the partisan way in which it blindly accepted the testimony of those against Anastasia while arbitrarily rejecting that of those in her favour, despite the fact that the type of evidence offered by both sides was much the same. He also argued that as it was now almost impossible to be able to furnish conclusive proof of identity, and as it has been decided legally that Anna Anderson was not the woman (Franziska Schankowska) the defendants had tried to prove she was, it was time the burden of proof was shifted to the other side. Instead of her always having to prove that she is Anastasia, they should now be made to prove that she is not. According to Stackelberg the overwhelming mass of evidence would make this impossible for them to do.

The outcome of the next stages of this seemingly endless legal battle will be awaited with great interest.

Meanwhile, however, in December 1968, Anna Anderson has married (at Charlottesville in Virginia) a forty-nine year-old former professor of history at the University of Virginia, Dr. John Manahan, whom she had met five months previously.

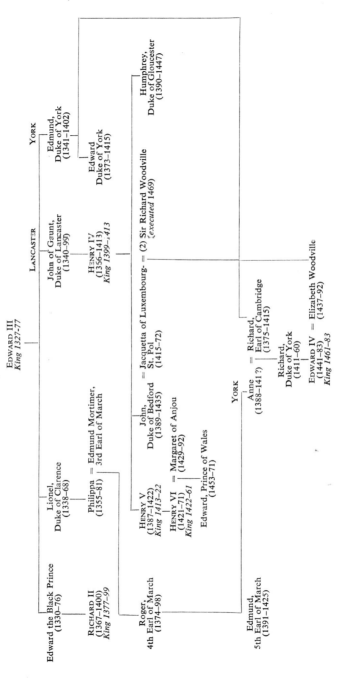

TABLE No. 1

Houses of Lancaster and York

G

TABLE No. 2
Descent of Henry VII

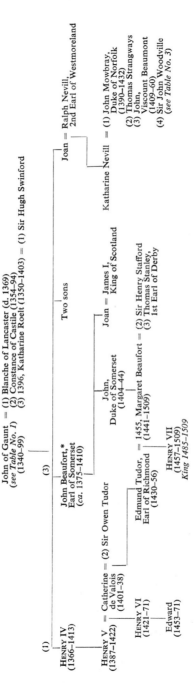

John of Gaunt = (1) Blanche of Lancaster (d. 1369)
(see Table No. 1) (2) Constance of Castile (1354–94)
(1340–99) (3) 1396, Katharine Roelt (1350–1403) = (1) Sir Hugh Swinford

(1)

(3)

HENRY IV
(1366–1413)

HENRY V = (2) Sir Owen Tudor
(1387–1422) Catherine
            de Valois
            (1401–38)

HENRY VI
(1421–71)

Edward
(1453–71)

John Beaufort,*
Earl of Somerset
(ca. 1375–1410)

Edmund Tudor,
Earl of Richmond
(1430–56)

John,
Duke of Somerset
(1404–44)

= 1455, Margaret Beaufort
        (1441–1509)

HENRY VII
(1457–1509)
King 1485–1509

Two sons

Joan = James I,
       King of Scotland

Margaret Beaufort = (2) Sir Henry Stafford
                    (3) Thomas Stanley,
                        1st Earl of Derby

Joan = Ralph Nevill,
       2nd Earl of Westmoreland

Katharine Nevill = (1) John Mowbray,
                       Duke of Norfolk
                       (1390–1432)
                   (2) Thomas Strangways
                   (3) John,
                       Viscount Beaumont
                       (1409–60)
                   (4) Sir John Woodville
                       (see Table No. 3)

* Beaufort, his two younger brothers and his sister were born before the marriage of their parents. They were legitimated by Act of Parliament in 1397 but expressly excluded from the succession.

TABLE No. 3
The Woodvilles

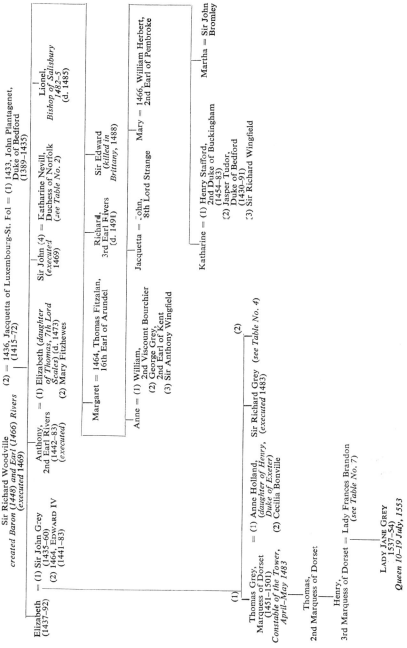

Sir Richard Woodville, created Baron (1448) and Earl (1466) Rivers (executed 1469) = 1436, Jacquetta of Luxembourg-St. Pol (1415–72) (2) = 1433, John Plantagenet, Duke of Bedford (1389–1435) (1)

Elizabeth (1437–92) = (1) Sir John Grey (1435–60) (2) 1464, EDWARD IV (1441–83)

Anthony, 2nd Earl Rivers (1442–83) (executed)

Sir John (4) (executed 1469) = Elizabeth (daughter of Thomas, 7th Lord Scales) (d. 1473) (2) Mary Fitzhewes

Sir John (4) (executed 1469) = Katharine Nevill, Duchess of Norfolk (see Table No. 2)

Lionel, Bishop of Salisbury 1482–5 (d. 1485)

Margaret = 1464, Thomas Fitzalan, 16th Earl of Arundel

Richard, 3rd Earl Rivers (d. 1491)

Sir Edward (killed in Brittany, 1488)

Anne = (1) William, 2nd Viscount Bourchier (2) George Grey, 2nd Earl of Kent (3) Sir Anthony Wingfield

Jacquetta = John, 8th Lord Strange

Mary = 1466, William Herbert, 2nd Earl of Pembroke

Katharine = (1) Henry Stafford, 2nd Duke of Buckingham (1454–83) (2) Jasper Tudor, Duke of Bedford (1430–91) (3) Sir Richard Wingfield

Martha = Sir John Bromley

(1)

Sir Richard Grey, (executed 1483)

(2)

(see Table No. 4)

Thomas Grey, Marquess of Dorset (1451–1501) Constable of the Tower, April–May 1483 = (1) Anne Holland, (daughter of Henry, Duke of Exeter) (2) Cecilia Bonville

Thomas, 2nd Marquess of Dorset

Henry, 3rd Marquess of Dorset = Lady Frances Brandon (see Table No. 7)

LADY JANE GREY 1537–54 Queen 10–19 July, 1553

TABLE No. 4
The Last of the Plantagenets

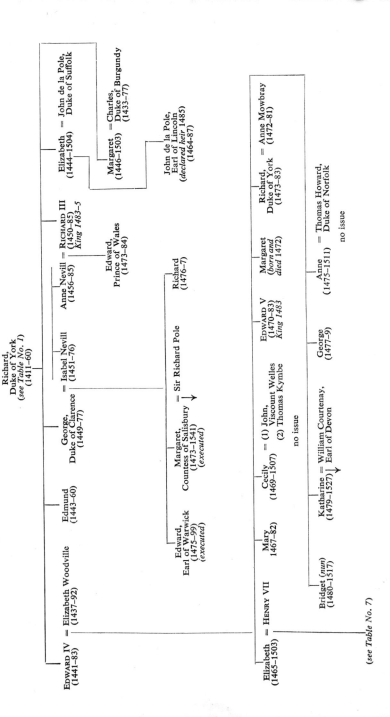

(see Table No. 7)

TABLE No. 5
Ancestry of Don Carlos

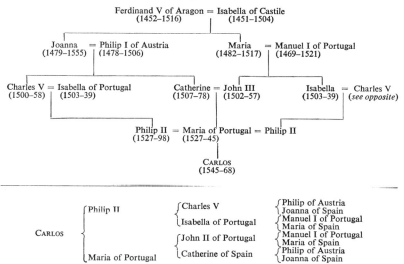

Ferdinand V of Aragon = Isabella of Castile
(1452–1516)   (1451–1504)

Joanna = Philip I of Austria   Maria = Manuel I of Portugal
(1479–1555) | (1478–1506)   (1482–1517) | (1469–1521)

Charles V = Isabella of Portugal   Catherine = John III   Isabella = Charles V
(1500–58) | (1503–39)   (1507–78) | (1502–57)   (1503–39) | (*see opposite*)

Philip II = Maria of Portugal = Philip II
(1527–98)   (1527–45)

CARLOS
(1545–68)

CARLOS
- Philip II
  - Charles V
    - Philip of Austria
    - Joanna of Spain
  - Isabella of Portugal
    - Manuel I of Portugal
    - Maria of Spain
- Maria of Portugal
  - John II of Portugal
    - Manuel I of Portugal
    - Maria of Spain
  - Catherine of Spain
    - Philip of Austria
    - Joanna of Spain

Whereas a normal person would have eight different great-grandparents, Don Carlos had only four. Of these, Manuel I was the child of first cousins, Philip of Austria, Joanna and Maria of Spain were the children of second cousins. Moreover, Joanna and Maria were sisters.

TABLE No. 5a
Family of Philip II

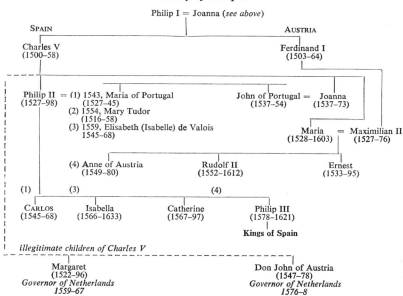

Philip I = Joanna (*see above*)

SPAIN   AUSTRIA

Charles V   Ferdinand I
(1500–58)   (1503–64)

Philip II = (1) 1543, Maria of Portugal   John of Portugal = Joanna
(1527–98)   (1527–45)   (1537–54)   (1537–73)
     (2) 1554, Mary Tudor
     (1516–58)
     (3) 1559, Elisabeth (Isabelle) de Valois   Maria = Maximilian II
     1545–68   (1528–1603)   (1527–76)

(4) Anne of Austria   Rudolf II   Ernest
(1549–80)   (1552–1612)   (1533–95)

(1)   (3)   (4)

CARLOS   Isabella   Catherine   Philip III
(1545–68)   (1566–1633)   (1567–97)   (1578–1621)

Kings of Spain

illegitimate children of Charles V

Margaret   Don John of Austria
(1522–96)   (1547–78)
Governor of Netherlands   *Governor of Netherlands*
1559–67   *1576–8*

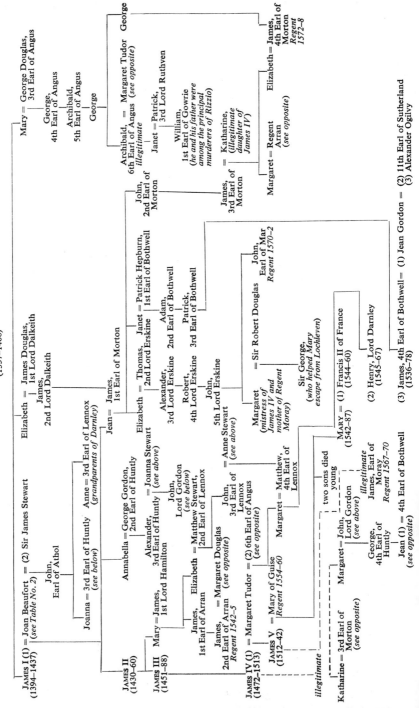

TABLE No. 6

Mary and the Scottish Nobility

TABLE No. 7

Claims of Mary Queen of Scots

HENRY VII
(1457–1509)

Arthur
(1486–1502)

Margaret = (1) James IV of Scotland
(1489–1541)   (1472–1513)
            (2) Archibald Douglas,
                6th Earl of Angus
                (1490–1556)

HENRY VIII
(1491–1547)

Mary = (1) Louis XII of France
(1496–1533)   (1462–1515)
            (2) Charles Brandon,
                Duke of Suffolk

(1)

(2)

James V = (2) Mary of Guise
(1512–42)   (1515–60)

Margaret = Matthew Stewart,
(1515–77)   4th Earl of Lennox

MARY = Philip II
(1516–58)   of Spain

ELIZABETH I
(1533–1603)

EDWARD VI
(1537–53)

Frances = Henry Grey,
(1517–59)   Marquess of Dorset,
            Duke of Suffolk
            (see Table No. 3)

Eleanor = Henry Clifford,
(1524–47)   2nd Earl of
            Cumberland

James
(born 1540,
died in
infancy)

Arthur
(born 1541,
died in
infancy)

MARY = (1) 1558, Francis II
(1542–87)   of France
            (1543–60)
        (2) 1565, Henry, Lord
            Darnley
            (1545–67)
        (3) 1567, James Hepburn,
            4th Earl of Bothwell
            (1536–78)

Charles,
5th Earl of
Lennox
(1555–76)

Jane = Lord Guildford
(1537–54)   Dudley

Katharine = (1) Henry Herbert,
(1540–69)   Earl of Pembroke
            (2) Edward Seymour,
                Earl of Hertford

Mary = Thomas Keys
(1543/5–78)

Arabella = 1610, William Seymour
(1575–1616)

JAMES VI and I
(1566–1625)

The Last of the Ruriks and the Early Romanovs

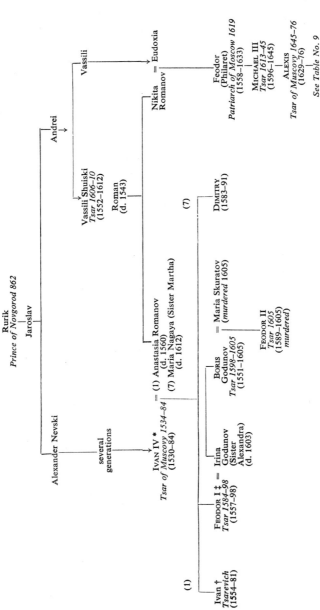

Rurik
Prince of Novgorod 862

Jaroslav

Alexander Nevski

several generations

IVAN IV *
Tsar of Muscovy 1534–84
(1530–84)

= (1) Anastasia Romanov (d. 1560)
(7) Maria Nagaya (Sister Martha) (d. 1612)

Andrei →

Vassili

Vassili Shuiski
Tsar 1606–10
(1552–1612)

Roman
(d. 1543)

Nikita Romanov = Eudoxia

(1)

Ivan †
Tsarevich
(1554–81)

FEODOR I ‡
Tsar 1584–98
(1557–98)

= Irina Godunov (Sister Alexandra) (d. 1603)

Boris Godunov
Tsar 1598–1605
(1551–1605)

= Maria Skuratov (*murdered 1605*)

(7)

Dimitry
(1583–91)

Feodor (Philaret)
Patriarch of Moscow 1619
(1558–1633)

Michael III
Tsar 1613–45
(1596–1645)

Alexis
Tsar of Muscovy 1645–76
(1629–76)

See Table No. 9

Feodor II
Tsar 1605
(1589–1605)
murdered

* Although married seven times he had surviving issue only by his first and seventh wives.
† Married three times but had no children.
‡ His only daughter died in infancy.

TABLE No. 9

Family of Peter the Great

ALEXIS, Tsar of Muscovy (see Table No. 8) (1629–76) = (1) Maria Miloslavsky (1626–69) (2) Natalia Narishkin (1651–94)

(1)
- Sophia (Sister Susanna) Regent 1682–9 (1657–1704)
- FEODOR III Tsar 1676–82 (1661–82)
- IVAN V Tsar 1682–96 (1666–96)

(2)
- PETER I Tsar 1682–1725 (1672–1725) = (1) Eudoxia Lapoukhin (Sister Helena) (1669–1731) (divorced 1698) (2) 1707 and 1712, CATHERINE I Tsarina 1725–7 (1689–1727)
- Natalia (1674–1716)

Children of Ivan V:
- Catherine = Charles Leopold of Mecklenburg (1692–1733)
- ANNA Tsarina 1730–40 (1693–1740) = Frederick of Courland

Children of Peter I:
(1)
- Alexis Tsarevich (1690–1718) = Charlotte of Brunswick (1694–1715)

(2)
- Natalia (1714–28)
- two sons (died in infancy)
- Catherine (1707–8)
- Anna (1708–28) = Charles Frederick, Duke of Holstein-Gottorp
- ELIZABETH Tsarina 1741–62 (1709–62) = Alexis Razumovsky
- Peter (1715–19)
- three daughters and a son (all died young)

Anna Regent 1740–1 1718–46 = Anton Ulric of Brunswick

IVAN VI Tsar 1740–1 (1740–61)

Natalia (1714–28)

Peter II Tsar 1727–30 (1715–30)

PETER III Tsar 1762 (1728–62)

see Table No. 10

TABLE No. 10
The Romanovs 1762–1881

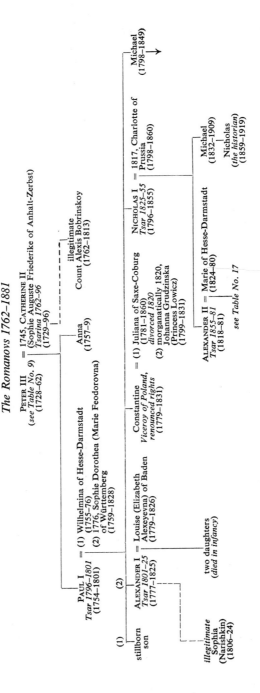

PETER III = 1745, CATHERINE II
(see Table No. 9)   (Sophie Auguste Friederike of Anhalt-Zerbst)
(1728–62)   Tsarina 1762–96
                   (1729–96)

Anna
(1757–9)

illegitimate
Count Alexis Bobrinskoy
(1762–1813)

PAUL I = (1) Wilhelmina of Hesse-Darmstadt
Tsar 1796–1801   (1755–76)
(1754–1801)   (2) 1776, Sophie Dorothea (Marie Feodorovna)
                  of Württemberg
                  (1759–1828)

(1) stillborn son

(2)

ALEXANDER I = Louise (Elizabeth Alexeyevna) of Baden
Tsar 1801–25   (1779–1826)
(1777–1825)

two daughters
(died in infancy)

illegitimate
Sophia (Narishkin)
(1806–24)

Constantine
Viceroy of Poland,
renounced rights
(1779–1831)

= (1) Juliana of Saxe-Coburg
       (1781–1860)
       divorced 1820
   (2) morganatically 1820,
       Johanna Grudzinska
       (Princess Lowicz)
       (1799–1831)

NICHOLAS I = 1817, Charlotte of
Tsar 1825–55   Prussia
(1796–1855)   (1798–1860)

ALEXANDER II = Marie of Hesse-Darmstadt
Tsar 1855–81   (1824–80)
(1818–81)

see Table No. 17

Michael
(1832–1909)

Nicholas
(the historian)
(1859–1919)

Michael
(1798–1849) →

TABLE NO. 11
The Elder Bourbon Line

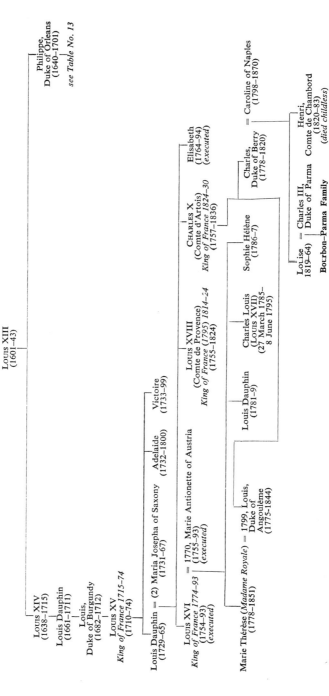

LOUIS XIII
(1601–43)

Philippe,
Duke of Orleans
(1640–1701)
see Table No. 13

LOUIS XIV
(1638–1715)

Louis Dauphin
(1661–1711)

Louis,
Duke of Burgundy
(1682–1712)

LOUIS XV
King of France 1715–74
(1710–74)

Louis Dauphin = (2) Maria Josepha of Saxony
(1729–65)   (1731–67)

Adelaide
(1732–1800)

Victoire
(1733–99)

LOUIS XVIII
(Comte de Provence)
King of France (1795) 1814–24
(1755–1824)

CHARLES X
(Comte d'Artois)
King of France 1824–30
(1757–1836)

Elisabeth
(1764–94)
(executed)

LOUIS XVI = 1770, Marie Antionette of Austria
King of France 1774–93   (1755–93)
(1754–93)   *(executed)*
(executed)

Marie Thérèse (*Madame Royale*) = 1799, Louis,
(1778–1851)   Duke of
                                             Angoulême
                                             (1775–1844)

Louis Dauphin
(1781–9)

Charles Louis
(Louis XVII)
(27 March 1785–
8 June 1795)

Sophie Hélène
(1786–7)

Charles,
Duke of Berry
(1778–1820)

= Caroline of Naples
  (1798–1870)

Louise = Charles III,
1819–64)   Duke of Parma
Bourbon–Parma Family

Henri,
Comte de Chambord
(1820–83)
(died childless)

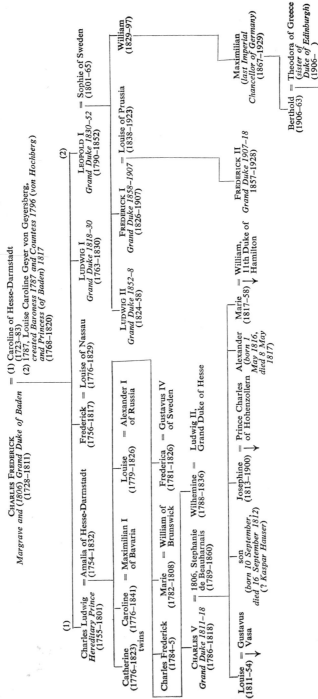

TABLE No. 12
The Baden Succession

CHARLES FREDERICK
Margrave and (1806) Grand Duke of Baden = (1) Caroline of Hesse-Darmstadt
(1728–1811) (1723–83)
(2) 1787, Louise Caroline Geyer von Geyersberg, *created Baroness 1787 and Countess 1796 (von Hochberg)* *and Princess (of Baden) 1817* (1768–1820)

(1)

Charles Ludwig
Hereditary Prince
(1755–1801)
= Amalia of Hesse-Darmstadt
(1754–1832)

Frederick = Louise of Nassau
(1756–1817)   (1776–1829)

(2)

Ludwig I
Grand Duke 1818–30
(1763–1830)

Leopold I
Grand Duke 1830–52
(1790–1852)
= Sophie of Sweden
(1801–65)

William
(1829–97)

Catherine
(1776–1823)
twins

Caroline
(1776–1841)
= Maximilian I
of Bavaria

Louise
(1779–1826)
= Alexander I
of Russia

Frederica
(1781–1826)
= Gustavus IV
of Sweden

Marie
(1782–1808)
= William of
Brunswick

Wilhemine
(1788–1836)
= Ludwig II,
Grand Duke of Hesse

Ludwig II
Grand Duke 1852–8
(1824–58)

Frederick I
Grand Duke 1858–1907
(1826–1907)
= Louise of Prussia
(1838–1923)

Charles Frederick
(1784–5)

CHARLES V
Grand Duke 1811–18
(1786–1818)
= 1806, Stephanie
de Beauharnais
(1789–1860)

son
(born 10 September,
died 16 September 1812)

Alexander
(born 1
May 1816,
died 8 May
1817)

Marie
(1817–58)
= William,
11th Duke of
Hamilton

Josephine
(1813–1900)
= Prince Charles
of Hohenzollern

Frederick II
Grand Duke 1907–18
(1857–1928)

Louise
(1811–54)
= Gustavus
Vasa

Maximilian
(*last Imperial
Chancellor of Germany*)
(1867–1929)

Berthold
(1906–63)
= Theodora of Greece
(*sister of
Duke of Edinburgh*)
(1906–)

Maximilian
(1933–)
present Head of House of Baden

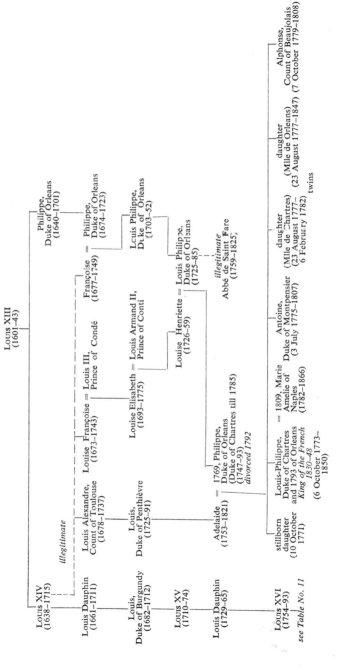

TABLE NO. 14
The Kings of Bavaria

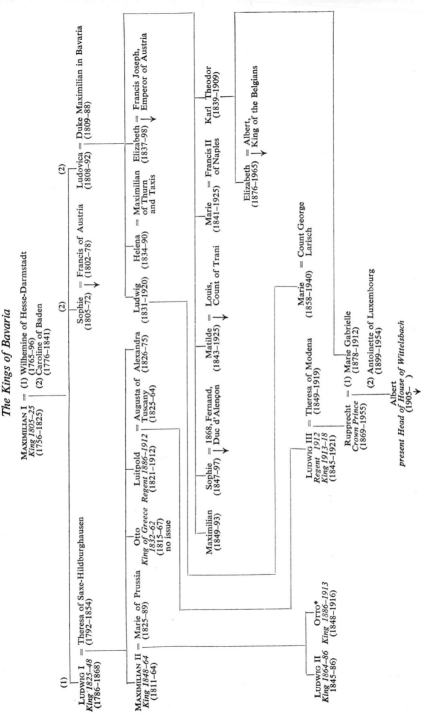

* In November 1913, as it was clear that Otto would never recover his reason, the throne was declared vacant by decree and the Regent succeeded as Ludwig III.

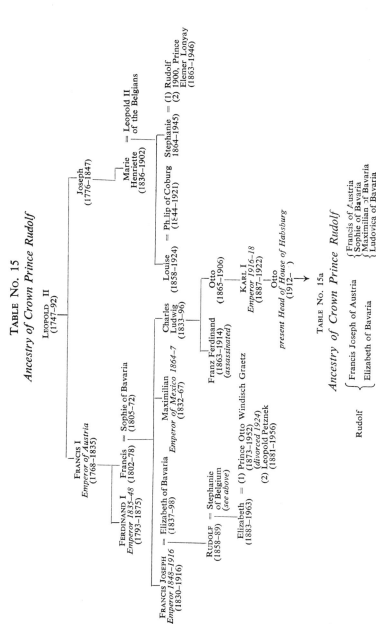

```
                                    LEOPOLD II
                                    (1747–92)

                          Joseph
                          (1776–1847)

                                              Marie    = Leopold II
                                              Henriette    of the Belgians
                                              (1836–1902)

FRANCIS I
Emperor of Austria
(1768–1835)

Francis    = Sophie of Bavaria                    Louise    = Philip of Coburg    Stephanie = (1) Rudolf
(1802–78)    (1805–72)                            (1858–1924)   (1844–1921)       1864–1945     (2) 1900, Prince
                                                                                                Elemer Lonyay
                                                                                                (1863–1946)

        Maximilian          Charles          Otto
        Emperor of Mexico 1864–7   Ludwig    (1865–1906)
        (1832–67)          (1833–96)
FERDINAND I
Emperor 1835–48
(1793–1875)

                Franz Ferdinand                 KARL I
                (1863–1914)                      Emperor 1916–18
                (assassinated)                   (1887–1922)

FRANCIS JOSEPH = Elizabeth of Bavaria                            Otto
Emperor 1848–1916   (1837–98)                                    (1912– )
(1830–1916)
                                                        present Head of House of Habsburg

RUDOLF = Stephanie
(1858–89)   of Belgium
            (see above)

Elizabeth = (1) Prince Otto Windisch Graetz
(1883–1963)    (1873–1952)
               (divorced 1924)
               (2) Leopold Petznek
               (1881–1956)
```

TABLE No. 15a

Ancestry of Crown Prince Rudolf

Rudolf {
    Francis Joseph of Austria { Francis of Austria
                                 { Sophie of Bavaria
    Elizabeth of Bavaria { Maximilian of Bavaria
                            { Ludovica of Bavaria
}

Thus three of Rudolf's four grandparents belonged to the House of Wittelsbach; and of these, Sophie and Ludovica were sisters, while Maximilian was their second cousin. Of his mother's eight great-grandparents, four were Wittelsbachs and one of those who was not had a Wittelsbach mother.

AUSTRIA

Francis I
(1768–1835)

Francis
(1802–78)

Francis Joseph
(1830–1916)

Rudolf
(1858–89)

LEOPOLD II
(see Table No. 15)

TUSCANY

FERDINAND III
Grand Duke of Tuscany
1790–1824
(1769–1824)

LEOPOLD II = Maria Antonia of Bourbon-Sicily
Grand Duke of Tuscany   (1814–98)
1824–59
(1797–1870)

Isabella = Francis of Bourbon-Sicily
(1834–1901) | Count of Trapani

Antoinette = Alfonso of Bourbon-Sicily,
(1851–1931) | Count of Caserta →

FERDINAND IV
Grand Duke of Tuscany
1859–60
(1835–1908)

Leopold ('Wolfling')
(1868–1935)
(married three times,
all to commoners)

AUSTRIA

Charles
(1771–1847)

Albert   William
(1817–95)   (1827–94)

Johann Nepomuk Salvator
(John Orth)
(1852–90)

Ludwig Salvator
(1847–1915)

Louise = (1) Frederick Augustus III
(1870–1947) | *Crown Prince and later*
              | *King of Saxony*
              | (1865–1932)
              | *(divorced 1903)*
              | (2) 1907, Enrico Toselli
              | (1883–1926)
              | *(divorced 1912)*

TABLE NO. 17
The End of the Romanovs

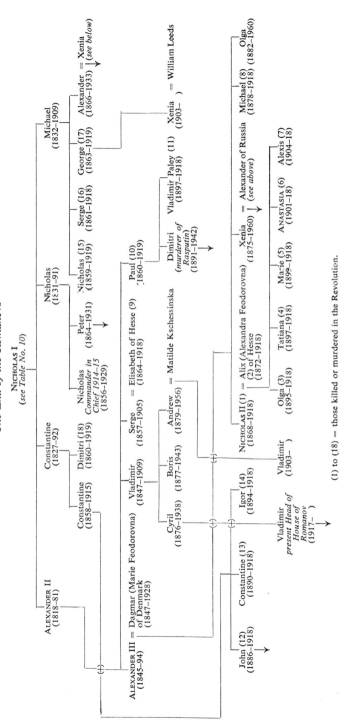

(1) to (18) = those killed or murdered in the Revolution.

TABLE No. 18
Relationship Between the British and Russian Royal Families

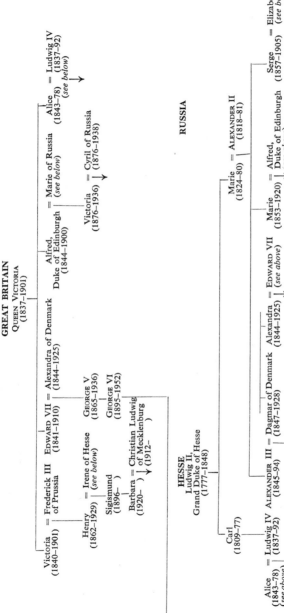

GREAT BRITAIN
QUEEN VICTORIA
(1837–1901)

Victoria = Frederick III
(1840–1901)   of Prussia

Henry = Irene of Hesse
(1862–1929)   (see below)

Sigismund
(1896–)

Barbara = Christian Ludwig
(1920–)   of Mecklenburg
(1912–)

EDWARD VII = Alexandra of Denmark
(1841–1910)   (1844–1925)

GEORGE V
(1865–1936)

GEORGE VI
(1895–1952)

Alfred, = Marie of Russia
Duke of Edinburgh   (see below)
(1844–1900)

Victoria = Cyril of Russia
(1876–1936)   (1876–1938)

Alice = Ludwig IV
(1843–78)   (1837–92)
(see below)

RUSSIA

Marie = ALEXANDER II
(1824–80)   (1818–81)

Marie = Alfred,
(1853–1920)   Duke of Edinburgh
(see above)

Serge = Elizabeth of Hesse
(1857–1905)   (see below)

HESSE
Ludwig II,
Grand Duke of Hesse
(1777–1848)

Carl
(1809–77)

Ludwig IV = Alice
(1837–92)   (1843–78)
(see above)

Victoria = Louis of
(1863–1950)   Battenberg

Alice = Andrew of Greece
(1885–)

ELIZABETH II = Philip
(1926–)   (1921–)

ALEXANDER III = Dagmar of Denmark
(1845–94)   (1847–1928)

Elizabeth = Serge of Russia
(1864–1918)

Irene = Henry of Prussia
(1866–1953)   (see above)

Ernst Ludwig,
Grand Duke of Hesse
(1868–1937)

Alix = NICHOLAS II
(1872–1918)   (1868–1918)

See Table No. 17

Bibliography

THERE is so much that has been written on most of the subjects included in this book that it is quite impossible to do more than indicate those authorities which I consider the reader will find most useful for further study.

On the whole I have confined myself to the latest works, only including those written some years ago when I consider them to be helpful.

Chapters 1 and 2
For background:

> E. F. JACOBS, *The Fifteenth Century*, Oxford, 1961.

For the Princes:
The best account is an article by—

> GEOFFREY WHITE, in *The Complete Peerage*, Vol. XII, Part II, Appendix J.

For recent investigations:

> L. E. TANNER and W. WRIGHT, 'Recent Investigations Regarding the Fate of the Princes in the Tower', in *Archaeologia*, Vol. lxxxiv (1934).

For them and for Simnel and Warbeck see also:

> SIR C. MARKHAM, *Richard III*, London, 1906.
> DAVID MACGIBBON, *Elizabeth Woodville*, London, 1938.
> A. R. MYERS, 'The Character of Richard III' (article in *History To-day*, Vol. IV, 1954).
> P. M. KENDALL, *Richard the Third*, London, 1955.
> E. N. SIMONS, *Henry VII*, London, 1968.

See also:

> *Dictionary of National Biography.*

Chapter 3

There exists no satisfactory biography of Don Carlos in English, but most works on Philip II deal with him.

MARTIN S. HUME, *Philip II*, London, 1897.

DR. A. S. RAPPOPORT, *Mad Majesties*, London, 1913.

SIR CHARLES PETRIE, *Philip II of Spain*, London, 1963.

Chapter 4

ANDREW LANG, *The Mystery of Mary Stuart*, London, 1901. (Still in many ways the best account.)

J. E. NEALE, *Queen Elizabeth*, London, 1934.

M. H. ARMSTRONG DAVISON, *The Casket Letters*, Washington, 1965.

GEORGE MALCOLM THOMSON, *The Crime of Mary Stuart*, London, 1967.

Chapter 5

For background:

B. PARES, *A History of Russia*, 3rd edition, revised, New York, 1937.

For the last Ruriks:

STEPHEN GRAHAM, *Boris Godunof*, London, 1933.

J. L. I. FENNELL, *Ivan the Great of Moscow*, London, 1961.

IAN GREY, *Ivan the Terrible*, London, 1964.

For Dimitry:

PHILIP L. BARBOUR, *Dimitry, Tsar and Great Prince of all Russia, 1605-1606*, London, 1967.

Chapter 6

For Peter the Great:

STEPHEN GRAHAM, *A Life of Peter the Great*, London, 1929.

IAN GREY, *Peter the Great*, London, 1962.

For Alexis:

VICOMTE E. M. DE VOGUÉ, *A Czarevitch of the Eighteenth Century* (English edition), London, 1913.

Chapter 7

For Catherine the Great:

The latest books in English are:

IAN GREY, *Catherine the Great*, London, 1961.

ZOE OLDENBOURG, *Catherine the Great*, London, 1965.

For Pugachov:

A. S. PUSHKIN, *History of the Pugachov Rebellion*, 1833–4.

A. S. PUSKKIN, *A Captain's Daughter* (fiction), 1836.

COUNT HENRY KRASINSKI, *Cossacks of the Ukraine*, London, 1848.

A. E. GAISINOVICH, *La Révolte de Pougatchev*, Paris, 1938.

Chapter 8

The latest books are:

H. R. MADOL, *The Shadow King*, London, 1930.

L. CREISSEL, *Louis XVII et les Faux Dauphins*, Paris, 1936.

A DECAUX, *Louis XVII Retrouvé Naundorff, Roi de France*, Paris, 1947.

MAURICE CONSTANTIN-WEBER, *Naundorff ou Louis XVII?* Paris, 1950.

LOUIS HASTIER, *La Double Mort de Louis XVII*, Paris, 1951.

J. P. ROMAIN, *L'enigme du Cimetière Sainte Marguerite*, Paris, 1953.

A. CASTELOT, *Louis XVII*, Paris, 1960.

RUPERT FURNEAUX, *The Bourbon Tragedy*, London, 1968.

Chapter 9

For background:

H. SETON-WATSON, *The Russian Empire, 1801–1917*, London, 1967.

For pro-Kuzmich view:

LEONID I. STRAKHOVSKY, *Alexander I of Russia*, London, 1949.

For opposite view:

E. M. ALMEDINGEN, *The Emperor Alexander I*, London, 1964.

Chapter 10

A good introduction to this tangled story is:

ELIZABETH E. EVANS, *The Story of Kaspar Hauser*, London, 1892.
    (It contains a bibliography of the main works to that date.)
and

ANDREW LANG, 'The Mystery of Kaspar Hauser' (in *Historical Mysteries*), London, 1904.

For the Stanhope side:

P. H. STANHOPE, *Tracts Relating to Caspar Hauser*, London, 1836.
DUCHESS OF CLEVELAND, *True Story of Kaspar Hauser*, London, 1893.

For the Baden Connection:

E. BAPST, *A la Conquète du Trône de Bade*, Paris, 1930.
E. BAPST, *Une Mère et son fils*, Paris, 1933.

Chapter 11

For Lord Newborough see:
Complete Peerage, Vol. IX, (1936).

For Stella's point of view see her memoirs (first published in French in 1830) and in English:
The Memoirs of Maria Stella, Lady Newborough, London, 1914.

See also:

SIR RALPH PAYNE-GALLWEY, *The Mystery of Maria Stella, Lady Newborough*, London, 1907. (On the whole favourable to her claims.)
MAURICE VITRAC, *Philippe Egalité et Monsieur Chiappini*, Paris, 1907. (Unfavourable.)
A. CASTELOT, *Philippe Egalité: le Prince Rouge*, Paris, 1950.

Chapter 12

D. CHAPMAN-HUSTON, *Bavarian Fantasy: the Story of Ludwig II*, London, 1955.

For Ludwig's relations with the Empress Elizabeth:
COUNT CORTI, *Elizabeth, Empress of Austria*, London, 1936.

For his relations with Wagner:
ANNETTE KOLB, *Le roi Louis II de Bavière et Richard Wagner*, Paris, 1947.

Chapter 13

BARON VON MITIS, *The Crown Prince Rudolf*, London, 1928.
COUNT CARL LONYAY, *Rudolf, the Tragedy of Mayerling*, London, 1950. (Reliable and has a good bibliography.)
RICHARD BARKELEY, *The Road to Mayerling: Life and Death of Crown Prince Rudolf*, London, 1958.

For lighter reading:
MARIE LARISCH, *My Past*, London, 1913.
STEPHANIE OF BELGIUM, PRINCESS OF LONYAY, *I Was to be Empress*, London, 1937.

Chapter 14

There is no biography in English of John Orth. There is a short study in French:

A DE FAUCIGNY-LUCINGE, *L'Archiduc Jean Salvator*, Paris, 1911.

There are references to him in the standard biographies of the Emperor Francis Joseph, Crown Prince Rudolf and the Emperor Karl. (COUNT ARTHUR POLZER-HODITZ, *The Emperor Karl*, London, 1930.)

See also:
LOUISA OF TUSCANY, EX-CROWN PRINCESS OF SAXONY (his niece), *My Own Story*, London, 1911.
LEOPOLD WÖLFLING (his nephew), *My Life Story from Archduke to Grocer*, London, 1930.

Chapter 15

For the Tsar and Tsarina:
ROBERT K. MASSIE, *Nicholas and Alexandra*, London, 1968.

For Ekaterinburg:
CAPTAIN PAUL BULYGIN, *The Murder of the Romanovs*, London, 1935.
VICTOR ALEXANDROV, *The End of the Romanovs*, London, 1966.

For those who escaped:
VICE-ADMIRAL SIR FRANCIS PRIDHAM, *Close of a Dynasty*, London, 1956.

For Anastasia's own story (originally published in German, 1957, and translated into English):
I, Anastasia, London, 1958.

Index

THIS is an Index of Names only. For the convenience of the reader I have grouped all royal personages (for whom alone I have supplied dates) under the country of their origin or that into which, in the case of women, they married. Appropriate cross references have been supplied.

The only exceptions I have made to this rule is where a royal prince or princess has a distinctive title by which they are usually remembered (e.g. Angoulême, Edinburgh, York, etc.) I have also placed those who form a separate study in this book under their Christian names (e.g. Alexander I of Russia, Ludwig II of Bavaria, etc.).

Acton, John, 1st Lord, 46
Alba, Fernando Alvarez de Toledo, Duke of, 23, 28, 29, 32 note
Alençon, Ferdinand Duc d' (1844–1910), 137
Alençon, Sophie of Bavaria, Duchesse d' (1847–97), 136–7 and note 11
Alexander I, Tsar of Russia (1777–1825), 95–108, 116, 118, 162
Alexandrov, Victor, 175 note
Alexis, Tsarevich of Russia, 54–66, 67, 97
Alfieri, Vittorio, 31
Almedingen, E. M., 106
Anastasia, Grand Duchess of Russia (1901–18), 168, 171–80
Anderson, Anna (Anastasia), 167, 175–80
Andrassy, Count Julius, 157
Angoulême, Louis, Duc d' (1775–1844), 87, 89 note 23
Angoulême, Marie Thérèse Charlotte (Madame Royale), Duchesse d' (1778–1851), 82, 83, 84, 85, 87, 89, 90, 93
Aragon, Catherine of (1485–1536), 21 and note 20
Arakcheyev, Count A. A., 95 and note 3
Arran, James Hamilton, 2nd Earl of, Regent of Scotland, 37, 38
Arthur, Prince, 11
Ashton, Christopher, 22 note 24
Astley, 19, 20, 21 and note 21
Atholl, John Stewart, 4th Earl of, 41
Auckland, William Eden, 1st Lord, 123
Audley, James, 7th Lord, 20
Audubon, John James, 89
Austria (House of Habsburg Family)
　Albert, Archduke (1817–95), 145, 149 note 13, 157–8, 159
　Charles V, Emperor, see Spain
　Charles VI, Emperor (1685–1740), 59, 61, 62
　Charles (1771–1847), 157
　Elizabeth of Bavaria, Empress (1837–98), 134, 136, 141 and note, 142, 143, 144, 146, 148, 151 and note 18, 152, 153 and note, 154

Elizabeth, Archduchess (1883–1963), 146, 155
Elizabeth Christine of Brunswick, Empress (1691–1750), 59, 61
Ernest, Archduke (1533–95), 27, 34
Ferdinand, Emperor (1793–1875), 153
Francis Ferdinand, Archduke (1863–1914), 143
Francis Joseph, Emperor (1830–1916), 143, 144, 147, 149, 150, 151, 152, 153 note, 154, 155, 156, 157, 158, 159, 160, 161, 163, 164
Frederick III, Emperor (1415–93), 18
Joseph II, Emperor (1741–90), 82, 145
Karl, Emperor (1887–1922), 143 and note, 163
Leopold II, Emperor (1747–92), 130
Maximilian I (1459–1519), 14, 16 note 11, 18 and note 14
Maximilian II, Emperor (1527–76), 27 and note 6, 33, 34
Otto, Archduke (1865–1906), 163
Otto, Archduke (born 1912), 145
Philip, Archduke, see Spain
Rudolf II, Emperor (1552–1612), 27, 34
Rudolf, Crown Prince (1858–89), see entry under Rudolf
Sophie of Bavaria, Archduchess (1805–72), 144 and notes 2 and 4
Stephanie of Belgium, Crown Princess (1864–1945), 146 and notes 7 and 8, 149 and note 14, 151, 153 note, 154, 155
Valerie, Archduchess (1868–1924), 150, 153 note
William, Archduke (1827–94), 149 note 13, 157, 158
see also France (Marie Antoinette), Mexico (Maximilian), Spain (Anna),
Tuscan Branch
Ferdinand IV, Grand Duke (1835–1908), 156
Francis Salvator, Archduke (1866–1939), 150
John Salvator, see entry under Orth, John

Leopold I, Grand Duke, *see* Leopold II, Emperor (*previous entry*)
Leopold II, Grand Duke (1797–1870), 156
Leopold Salvator, Archduke (1868–1935), 165
Ludwig Salvator, Archduke (1847–1915), 165–6
see also Saxony (Louise)
Azpilcueta, Martin, 29

Backen, Judge, 178
Bacon, Sir Francis, 16 note 9
Baden, House of
Alexander, Prince (1816–17), 118
Amalia of Hesse, Princess (1754–1832), 104, 115
Charles V, Grand Duke (1786–1818), 116, 118
Charles Frederick, Grand Duke (1728–1811), 115–16
Charles Ludwig, Prince (1755–1801), 115–16
Frederick I, Grand Duke (1826–1907), 120
Frederick, Prince (1756–1817), 116
Leopold, Grand Duke (1790–1852), 118
Louisa of Prussia, Grand Duchess (1838–1923), 120
Ludwig (Louis), Grand Duke (1763–1830), 115 note 14, 116, 118
Stephanie de Beauharnais, Grand Duchess (1789–1860), 116, 117–18, 119–20
see also Hamilton (Marie), Hochberg, Russia (Elizabeth) and Sweden (Frederica)
Baltazzi, Alexander, 152
Bapst, E., 116 note 18
Barbour, Philip, 52 and note
Bariatinsky, Prince Feodor, 73, 74–6
Barras, Paul, Comte de, 86 and note 17
Basmanov, Peter, 51 and note 9
Battenberg, Julia, Princess (1825–95), 180
see also Bulgaria (Alexander)
Bavaria (*House of Family of Wittelsbach*)
Alexandra, Princess (1826–75), 133
Joseph Ferdinand, Electoral Prince (1692–9), 131
Karl Theodor, Duke (1839–1909), 136
Ludovica, Princess (1808–92), 136
Ludwig I, King (1786–1868), 113 note 9, 119, 132–3
Ludwig II, King, *see separate entry as* Ludwig II
Ludwig III, King (1845–1921), 142
Ludwig, Duke (1831–1920), 136, 148
Luitpold, Prince Regent (1821–1912), 138, 142
Marie of Prussia, Queen (1825–89), 133, 134 and note 4
Maximilian I, King (1756–1825), 132, 136
Maximilian II, King (1811–64), 133
Maximilian, Duke (1849–93), 133
Otto, King (1848–1916), 133, 138, 140, 142, 154
Theresa of Saxe-Hildburghausen, Queen (1792–1854), 113 note 9
see also Alençon (Sophie), Austria (Elizabeth and Sophie), Belgium (Eliza-
beth), Naples (Marie), Thurn and Taxis (Helena), Trani (Mathilde)
Bayreuth, Wilhelmina of Prussia, Margravine of (1709–58), 57
Bedford, John, Duke of (1389–1439), 3
Belgium (*House of Saxe-Coburg*)
Elizabeth of Bavaria, Queen (1876–1965), 136 note 9
Leopold II, King (1835–1909), 146
see also Austria (Stephanie) and Saxe-Coburg (Louise)
Benbow, Admiral John, 55
Benedek, General Ludwig von, 158 and note
Benningsen, General Count Levin von, 98–9, 100
Berry, Charles, Duc de (1778–1820), 89 and note 23, 90
Bie, Jacob de, 66
Bieberbach, Herr and Frau, 111
Bigot, Remy, 88
Biron, Ernest Ludwig (later Duke of Courland), 68
Bismarck, Prince Otto von, 141, 157
Blessington, Margaret, Countess of, 122 and note 6
Blochmann, Christoph, 116–17, 118
Bobrinskoy, Count Alexis, 72 note 14
Boglich, José, 163
Bohemia, Elizabeth Stuart, Queen of (1596–1662), 131 and note
Frederick of the Palatinate, King of (1596–1632), 131
John of Luxembourg, King of (1296–1346), 3
Bombelles, Count Karl, 145, 160
Borghi, Countess Camilla, 122
Borghi, Count Pompeio, 122
Borgia, St. Francis, 25 note 4
Bormann, Martin, 164
Bothwell, James Hepburn, 4th Earl of, 39–40, 41, 43, 44
Bourbon, Louis Henri, Duc de (1756–1830), 128
Bourchier, Thomas, Cardinal Archbishop of Canterbury, 7
Bourgeois, A., 120
Brackenbury, Sir Robert, 8
Braganza, Miguel of Portugal, Duke of (1853–1927), 153 note, 160
Brampton, Sir Edward, 17
Brampton, Lady, 17
Brantôme. Pierre de Bourdeille, Seigneur de, 27
Bratfisch, Josef, 146 and note 9, 149, 151
Brehm, Professor Alfred, 144
Brémond, 90
Bruneau, Mathurin, 88
Brunswick
Anton Ulric, Duke of (1714–74), 68 note 88
Frederick William, Duke of (1771–1815), 90
see also Austria (Elizabeth Christine) Denmark (Juliana) and Russia (Charlotte and Ivan VI)
Buckingham, Henry Stafford, 2nd Duke of, 6 and note

Buckingham, Katharine Woodville, Duchess of, 6
Bulgaria, Alexander of Battenberg, Prince of (1857–93), 159, 166
Bulgaria, Ferdinand of Saxe-Coburg, Tsar of (1861–1948), 159, 166
Bülow, Cosima von, 135
Burgundy, Charles the Bold, Duke of (1433–77), 16 note 11
  Margaret Plantagenet, Duchess of (1446–1503), 14, 16, 17, 18
  Mary, Princess of (1457–82), 16 note 11, 18 note 14
Burnet, Gilbert, Bishop of Salisbury, 55
Bute, Maria, Marchioness of, 125, 127
Butler, Lady Elizabeth, 8 and note 5
Buxhoeveden, Baroness Sophie, 177

Calvet, Melanie, 91
Cambridge, Richard, Earl of (1375–1415), 1
Campistron, Jean Galbert de, 31
Capteline, Sister, 63
Carlos of Spain (1545–68), 23–34, 38
Carlyle, Thomas, 71 note 10
Caserta, Marie Antoinette of Bourbon-Sicily, Countess of (1851–1938), 165
Castelot, André, 128, 129
Castlereagh, Robert Stewart, Viscount, 101
Cathcart, William, 1st Earl, 104
Chaliapin, Feodor, 48
Chambord, Henri, Comte de (1820–83), 127
Chapman-Huston, Major D., 134 note 5
Chartres, see Orleans
Chiappini, Lorenzo, 121–2, 123 and note 8, 124 and note 10, 125, 129
Chiappini, Maria Stella Petronilla, 121–30
Chiappini, Vincenzia, 121–2
Choiseul, Etienne François, Duc de, 81
Clarence, George, Duke of (1449–77), 7, 8 and note 15, 13, 17
  Lionel, Duke of (1338–68), 1
Clery, J. H., 84 and note 10
Coburg, see Saxe-Coburg
Comines, Philippe de, 4
Condé, Louis Joseph, Prince de (1736–1818), 128
Consalvi, Cardinal Ercole, 126
Conti, Louis François, Prince de (1717–76), 128
Cooper, Henry Driver, 127 and note 22
Courland, Anna, Duchess of, see Russia (Anna)
Cradock, Sir Matthew, 22 note 24
Crichton of Sanquhar, 41
Czartoryski, Prince Adam, 95 and note 1

Dalgleish, Geordie, 41
Darnley, Henry Stuart, Lord (1545–67), 38–40, 41, 42 note 10, 43–4
Dashkov, Princess Catherine, 73 and note 17
Daubeney, Giles, Lord, 20
Daumer, Professor Georg Friedrich, 110–11
Daun, Count Wirich Philipp Lorenz von, 62
Demidova (maid), 174, 175
Denmark, Dagmar, Princess of, see Russia (Marie Feodorovna)

Juliana of Brunswick, Queen of (1729–96), 69 note 2
Dennery, A., 120
Derby, Margaret Beaufort, Countess of (1441–1509), 18 note 15
Derby, Thomas Stanley, 1st Earl of, 18 note 15
Desault, Doctor Pierre Joseph, 86–7
Desmond, Maurice Fitzgerald, 10th Earl of, 17, 18, 19
Diego, St., 27 and note 5, 30
Dietrichstein, Count Adam von, 27, 30 note
Dighton, John, 8
Dimitry (the first), 48–52, 53
Dimitry (the second), 52–3
Dimitry (the third), 53
Dolgoruki, Prince, 76
Dolgoruki, Princess Catherine, 67
Dorset, Thomas Grey, 1st Marquis of, 4, 5, 6
Dostoievsky, F. M., 50
Douglas, Sir George, 41
Douglas, Margaret Erskine, Lady, 40 and note 7
Douglas, Willie, 41
Drouet, Jean Baptiste, 83 note 5
Dubarry, Jeanne Bécu, Comtesse, 133
Dudley, Robert, Earl of Leicester, 38
Dumangin, Doctor Jean Baptiste Eugène, 87
Dumas, Alexandre, 126, 132
Dumouriez, Charles Frederic du Perier, General, 87 note 21
Dussert (Police Commissioner), 88

Edinburgh, Philip, Duke of (born 1921), 118 note 20, 180
Edward V (1470–83), 2, 3–12, 16 note 8
Egmont, John Perceval, 2nd Earl of, 122 note 5
Egmont, Lamoral, Count, 32 note
Einert, Johanna, 89
England (Houses of Plantagenet, Tudor, Stuart, Hanover, Saxe-Coburg and Windsor)
  Albert, Prince Consort (1819–61), 113 note 8
  Caroline of Brunswick, Queen (1768–1821), 113 note 3
  Catherine of Aragon, Queen (1485–1536), 21 and note 20
  Charles I, King (1600–49), 131
  Charles II, King (1630–85), 9
  Edward III, King (1312–77), 1
  Edward IV, King (1441–83), 1, 2–5, 6 note 7, 11, 14, 16, 21, note 22, 47
  Edward V, King, see separate entry Edward V
  Edward VI, King (1537–53), 26, 37
  Elizabeth I, Queen (1533–1603), 38, 41, 43, 44 and note, 47
  Elizabeth II, Queen (born 1926), 131 note
  Elizabeth Woodville, Queen (1437–92), 2–7, 15–16 and note 7
  Elizabeth of York, Queen (1465–1503), 7, 9 note 11
  George III, King (1738–1820), 31 and note
  George V, King (1865–1936), 168, 170 note 7

Henry IV, King (1366–1413), 1
Henry V, King (1387–1422), 1, 5
Henry VI, King (1421–71), 1, 2, 3, 5, 11
and note 16
Henry VII, King (1457–1509), 7, 8 note 7, 9
and note 11, 10–12, 13, 15, 16, 17, 18 and
note 15, 19 and note 17, 20, 21
Henry VIII, King (1491–1547), 15, 22, 37
James I, King (1566–1625), 131
see also Scotland (James VI)
John, King (1166–1216), 11
Margaret of Anjou, Queen (1429–82), 1, 2,
3
Mary I, Queen (1516–82), 26
Richard II, King (1387–1400), 1, 11
Richard III, King (1450–85), 2, 5–8, 10–12,
13, 14, 16, 17
Victoria, Queen (1819–1901), 168 and note
3, 179
William III, King (1650–1702), 55 note 1
see also Bedford, Bohemia (Elizabeth),
Cambridge, Clarence, Edinburgh,
Gloucester, Romania (Marie), Wales,
Warwick and York
Escovedo, Juan de, 33 and note 17
Espinosa, Cardinal Diego de, 31
Eufrosina, 59, 61–2, 64, and note 19
Evelyn, John, 55

Farmer, Maurice, 122 note 6
Faro, Catherine de, 17
Favre, Jules, 91, 92
Fawcett, Colonel, 164
Feria, Gomez Suarez de Figueroa, Duke of,
29
Fersen, Count Axel, 83, 94, 171 note
Fersen, Count, 171 note
Feuerbach, Anselm von, 110–11, 113 and
note 7
Fitzgerald, Sir Thomas, 14
Flake, Otto, 120
Flavitzki, 107
Foix, Louis de, 28 note 9
Forest, Miles, 8
France (*Houses of Valois, Bourbon and
Orleans*)
Adelaide, Princess (1732–1800), 82
Catherine de Medici, Queen (1519–89),
26, 37
Charles VII, King (1402–61), 29 and note
11
Charles VIII, King (1470–98), 17
Charles IX, King (1550–74), 37
Charles X, King (1757–1836), 82, 87, 127
Elisabeth, Princess (1764–94), 83–5, 87,
90
Francis II, King (1543–60), 37, 39, 44 note
Henry II, King (1519–59), 26, 37
Louis XI, King (1423–83), 4, 29
Louis XIV, King (1638–1715), 126 note 17,
137, 143
Louis XV, King (1710–74), 81 note 2, 82
Louis XVI, King (1754–93), 81–5, 86 note
17, 87 and note 19, 88, 90, 91, 92, 93,
94, 127 note 21, 129, 168
Louis XVII, *see separate entry* at Louis
XVII

Louis XVIII, King (1755–1824), 83, 84
note 9, 87 note 19, 88, 91
Louis, Dauphin (1729–65), 81 note 2
Louis Joseph Xavier François, Dauphin
(1781–9), 82
Louis-Philippe, King (1773–1850), 125,
127, 128–9
Marie Antoinette of Austria, Queen
(1755–93), 81–5, 87, 88, 94, 168
Marie Josepha of Saxony, Dauphine
(1731–67), 94
Marguerite, Princess (1553–1615), 26
Victoire, Princess (1733–99), 82
see also Alençon (Duc), Angoulême (Duc
and Duchesse), Berry (Duc) Bourbon
(Duc), Chambord (Comte), Condé
(Prince), Conti (Prince), Joinville
(Prince), Orleans, Penthièvre (Duc),
Spain (Isabella), Toulouse (Comte)
Fuhrmann, Pastor, 114

Gautier, Abbé, 128
Genlis, Stephanie Duciest de Saint Aubin,
Comtesse de, 127
Gillard, Pierre, 177
Glebov, Stephen, 63
Glencairn, Alexander Cunningham, 5th
Earl of, 41
Gloucester, Humphrey, Duke of (1390–
1447), 5
Richard, Duke of, *see* Richard III
Godunov, Boris, Tsar of Muscovy (1551–
1605), 47, 48, 49, 51
Golitzin, Prince Alexander, 107
Golovkin, Gavril, Chancellor of Russia, 65
and note 22
Gomez de Silva, Ruy, 29
Gomin, 86, 93
Gondrecourt, Major-General Count
Leopold, 144 and notes 4 and 5, 145
Gordanov, Colonel, 98–9
Gordon, Lady Catherine, 19, 22 and notes
23 and 24
Gordon, Lady Jean (Countess of Bothwell,
then of Sutherland), 39, 40 note 6, 43
Gowrie, William, 1st Earl of, 42
see also Ruthven
Green, John, 8
Gregory XVI, Pope, 91
Grey, Sir John, 3 and note
Grey, Sir Richard, 6, 10 and note 12
Grey, Sir Thomas, *see* Dorset
Griesenbeck, Baron von, 119
Gudden, Doctor Richard Aloys von, 138–41
Guise, Antoinette de Bourbon, Duchess of
(1493–1583), 37
Guise, Mary of, *see* Scotland

Hamilton, Emma, Lady, 106, 122
Hamilton, Marie of Baden, Duchess of
(1817–88), 120
Hamilton, Sir William, 106
Hardenberg, Prince Carl August, von, 90
Harmand de la Meuse, Jean Baptiste, 86 and
note 16, 87, 93
Harrach, Count Franz, 165
Hastings, Lady Mary, 47

Hastings, William, 1st Lord, 5–6, 7, 10 and note 13
Hauser, Kaspar, 89, 91, 109–20
Heine, Heinrich, 174
Hennenhofer, Major von, 119
Heron, 19, 20
Hervagault, Jean Marie, 88
Hervey, 123
Hesse, Ernest Ludwig, Grand Duke of (1868–1937), 178
  see also Baden (Amalia) Prussia (Princess Henry), and Russia (Alexandra Feodorovna and Serge)
Hickel, Lieutenant, 113–14
Hitler, Adolf, 71 note 10, 164
Hochberg, Louisa, Countess of (later Princess of Baden) (1768–1820), 115–18, 119
Hofmann, Doctor, 151 note 20
Holstein, Anna of Russia, Duchess of (1708–28), 67
Home, Alexander, Earl of, 41
Horn, Philippe de Montmorency, Count of, 32 note
Horning, Richard, 135, 137
Hoyos, Count Joseph, 149–51
Hue, François, 84 and note 9
Hume, Daniel, 120 note 21
Hunolstein, Comte d', 128
Hunter, Doctor Richard, 31 note
Huntly, George Gordon, 2nd Earl of, 19 and note 18
  George Gordon, 4th Earl of, 39
Huyssen, Baron Heinrich von, 57 and note 8

Ignatiev, Jacob, 65
Irkutsk, Archbishop of, 105

Jeanroy, Doctor Nicolas, 87
Jenkins, Captain, 122 note 6
John of Austria, see Spain
Joinville, Comte and Comtesse of, 121–2, 125, 126, 129–30
Joinville, François de Bourbon-Orleans, Prince de (1818–1900), 125 note 12
Joinville, Sire de, 125 note 11
Josephine, Empress (1763–1814), 86 note 17, 89
Juan, Honorato, Bishop of Cartagena, 23

Kainz, Josef, 135
Kalnoky, Count Gustav, 147, 160
Karolyi, Count Stephen, 154
Kaspar, Marie, 149, 153 and note 21
Kaunitz, Prince Wenzel Anton von, 81
Kerensky, Alexander, 170 and note 9, 172, 173
Kharitonov (cook), 174, 175
Kikine, Alexander, 61, 63
Kildare, Gerald Fitzgerald, 8th Earl of, 14–15, 17, 19
Kleist, Baron, 175
Kneller, Sir Godfrey, 55
Knollys, Sir Francis, 42 note 12
Knox, John, 37
Kobylinsky, Colonel Eugene, 172, 173 and note 13

Koehler, Hugo, 166
Kolchak, Admiral Alexander, 174, 175
Kornilov, General Lavr, 171, 172
Kramer, Doctor, 116
Krüdener, Julia von Vietinghoff, Baroness, 100
Kschessinska, Matilde, 176
Kundrat, Doctor, 151 note 20
Kurbsky, Prince Andrew, 45 and note
Kuzmich, Feodor, 104–8

Lacher, Rudolf, 174, 178
La Harpe, Jean François de, 95
Lamballe, Marie Thérèse de Savoie-Carignan, Princesse de (1748–92), 84 and note 7
Lapoukhin, Eudoxia (1669–1731), 56, 57, 58, 63 and note 18
Larisch von Moennich, Count Georg, 148 note 11
Larisch von Moennich, Countess Marie, 136, 148, 149, 151, 154
La Rochefoucauld, Sosthène de, 90, 92
Lasne, Etienne, 88, 93
Lassus, Doctor Pierre, 87
Latour von Thurnbruck, General Joseph, 144
Laurent, Jean Jacques, 86
Lenin, V. I., 64 note 20, 172
Lennox, Matthew Stuart, 4th Earl of, 39 and note 4
Leo XIII, Pope, 151, 152, 155
Leopold, Salvator of Tuscany, see Orth, John
Leslie, John, Bishop of Ross, 42 and note 12, 44 note
Lincoln, John de la Pole, Earl of, 13, 14
Liszt, Franz, 133, 135
l'Isle, Arthur Plantagenet, Viscount, 21 note 22
Locke, John, 112
Loschek, Johann, 146, 150, 153 note
Louis XVII, Dauphin and Titular King, 82–8, 89 et seq., 92–4
Lovel, John, Lord, 14 note 4
Lovell, Sir Thomas, 15 and note 5
Lowicz, Johanna Grudzinska, Princess of (1799–1831), 102
Ludwig II, King of Bavaria (1845–86), 131, 133–42, 154
Lvov, Prince George, 170 and note 9, 172

Macalpine, Doctor Ida, 31 note
Maciejowski, Cardinal, 50
Malesherbes, Chrétien Guillaume de Lamoignon, Comte de, 85 and note 12
Manahan, Doctor John, 180
Mancini, 11
Mann, Sir Horace, 123
Mar, John Erskine, 1st Earl of, Regent of Scotland, 41
Marina, see Mniszech
Mary, Queen of Scots (1542–87), 35–44
Martin of Gallardon, Thomas, 91
Maskov (courier), 103, 104 and note
Maslov (lackey), 75, 78
Maurice, Prince of the Rhine (1620–52), 131

Mecklenburg, Anna Leopoldovna, Princess of, *see* Russia (Anna Leopoldovna)

Mecklenburg, Barbara of Prussia, Duchess of (born 1920), 177

Menger, Professor Anton, 144

Meno, Prigent, 17

Menshikov, Prince Alexander, 57 and note 7, 63, 65, 67

Metternich, Prince Clemens Lothar Wenzel von, 101

Mexico, Maximilian of Austria, Emperor of (1832–67), 143, 159

Meyer, Pastor, 113–14

Millot (accoucheur), 128

Mirovich, Lieutenant, 68–9

Mniszech, George, 49, 50

Mniszech, Marina (wife of Dimitry), 49, 50–1, 53

Moltke, Field Marshal, Count Helmuth, 157, 158

Monk, General George, 21 note 22

Montenegro, Prince Sava of (1702–86), 76

Montespan, Françoise Athenaïs de Rochechouart, Marquise de, 126 note 17

Montez, Lola, 132–3

Montgelas, Count Maximilian, 132

Montigny, Floris de Montmorency, Baron de, 32 and note

Moray, James Stuart, Earl of (1531–70), Regent of Scotland, 37 note, 38, 40, 41, 42, 44

More, Sir Thomas, 8, 10, 17 note 12

Morton, James Douglas, 4th Earl of, Regent of Scotland, 38, 40, 41

Morton, John, Cardinal Archbishop of Canterbury, 8–9, 10

Mowbray, Anne (Duchess of York), (1472–81), 12

Mugnatones, Don Bribiesca, 32

Mussorgsky, M. P., 48

Nagaya, Maria, 46, 47–8, 49

Naples, Marie of Bavaria, Queen of (1841–1925), 136

Napoleon I, Emperor (1769–1821), 88, 100, 116, 131, 157

Napoleon III, Emperor (1808–73), 91, 119

Narishkin, Natalia (1651–94), 56

Narishkin, Sophia (1808–24), 101, 102

Naundorff, Karl, 89–94, 179

Neale, Professor J. E., 44 note

Newborough, Spencer Wynne, 3rd Lord, 123

Newborough, Stella, Lady, *see* Chiappini

Newborough, Thomas, 1st Lord, 122–4

Newborough, Thomas, 3rd Lord, 123

Nikhon, Patriarch of Moscow, 77 note 21

Norfolk, Elizabeth (Talbot), Duchess of, 12

   John (Mowbray), Duke of, 12

   Katherine (Nevill), Duchess of, 5

   Thomas, Howard, Duke of, 41

North, Frederick, Lord, 122

Novosiltzov, N. N., 95 and note 2

Orange, Wilhelmina of Prussia, Princess of (1751–1820), 123

   William, Prince of (1748–1806), 123

Orleans (*Branch of French Royal House*)

   Adelaide, Princess (1777–1847), 129

   Adelaide de Bourbon-Penthièvre, Duchess (formally styled Duchess of Chartres) (1753–1821), 126, 128–9

   Alphonse, Prince (1779–1808), 129

   Antoine, Prince (1775–1807), 129

   Louis-Philippe, Duke (1725–85), 125

   Louis-Philippe, Duke, *see* France, King of

   Louis-Philippe Joseph, Duke (formerly of Chartres and nicknamed Égalité) (1747–93), 125, 126, 128–9 169 note 4

   Louise, Princess (1777–82), 129

Orlov, Count Alexis, 73–5

Orlov, Prince Grigori, 68–9, 72–3

Orth, John, 134, 145, 152, 156–66

Orton, Arthur, 178

Osbeck, John, 16

Otrepyev, Grigori, 52

Otway, Thomas, 31

Oxford, John de Vere, 13th Earl of, 21

Pahlen, Count Peter von der, 97–100

Palmerston, Henry John Temple, 3rd Viscount, 112 note 3

Panin, Count Nikita, Foreign Minister, 73 and note 18, 74, 79, 96

Panin, Count Nikita, Vice-Chancellor, 96–7, 100

Panin, Count Peter, 79

Paoli, Pasquale, 123

Parma, Louise of Bourbon, Duchess of (1819–64), 87

   Margaret of Austria, Duchess of (1522–86) 28 and note 7

Passek, Captain, 73

Payne, John, Bishop of Meath, 14 and note 3

Peel, Sir Robert, 112 note 3

Pelletan, Doctor Philippe Jean, 87

Penn, William, 55

Penthièvre, Louis Jean Marie de Bourbon, Duc de (1725–91), 126 note 17, 128

Perez, Antonio, 33 note 17, 34 and note 18

Peter III, Tsar of Russia (1728–62), 56 note, 67–78, 80, 96

Philaret, Patriarch of Moscow, *see* Romanov, P.

Pleyer, 65–6

Poland, Sigismund III, King of (1566–1632), 49

Pole, Katharine, 47

Polzer-Hoditz, Count Arthur, 165

Pompadour, Jeanne Antoinette Poisson, Marquise de, 133

Poniatowski, Stanislaus, later King of Poland (1732–98), 71

Portugal, Catherine of Spain, Queen of (1507–78), 24, 25 and note 3

   John III, King of (1502–57), 25 note 3

   Manuel I, King of (1469–1521), 24

   see also Spain (Maria and Isabella), and Braganza

Poynings, Sir Edward, 18

Prussia (*and Germany*) (*House of Hohenzollern*)

   Charlotte (later Tsarina of Russia), 103

Frederick II (the Great) (1712–86), King, 70, 71 and note 10, 74
Frederick William IV, King (1795–1861), 133
Henry, Princess (Irene of Hesse) (1866–1953), 176, 177
William I, King and German Emperor (1797–1888), 120, 134 note 3
William II, King and German Emperor (1859–1941), 145, 149, 169, 173 note 12
see also Bavaria (Marie), Bayreuth, Mecklenburg (Barbara) and Orange (Wilhelmina)
Pugachov, E. I., 77–80
Pushkin, A. S., 48, 80, 95 and note 4

Radziwill, Prince, 107
Rambaud, Madame de, 90
Rampolla, Cardinal Mariano, 152
Rasputin, Grigori, 77, 168, 171 note 11, 172, 174
Razan, Stenka, 79 and note 25
Razumovsky, Count Alexis, 73 note 16, 106
Razumovsky, Count Cyril, 73
Reuss, Prince Henry VII (1825–1906), 149
Richard, Duke of York (1473–83), 2, 6, 7–12
Richemont (V. Hébert), Baron de, 88–9, 94
Richmond, Margaret Beaufort, Countess of, 18 note 15
Richter, Franz, 119
Rivers, Anthony Woodville, 12th Earl, 5, 6, 10 and note 12
Rivers, Jacqueline de Luxembourg-St. Pol, Countess (1415–72), 3–4
Rivers, Richard Woodville, 1st Earl, 3, 4, 5
Rizzio, David, 38, 39, 42
Robespierre, Maximilien, 86 and notes 14 and 17
Robin, 88
Rodzianko, Michael, 170
Romania, Marie of Edinburgh, Queen of (1875–1938), 179
Romanov, Anastasia (died 1560), 46, 53
Romanov, Philaret (Feodor), Patriarch of Moscow (1558–1633), 53
Rostov, Dositheus, Bishop of, 63
Rousseau, Jean Jacques, 112
Rudolf, Crown Prince of Austria (1858–89), 134, 142, 143–55, 160–1
Rumiantsev, Captain, 61, 65
Rupert, Prince of the Rhine, (1619–82), 131
Russia (*Houses of Rurik and Romanov*)
Alexander I, Tsar, *see separate entry*
Alexander II, Tsar (1818–81), 103
Alexander III, Tsar (1845–94), 106
Alexandra Feodorovna (Alix of Hesse), Tsarina (1872–1918), 168–75, 176, 178
Alexandra Feodorovna (Charlotte of Prussia), Tsarina (1798–1860), 103
Alexis, Tsar (1629–76), 54, 58
Alexis, Tsarevich, *see separate entry*
Alexis, Tsarevich (1904–18), 168 *et seq.*, 170, 171, 173, 174–5
Anastasia, Grand Duchess, *see separate entry*
Andrew, Grand Duke (1879–1956), 176

Anna, Tsarina (1693–1740), 67, 68, 72
Anna Leopoldovna of Mecklenburg and Brunswick, Regent (1718–46), 68 and notes
Catherine I, Tsarina (1689–1727), 56–7, 67
Catherine II, Tsarina (1729–96), 67, 68, 69–76, 78, 79, 80, 96, 97, 106, 107
Charlotte of Brunswick (1694–1715), 59–60, 61
Constantine Constantinovitch, Grand Duchess (Elizabeth of Saxe-Altenburg), (1865–1927), 175
Constantine Pavlovitch, Grand Duke (1779–1831), 98, 100, 102–3
Cyril, Grand Duke (1876–1938), 169 note 4, 176
Dimitry, Prince (1583–91), 46 *et seq.*
see also Dimitry
Elizabeth, Tsarina (1709–62), 68, 69, 71–1, 96, 106
Elizabeth Alexeyevna (Marie of Baden), Tsarina (1779–1826), 67, 100, 101–2, 103–4, 107, 116
Feodor I, Tsar (1557–98), 45, 46, 47, 48, 50
Feodor II, Tsar (1589–1605), 49–50
Feodor III, Tsar (1661–82), 54
Ivan IV, Tsar (1530–84), the Terrible, 45–7, 48, 49 note 5, 50, 51, 52
Ivan V, Tsar (1666–96), 54, 68
Ivan VI, Tsar (1740–64), 67, 68–9, 76
Ivan, Tsarevich (1554–81), 46–7
Marie Feodorovna (Dagmar of Denmark) Tsarina (1847–1928), 168, 171, 176
Marie Feodorovna (Sophie Dorothea of Württemberg), Tsarina (1759–1828), 96, 98, 99, 100, 102, 106
Marie, Grand Duchess (1899–1918), 168 *et seq.*, 173, 174–5
Michael III, Tsar (1596–1645), 45, 53, 54
Michael Alexandrovitch, Grand Duke (1878–1918), 169, 170 and note 8, 172
Michael Pavlovitch, Grand Duke (1798–1849), 102, 105
Nathalia, Princess (1674–1716), 57
Natalia, Princess (1714–28), 60 and note 13
Nicholas I, Tsar (1796–1855), 102, 103, 106
Nicholas II, Tsar (1868–1918), 84, 106, 167–75, 176, 177, 178, 180
Nicholas Michaelovitch, Grand Duke (1859–1919), 106
Nicholas Nicholaevitch, Grand Duke (1856–1929), 170, 171 note 11
Olga, Grand Duchess (1882–1960), 176
Olga, Grand Duchess (1895–1918), 168 *et seq.*, 171, 173, 174–5
Paul, Tsar (1754–1801), 67, 70, 71, 75, 96–9, 102
Peter, the Great Tsar (1672–1725), 54–66, 67, 68, 70, 72, 97
Peter II, Tsar (1715–30), 60, 67
Peter III, Tsar (1728–62), *see separate entry*
Peter, Prince (Tsarevich) (1715–19), 60, 62
Peter, Grand Duke (1864–1931), 171 note 11

Serge (Elizabeth of Hesse), Grand Duchess (1864–1918), 169 and note 5
Sophia, Regent (1657–1704), 54, 56
Tatiana, Grand Duchess (1897–1918), 168 *et seq.*, 171, 173, 174–5
Xenia, Grand Duchess (1875–1960), 171 note 11, 176
Xenia, Princess (Mrs. Leeds) (1903–65), 175
see also Godunov (Boris), Romanov (Anastasia and Philaret), Shuiski (Vassili) and Württemburg (Catherine)
Ruthven, Patrick, 3rd Lord (Father of Gowrie), 42 and note 10
Ruzky, General, 170

Saint-Didier, Morel de, 90
Saint-Fare, Abbé de, 125 and note 14
Saint-Hilaire, Marco de, 90
Saltykov, Serge, 71, 96 and note
Savoy, Bona of, 4
Saxe Altenburg, Prince Frederick Ernest (born 1905), 175
see also Russia (Constantine Constantinovitch)
Saxe-Coburg (and Gotha)
Antoinette of Württemberg, Duchess of (1799–1860), 113
Ernest I, Duke of (1784–1844), 113
Louise of Belgium, Princess of (1858–1924), 146 note 8, 149 note 14
Philip, Prince of (1844–1921), 149–51, 155, 160
see also Belgium, Bulgaria (Ferdinand), England (Albert)
Saxony
Ernest August, Elector (and King of Poland) 1670–1733), 59 and note 9
Louise of Tuscany, Crown Princess (1870–1947), 162, 165
see also France (Maria-Anna Josepha)
Schankowska, Franziska, 177, 178, 180
Schiller, Johann Christoph Friedrich von, 31
Schönborn, Count, 61
Schratt, Katharina, 149, 151 and note 19
Scotland
Alexander III, King (1241–86), 36 note
James I, King (1394–1437), 19 note 18, 35–6
James II, King (1430–60), 36
James III, King (1451–88), 36
James IV, King (1472–1513), 19, 20, 22 note 23, 36
James V, King (1512–42), 35, 36, 37 and note, 40 note 7
James VI, King (1566–1625), 39, 40, 41 note 9, 42, 43
Margaret (the Fair Maid of Norway), (1283–90), 36 note
Mary, Queen of Scots (1542–87), *see separate entry*
Mary of Guise, Queen and Regent (1515–60), 37
Robert I (1274–1329), 19 note 18
Selivanov, 76–7
Sempill, Robert Forbes, 3rd Lord, 41

Shakespeare, William, 7, 8
Shaw, Doctor Ralph, 7
Shore, Jane, 7
Shuiski, Vassili (Tsar of Russia) (1552–1612), 48–9, 50, 51, 52, 53
Sidorka, 53
Simnel, Lambert, 11, 13–15, 19, 20, 21
Simnel, Richard, 15
Simon, Antoine, 85–6 and note 14
Simon, Madame Marie Jeanne, 85–6, 93 and note 29
Skariatin, J. F., 98–9
Skelton, 19, 20
Skuratov, Malyuta, 48, 50 and note 7
Sodich, Captain, 162, 163
Sokolov, Nicholas, 175
Somerset, Edward, 1st Duke of, 37
Spain (Houses of Castile, Aragon, Habsburg and Bourbon),
Alfonso XIII, King (1886–1941), 168 note 3
Anna of Austria, Queen (1549–80), 27 note 4, 34
Carlos, Prince of the Asturias, *see separate entry*
Charles V, Emperor (Charles I, King of Spain) (1500–58), 18 note 14, 25 and note 4, 28 note 7
Charles II, King (1661–1700), 34, 131
Ferdinand II, King of Aragon (1452–1516), 23, 24
Isabella, Queen of Castile (1451–1504), 23, 24
Isabella of Portugal, Queen of Castile (died 1496), 24
Isabella (Elizabeth de Valois), Queen (1545–68), 26, 31
Joanna of Castile (wife of Philip I) (1479–1555), 24–5 and note 4
Joanna, Infanta (1537–73), 23, 25, 26, 30
John of Austria, Don (1547–78), 28 and note 8, 33 and note 16, 34
Maria of Portugal, Princess (1527–45), 23
Philip I (Archduke and titular King) (1478–1506), 18 and note 14, 24–5
Philip II, King (1527–98), 23, 25 note 4, 26–34
Philip III, King (1578–1621), 27 note 6, 34
see also Portugal (Catherine)
Stackelberg, Baron, 180
Stalin, J. V., 46, 63
Stanhope, Charles, 3rd Earl, 112
Stanhope, James Richard, 7th Earl, 112 note 6
Stanhope, Philip Henry, 4th Earl, 112–14 and note 3, 4, 5, 6, 118, 119, 120
Stanley, Sir William, 18 and note 15
Stcherbatov, Prince, 63
Stephen, Ruler of Montenegro, 76
Stillington, Robert, Bishop of Bath and Wells, 7
St. Pol, Peter of Luxembourg, Count of, 3
Stockau, Count George, 162
Strangways, James, 22 note 24
Stuart, Esmé, 41 note 9
Stuart de Rothesay, Charles, Lord, 127
Stubel, Milly, 161, 162

212 · INDEX

Suffolk, Edmund de la Pole, Earl of, 8
Elizabeth, Plantagenet, Duchess of (1444–
1504), 13
Sverdlov, Jacob, 173 and note 14
Svoboda, Frank, 178–9
Sweden, Charles XI, King of (1655–97), 69
note 4
Sweden, Christina, Queen of (1626–89), 95,
134
Frederica of Baden, Queen of (1781–
1826), 166
Szeps, Moritz, 145, 147
Szogenyi-Marich, Laszlo, 153 note

Taafe, Count Eduard, 155 and note
Tamburlane, 79
Tarakanova, Princess, 106–7
Tarassov, Doctor Dimitry, 101 note, 104
and note
Tatarinov, Colonel, 98, 99
Tchaikovski, Alexander, 176
Tchaikovski, Alexis, 176, 180
Tchaikovski, Serge, 176
Thou, Jacques Auguste de, 28
Thurn and Taxis, Helena of Bavaria,
Princess (1834–90), 135 and note, 7,
136
Thurn and Taxis, Prince Paul, 135 and note, 6
Toledo, Garcia Alvarez de, 23
Tolstoy, Count Leo, 62 note, 102 note
Tolstoy, Count Peter, 62, 64, 65, 67
Toulouse, Louis Alexandre de Bourbon,
Comte de (1678–1737), 126 note 17
Tourzel, Louise Elisabeth, Duchesse du, 83,
84
Trani, Mathilde of Bavaria, Countess of
(1843–1925), 136
Troiekurov, Princess, 63
Trotsky, Leo, 168
Trupp (valet), 174, 175
Tucher von Simmelsdorf, Baron Gottfried
von, 112–13
Tuscany, see Austria
Tyrell, Sir James, 8 and note 7, 10

Ungern-Sternberg, Baron Edward, 124, 125,
126
Ungern-Sternberg, Baron Edward (Ned),
125 and note 15, 126
Uz, Johann Peter, 114

Van den Gheynst, Katharina von, 28 note 7
Varicourt, Baron von, 135
Verlaine, Paul, 120
Vesalius, Andreas, 27
Vetsera, Baron Albin, 147–8
Vetsera, Baroness Helena, 148 and note 10,
151–2, 153 note
Vetsera, Baroness Marie, 147–55
Vienna, Archbishop of (Cardinal Joseph
Othmar Rauscher), 149

Villa Rey, Signor, 163–4
Virgil, Polydore, 15
Volkhonsky, Prince, 103
Voltaire, François Marie Arouet de, 79
Vorontsov, Catherine, see Dashkov
Vorontsov, Elizabeth, 72 and note 12, 73,
74
Vorontsov, Count Michael, Chancellor of
Russia, 72 note 12
Vryubova, Anna, 172

Wagner, Richard, 135–6, 138 note, 139
Wales, Princes of: Arthur Tudor (1486–
1502), 21
Edward Plantagenet (1453–71), 2
Edward Plantagenet, Black Prince (1330–
76), 1
Edward Plantagenet, see Edward V
(England)
Edward Plantagenet (1473–84), 10, 11
Walters, John, 19, 21
Warbeck, Perkin, 11, 13, 16–22
Warwick, Edward Plantagenet, Earl of
(1475–99), 11, 13, 14, 17 and note 12,
21–2, 68
Warwick, Richard Nevill, Earl of, 2, 4, 5
Wassermann, Jacob, 120
Weichmann, Georg, 109, 110
Werg, Carl Benjamin, 94
White, Mr. Geoffrey, 9 note 9
Wiasemsky, Prince, 57, 59, 63
Wiasemsky, Prince, 98–9
Widerhofer, Doctor, 151 note 20
Wilford, Ralph, 21
Wisniowiecki, Prince Adam, 49
Wisniowiecki, Prince Constantine, 49
Woodville, Anthony, see Rivers
Woodville, Sir Edward, 5, 7
Woodville, Elizabeth, see England
Woodville, Sir John, 5
Woodville, Lionel, Bishop of Salisbury, 5, 6
Woodville, Sir Richard, see Rivers
Woodville, see also Buckingham, Duchess of
Wren, Sir Christopher, 9, 55
Württemberg, Catherine of Russia, Queen of
(1788–1819), 101
see also Russia (Marie Feodorovna) and
Saxe-Coburg (Antoinette)
Wylie, Sir James, 101 and note, 102, 104

Yashvili, Prince, 98–9
York, Edmund, Duke of (1341–1402), 1
Edward, Duke of, see Edward IV
Richard, Duke of (1411–60), 1
Richard, Duke of (1473–83), see separate
entry under Richard
Yurovsky, Jacob, 174
Yussopov, Prince Felix, 171 note 11

Zubov, Count Nikita, 97, 98, 100
Zubov, Prince Plato, 97, 98–9, 100